Pastor Barch -

Thank you for your
ministry of the WORD

Mary Werner

INSPIRATIONAL GOLD

Thought-provoking meditations
from Great Christian authors

edited by
Mary Werner

CHRISTIAN FOCUS

© Copyright Mary Werner 2005

ISBN 1-84550-060-1

10 9 8 7 6 5 4 3 2 1

Published in 2005
by
Christian Focus Publications, Ltd.
Geanies House, Fearn, Tain,
Ross-shire, IV20 1TW, Great Britain.

www.christianfocus.com

Cover Design by Jonny Sherlock

Printed and bound by
WS Bookwell, Finland

Contents

Biography

Mary Werner and her husband were career missionaries in Bolivia, Cuba, St Lucia, St Vincent and the Grenadines, Grenada, and Canada. Their work included evangelism, church planting, pastoral training, and administration, although their primary interest was in seminary teaching that equipped indigenous leadership. She is also an author, a lover of handwork and old books, and a grandmother who now lives in Calgary, Canada.

Introduction

David devoted himself to God's two great books – nature and Scripture. And we can truly say, "Our Father wrote them both." In summarizing the merits of Scripture, he says, "the law of the Lord is perfect... the testimony of the Lord is sure... the statutes of the Lord are right... the commandment of the Lord is pure... the judgments of the Lord are true and righteous altogether. More to be desired are they than gold, yea, than much fine gold." The Scripture is pure gold, and through the ages authors have drawn their inspirational truth from it.

The idea for this collection arose during my husband's last lengthy illness. Our practice was to read out loud from various books, and I began copying selections that inspired faith and encouraged reflection. The collection grew, and this provided an initial source from which to edit inspirational quotations. The result is this book.

Nearly 900 quotes are included from about 425 writers spanning every one of the centuries from the first to the twentieth, although the majority are from the past 400 years. Here is Clement of Rome (30-100), a contemporary of the Apostles, followed by two millennia of great words from letters, sermons, commentaries, poems, prayers, hymns, and creeds. Some belong to well-known letter writers the likes of Francois Fenelon (1651-1715) or the Abbess Hildegarde (1090-1179), great preachers such as C.H. Spurgeon (1834-1892) and Jerome (340-420), or writers of mystical verse like Jeanne Marie Guyon (1648-1717) and Catherine of Siena (1349-1370). Many others are anonymous or little known. But all speak from a common Hope that transcends their own time and place, and so continue to inspire. Though a number of Christian traditions are represented, no attempt was made to be inclusive. The largesse of the universal church cannot be fitted within one small volume. I regret that the devotional richness of Eastern Orthodoxy's long literary history is barely represented, and references from non-Western countries are largely absent. I could only select from that narrow place that I know best.

For each day quotations are arranged around a theme announced by a Scriptural phrase rather than an entire verse. Most themes point us to God's attributes, and remind us that access to Him comes through His invitation and His work on our behalf. Their primary purpose is devotional rather than doctrinal, brief words to encourage praise and contemplation rather than provide systematic instruction. An obvious shortcoming of the selections is that they are shorn of original contexts and purposes, but it is hoped that this new context and the juxtaposition of words from different centuries, gives them opportunity to speak in fresh ways and stir reflection. Not all of the sentiments expressed will meet the approval of every reader; I trust this will not distract from the broader themes shared by God's people across time and place.

Each era has idiomatic turns of phrase and uses of punctuation that are foreign to modern sensibilities. This makes some quotations difficult to read quickly. But sometimes reading slowly is worth the effort. I edited for clarity of meaning, ease of readability, and sensitivity to gender inclusive language. Thanks to those who helped with the many tasks involved.

January

January 1st

The eyes of the LORD your God are always upon it, from the
beginning of the year unto the end of the year.
Deuteronomy 11:12

The word that glitters before us like a jewel in a crown is the word
"eyes." This is not mere omniscience. *The Lord knows the righteous*
with a knowledge which is over and above that of omniscience. The
eyes of the Lord are upon the righteous not merely to see them, but
to view them with delight. The big heart of Deity is set upon us poor,
insignificant, undeserving, worthless beings. The loving eyes of God
are always upon us... *from the beginning of the year even to the end of the
year.* The expression teaches that the Lord takes a personal interest in
us. Never, never, never, does He delegate to others, however good
or kind, or to any secondary agents, however active or powerful, the
care of His people; His own eyes, without a substitute, must watch
over us. And the text declares *always... from the beginning of the year
even to the end of the year.* This is so pointed that we may not imagine
that any one single hour of the day or minute of the hour are we
removed from the eyes or heart of God.

C.H. Spurgeon (1834-1892)

Another year is dawning! Dear Father let it be,
In working or in waiting, another year with Thee;
Another year of progress, another year of praise,
Another year of proving Thy presence all the days.
Another year of mercies, of faithfulness and grace,
Another year of gladness in the shining of Thy face;
Another year of leaning upon Thy loving breast,
Another year of trusting, of quiet, happy rest.
Another year is dawning! Dear Father, let it be,
On earth, or else in heaven, another year for Thee.

Frances Havergal (1836-1879)

January 2nd

Forgetting those things which are behind, and reaching forth
unto those things which are before, I press toward the mark
for the prize of the high calling of God in Christ Jesus.
Philippians 3:13, 14

The Apostle is letting us see the secret of his own life, and counsels wise obliviousness, wise anticipation, strenuous concentration....He aims at the *mark for* the sake of the *prize.* The crown hangs on the winning post, and the one who touches the goal clutches the garland. The aim of God is the production in us of a God-pleasing character. For this sorrows and joys are experienced; for this hopes and fears and loves are kindled. For this all the discipline of life is set in motion; for this we were created; for this we have been redeemed. For this Jesus Christ lived and suffered and died. For this God's Spirit is poured out upon the world. God means to make us like Himself. Let us forget our failures so far as these might paralyse our hopes, or make us fancy that future success is impossible. At the last we shall reach the mark, and as we touch it, we shall find dropped on our surprised and humble heads the crown of life which they receive who have so run, not as uncertainly, but doing this one thing: pressing towards the mark for the prize.

Alexander Maclaren (1826-1910)

Run the straight race through God's good grace,
Lift up thine eyes, and seek His face,
Life with its path before us lies,
Christ is the Path, and Christ the Prize.
Cast care aside, lean on thy Guide;
His boundless mercy will provide;
Trust, and the trusting soul shall prove
Christ is its life, and Christ its love.

John S. Monsell (1811-1875)

January 3rd

He knows the way that I take.
Job 23:10

We may not always see the way. There is probably no other thing about which we display equal impatience. Job didn't understand God's way when he was led to the ash-heap. But God knew! There were many times David was left in darkness, yet he could say, *The Lord knows the way of the righteous.* It is God *alone* that knows the way of the righteous, so hidden is it to the righteous themselves. For His right hand leads them on in a wonderful manner, not in a way of sense or reason, but of faith; even of that faith that sees in darkness and beholds things that are invisible.

Martin Luther (1483-1546)

The future is in God's Hands, not yours; God will rule it according to your need. But if you seek to forecast it in your own wisdom, you will gain nothing but anxiety and anticipation of inevitable trouble.... Sometimes what seems evil becomes good if we leave it to God, and do not forestall Him in our impatience.

François de la Mothe Fénelon (1651-1715)

Your Guide is good company, and knows all the ups and downs in the way; therefore trust, the nearer the morning the darker.

Samuel Rutherford (1600-1661)

O my God, I know not what must come to me today, but I am certain that nothing can happen to me which Thou has not foreseen and ordained from all eternity; that is sufficient for me. I adore Thy impenetrable and eternal designs to which I submit with all my heart; I accept them all. I ask in the Saviour's name and through His infinite merits, patience in my trials, and perfect submission to all that comes to me by Thy good pleasure. Amen.

Joseph Pignatelli (1737-1811)

January 4th

Lord, Thou hast been our dwelling place in all generations.
Psalm 90:1

God who is eternal is our habitation, our place of refuge, to whom fleeing we may be in safety.... It is a remarkable expression, that God is a *dwelling-place*. Because the believer is in God, we cannot be moved or transferred, for God is a habitation that cannot perish. God is our dwelling-place, not the earth, nor heaven, nor paradise, but simply God Himself.

Martin Luther (1483-1546)

> O Lord, Thou art our home, to whom we fly,
> And so hast always been, from age to age;
> Before the hills did intercept the eye,
> Or that the frame was up on earthly stage,
> One God Thou wert, and art, and still shall be;
> The line of time, it doth not measure Thee.

Francis Bacon (1560-1626)

Has there ever been a human creature that could stand on earth while clothed in the flesh and say, "I am satisfied"? Sufficiently filled; filled up in every part. When God's work is complete, we shall stand before Him, and with the bright ideal and glorified conception of heavenly aspiration upon us, we shall say, "I am satisfied"; for we shall behold His face in righteousness and we shall be like Him.

Henry Ward Beecher (1813-1887)

> Oh, rest of rest! Oh, peace serene, eternal!
> Thou ever livest; and Thou changest never,
> And in the secret of Thy presence dwelleth
> Fulness of joy, forever and forever.

Harriet Beecher Stowe (1812-1896)

January 5th

You were not redeemed with corruptible things, as silver and gold....
but with the precious blood of Christ.

I Peter 1:18, 19

He gave His own Son the ransom for us: the holy for the transgressors; the good for the bad; the just for the unjust; the incorruptible for the corruptible; the immortal for the mortal. For what, save His righteousness, could cover our sins? In whom was it possible that we, transgressors and ungodly as we were, could be justified save in the Son of God alone? O sweet interchange! O unsearchable operation! O unexpected benefits! that the transgression of many should be hidden in one righteous person, and that the righteousness of one should justify many transgressors.

Mathetes (130)

There is a fountain filled with blood
Drawn from Immanuel's veins,
And sinners plunged beneath that flood
Lose all their guilty stains.

The dying thief rejoiced to see
That fountain in his day,
And there am I, though vile as he,
Wash all my sins away.

Dear dying Lamb, Thy precious blood
Shall never lose its pow'r,
Till all the ransomed Church of God
Be saved to sin no more.

E'er since by faith I saw the stream
Thy flowing wounds supply,
Redeeming love has been my theme
And shall be till I die.

William Cowper (1731-1800)

When Jesus was born in Bethlehem... there came wise men from the east to Jerusalem, saying, Where is He that is born King of the Jews? for we have seen His star in the east and are come to worship Him.

Matthew 2:1, 2

We see the glory of the Lord even in His humiliation. He is born of lowly parents, laid in a manger, wrapped in swaddling bands; but, lo! the principalities and powers in the heavenly places are in commotion. An angel descends to proclaim the advent of the new-born King, and suddenly there is with him a multitude of the heavenly host. Nor was the commotion confined to the spirits above; for in the heavens which overhang this earth there is a stir. A star is deputed on behalf of all the stars, as if it were the envoy.... to represent them before their King. This star is put in commission to be His herald to people afar off, to conduct them to His cradle. Shepherds have come, and with all love and joy they bow before this mysterious child; and after them from afar come the choice and flower of their generation, the most studious minds of the age. Making a long and difficult journey, they too arrive, the representatives of the Gentiles. There are many questions regarding this star, but "Remember that Omnipotence, has servants everywhere." We do not know the colour, shape or magnitude of the star, but what is recorded is more important. *We have seen HIS star,* always, only, altogether. There is no note taken of any peculiarity that it had except that it was the star of the King. And may you and I, whatever our eccentricities or personalities, never attract people's attention to us. May people never dwell upon our attainments or deficiencies, but may they always observe that we are men and women of God, who labour to shine for Him, that His way may be known upon earth.

C.H. Spurgeon (1834-1892)

January 7th

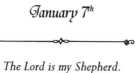

The Lord is my Shepherd.

Psalm 23: 1

David has left us no sweeter Psalm. It is the nightingale of psalms.... it has filled the air of the whole world with melodious joy. What would you say of a pilgrim commissioned of God to travel up and down the earth singing a strange melody, which when heard caused people to forget whatever sorrow they had? And so the singing angel goes through all lands, singing in the language of every nation. Behold just such a one! This pilgrim God has sent to speak in every tongue. It has charmed more griefs to rest than all the world's philosophy. It has remanded to their dungeon more felon thoughts, more black doubts, more thieving sorrows, than there are sands on the sea-shore. It has comforted the host of the poor. It has sung courage to the army of the disappointed. It has poured balm and consolation into the heart of the sick, of captives in dungeons, of widows in their pinching griefs, of orphans in their loneliness. Dying soldiers have died easier as it was read to them; hospitals have been illuminated; it has visited the prisoner and broken chains.... Nor is its work done. It will go on singing to your children and my children, and to their children through all the generations of time; nor will it fold its wings till the last pilgrim is safe, and time is ended; and then it shall fly back to the bosom of God whence it issues, and sound on, mingled with all those sounds of celestial joy which make heaven musical forever.

Henry Ward Beecher (1813-1887)

The God of love my Shepherd is, and He that doth me feed:
　While He is mine and I am His, what can I want or need?
Surely Thy sweet and wondrous love shall measure all my days;
　And as it never shall remove, so neither shall my praise.

George Herbert (1593-1632)

January 8ᵗʰ

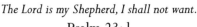

The Lord is my Shepherd, I shall not want.
Psalm 23: 1

Not was, not may be, nor will be. *The Lord is my Shepherd* -- is on Sunday, is on Monday, and is through every day of the week; is in January, is in December and every month of the year; is at home and is in China; is in peace and is in war; in abundance and in penury.

J. Hudson Taylor (1832-1905)

> The Lord my Shepherd is, I shall be well supplied;
> Since He is mine and I am His, what can I want beside?

Isaac Watts (1674-1748)

Our Shepherd the All-Sufficient! Nothing can add to His satisfying nature, nothing diminish from His fullness. There is a peace and fullness of expression in this little sentence, known only to the sheep. In the unfolding of it we find repose, refreshment, restoring mercies, guidance, peace in death, triumph, overflowing blessings, future confidence, eternal security in life or death, prosperity for time or eternity. Our wealth is His riches and glory. Eternal life is ours, with the promise that all shall be added. Our Shepherd has learned the wants of His sheep by experience, for He was Himself *led as a sheep to the slaughter.* Does not this imply a promise, when connected with His words *I know my sheep?* By what painful discipline was He instructed in this knowledge that He might be able to be touched with a feeling of our infirmities? The timid sheep has nothing to fear.

Theodosia A. Howard (1830)

Lord, when harder things shall rise and gather, and overshadow me, I shall have comfort in Thy strengthenings.

George Macdonald (1824-1903)

He makes me lie down in green pastures; He leads me beside the still waters.
Psalm 23:2

Here are many pastures; and every pasture rich so that it can never be eaten bare; here are many streams, and every stream so deep and wide that it can never be drawn dry. The sheep have been eating in these pastures ever since Christ had a church on earth, and yet they are as full as ever. The sheep have been drinking at these streams ever since Adam, and yet they are brim full to this very day, and will continue till the sheep are above and use them in heaven!

Ralph Robinson (1614-1655)

The Christian life has two elements to it, the contemplative and the active, and both are richly provided for. What are these *green pastures* but the Scriptures of truth -- always fresh, always rich and never exhausted? There is no fear of biting the bare ground where the grass is long enough for the flock to lie down in it. Sweet and full are the doctrines of the gospel; fit food for souls, as tender grass is natural nutriment for sheep. When by faith we are enabled to find rest in the promises, we are like sheep that lie down in the midst of the pasture; we find provender and peace, rest and refreshment, serenity and satisfaction. We can appropriate the promises!

And what are these *still waters* but the influences and graces of his blessed Spirit? His Spirit attends us in various operations, like waters -- in the plural -- to cleanse, to refresh, to fertilize, to cherish. They are *still waters*, for the Holy Spirit loves peace, and sounds no trumpet of ostentation in His operations. The Holy Spirit meets with the souls of His saints, not in raging waves of strife, but in peaceful streams of holy love where He conducts the chosen sheep.

C.H. Spurgeon (1834-1892)

He restores my soul: He leads me in the paths of righteousness for His name's sake.
Psalm 23:3

The Shepherd *restores* my soul to its original purity, what was grown foul and black with sin. He *restores* it to its natural temper in affections, what was grown distempered with violence of passions.... He *restores* it to life, what was grown quite dead; and who could *restore my soul* to life, but He only that is the Good Shepherd and gave His life for His sheep?

Richard Baker (1568-1645)

He leadeth me in the paths of righteousness. The Lord can lead us in no other paths than such as He walks in Himself.... The paths of providence in which God walks before us are paths of righteousness. People never question it when He goes before them in the glow of sunshine, dropping rich bounties every step He takes. But when the Lord walks before us covered with clouds, and a rod in His hand, how common then to talk of "mystery." In whatever way the Lord is going before you, the way is absolutely, constantly and without exception, a righteous one. The paths of Christian faith, obedience, self-denial, purity, truth, honesty, and love, are all straight. There is a world of comfort contained in the words *He leadeth me.* There is a Divine hand and purpose in all that befalls us. He leads in righteousness.

John Stoughton (1860)

For His name's sake. Seeing He has taken upon Him the name of a *Good Shepherd*, He will discharge His part, whatever His sheep be. It is not their being bad sheep that can make Him leave being a Good Shepherd, but He will be *good* and maintain the credit of *His name* in spite of all their badness.

Richard Baker (1568-1645)

January 11th

Though I walk through the valley of the shadow of death, I will fear no evil:
for Thou art with me; Thy rod and Thy staff they comfort me.

Psalm 23:4

In pastures green? Not always; sometimes He who knoweth best, in kindness leadeth me in many ways where heavy shadows be.

Henry H. Barry (1921)

Do we know the security, the strength of *Thou art with me?* "There is nothing in death to harm me, while Thy love is left to me." Death has left its sting in the humanity of Christ, and it has no more power to harm His child. Christ's victory over the grave is His people's. "At that moment I am with you. The same arm you have proved strong and faithful all the way up through the wilderness, will be there," whispers Christ. How can it be dark to come in contact with the light of life? It is *His rod* and *His staff;* therefore *they comfort.* It is our privilege to prove Him.

Theodosia A. Howard (1830)

> The King of Love my Shepherd is,
> whose goodness faileth never;
> I nothing lack if I am His
> and He is mine forever.
> In death's dark vale I fear no ill,
> with Thee, dear Lord, beside me;
> Thy rod and staff my comfort still,
> Thy Cross before to guide me.

Henry W. Baker (1821-1877)

The only saving faith is that which casts itself on God for life or death.

Martin Luther (1483-1546)

In His good time, I shall arrive: He guides me in His good time!

Robert Browning (1811-1889)

January 12th

You prepare a table before me in the presence of my enemies.
You anoint my head with oil.

Psalm 23:5

This is a desert scene. A panting fugitive is fleeing for his life, pursued by the forces of a fierce revenge. At last he touches the tent-rope of a desert man, and now he is a guest, and a guest is safe.... So the soul is a fugitive in flight across the plains of time. The soul is pursued by enemies which disturb its peace and threaten its destruction. What are these enemies that chase the soul across the ways of time? The sin of yesterday: I cannot get away from it. The temptation of today: sometimes it approaches me in deceptive deliberateness; sometimes its advance is so stealthy that in a moment I am caught in its snare. The death that awaits me tomorrow: we seek to banish that presence from our conscience, but we fail. Whither can we turn? In the whole vast plain is there one tabernacle whose tent-ropes we may touch and in whose circle of hospitality we may find food, refuge and rest? In the Lord our God is the fugitive's refuge. In our God we are secured against the destructiveness of our yesterdays, the menaces of today, and the darkening fears of the morrow. We are the Lord's guests, and our sanctuary is inviolable.

J.H. Jowett (1863-1923)

Other refuge have I none; hangs my helpless soul on Thee;
Leave, ah! leave me not alone, still support and comfort me.
All my trust on Thee is stayed; all my help from Thee I bring;
Cover my defenseless head with the shadow of Thy wing.

Jesus, Lover of my soul, let me to Thy bosom fly;
While the nearer waters roll, while the tempest still is high:
Hide me, O my Savior, hide, till the storm of life is past;
Safe into the haven guide, O receive my soul at last.

Charles Wesley (1707-1788)

January 13th

Surely goodness and mercy shall follow me all the days of my life,
and I will dwell in the house of the Lord forever.

Psalm 23:6

Someone has suggested that this is a psalm of David's later years. There is a fullness of experience and a tone of subdued, quiet confidence which speaks of a heart mellowed by years and of a faith made sober by many a trial.... The psalmist is looking at his yesterdays. He is gazing at the panorama of his past life. It may be upon a bed of illness that the memory wanders back the path of the years. Or it may be at the graveside of a comrade that the memory tugs us backward. Or sometimes a little commonplace incident unlocks the doors of the past and in vivid recollection we pass through all its rooms. To the psalmist, the retrospect oppressed him; yesterday became the burden of today. The burden of conscience never comes from tomorrow; it is rolled up from our yesterdays. It is not prospect, but retrospect, that lays the heaviest weight on the heart. But here we have a God in the rear, a Father coming up behind with His goodness and mercy. It is as if the sands of past years, in which we have the track of our sin, the tidal waves of Divine goodness and mercy roll up, and the unseemly track is smoothed away.

And I shall dwell.... We can only get out of the deep ruts of today by the powerful tug of to-morrow. Life grows heavy and stagnant when tomorrow ceases to pull, when the "forever" has lost its power.

J.H. Jowett (1863-1923)

Chance and change are busy ever;
Man decays and ages move;
But His mercy waneth never:
God is wisdom, God is love.

John Bowring (1792-1872)

I will never leave you nor forsake you.

Hebrews 13:5

When the Lord Jesus comes to you and covers you with His garment and says *Fear not*, He will never forsake that soul. When once the Lord Jesus comes to sinners to be their righteousness, He will never leave them. *I am with you always.* It is this that makes Him a friend that sticks closer than a brother. His love is everlasting. It is not like the love of a creature – it is unchangeable. He has died for that soul: He has borne all for that soul. Will He ever leave a soul that He has died for? You may also take these words as those of the Spirit. *He shall give you another Comforter that He may abide with you for ever.* When God the Holy Spirit comes to a soul, He will never leave it, never forsake the temple in which He dwells.... Remember that the word *never* reaches to death. And when the judgment is past, these words will be the eternal solace of all those who have believed – *I will never leave you, nor forsake you.* Eternity alone will unfold the riches of this promise. He who died for us will be our eternal friend; and He who sanctifies us will for ever dwell in us; and then God, who loved us, will be ever with us.

Robert Murray M'Cheyne (1813-1843)

> Abide with me! Fast falls the eventide;
> The darkness deepens: Lord, with me abide!
> When other helpers fail, and comforts flee,
> Help of the helpless, O abide with me.
>
> Hold Thou Thy cross before my closing eyes,
> Shine through the gloom, and point me to the skies;
> Heaven's morning breaks, and earth's vain shadows flee;
> In life, in death, O Lord, abide with me.

Henry Francis Lyte (1793-1847)

*Eye has not seen, nor ear heard, neither has entered into the heart of man
the things which God has prepared for those that love Him.*
1 Corinthians 2:9

What presumption would it have been to have thought of such things, if God had not spoken them before us! What arrogance would it have been to talk of being children of God; of having fellowship and communion with Him; or dwelling in Him and He with us -- if this had not been God's own language! How much less would we have thought of shining as the sun; of being joint-heirs with Christ; of judging the world; of sitting on Christ's throne; of being one with Him -- if we had not all this from the mouth and under the hand of God!

But *has He not said it, and shall He not do it? Has He not spoken, and shall He not make it good?* Yes, as the Lord God is true, *Thus shall it be done to the one whom Christ delights to honour.* Be of good cheer, Christian, the time is near when God and you shall be near, as near as you can desire. You shall be His child and He your Father; you shall be an heir of His kingdom. And what more can you desire? You shall be one with Christ who is one with the Father....

It will be the everlasting work of the saints to stand before the throne of God and the Lamb, and to praise Him for ever and ever. As their eyes and hearts shall be filled with His knowledge, and with His glory, and with His love, so shall their mouths be filled with His praise. Oh blessed employment – to sing for ever, *You are worthy, O Lord, to receive honour, glory and power, for You created all things, and for Your pleasure they are and were created....* Go on, O you saints, while you are on earth, in this divine exercise of praise!

Richard Baxter (1615-1691)

I look for the resurrection of the dead, and the life of the world to come. Amen

Nicene Creed (325)

January 16th

⌘ ——————◇—————— ◈

The preaching of the cross is to them that perish foolishness;
but unto us who are saved it is the power of God.
1 Corinthians 1:18

The Cross became a power which went forth like the light, noiselessly yet irresistibly... *the power of God unto salvation.* This power remains in its mystery, its silence, its influence. The Cross has not become obsolete; the preaching of the Cross has not ceased to be effectual. There are those who would persuade us that the Cross is out of fashion, time-worn, not time-honored; that Golgotha witnessed only a common martyr scene; that the great sepulchre is but a Hebrew tomb; that the Christ of the future and the Christ of the past are widely different. But this only leads us to clasp the Cross more fervently and to study it more profoundly, as embodying that Gospel which is at once the wisdom and the power of God.

Yet the Cross is not without its mysteries.... It illuminates, yet it darkens; it interprets, yet it confounds. It raises questions but refuses to answer all that is raised. It solves difficulties, but it creates them too. It locks as well as unlocks. It opens and no one shuts; it shuts and no one opens. It is life and yet it is death. It is honor, yet it is shame. It is wisdom, but also foolishness. It is both gain and loss; both pardon and condemnation; both strength and weakness; both joy and sorrow; both love and hatred; both medicine and poison; both hope and despair. It is grace and yet it is righteousness. It is law, yet it is deliverance from law. It is Christ's humiliation, yet it is Christ's exaltation. It is Satan's victory, yet it is Satan's defeat. It is the gate of heaven and the gate of hell. Let us look at the Cross as the divine proclamation and interpretation of the things of God; the key to His character, His word, His ways, His purposes.

Horatio Bonar (1808-1887)

January 17th

Now the God of hope fill you with all joy and peace in believing.
Romans 15:13

When Madame Guyon (1648-1717) was imprisoned in the Castle of Vincennes in 1695, she wrote: It sometimes seems to me as if I were a little bird whom the Lord has placed in a cage, and that I had nothing now to do but to sing. The joy of my heart gave brightness to the objects around me. The stones of my prison looked to my eyes like rubies.

I have neither tongue nor pen to express to you the happiness of such as are in Christ. When you have sold all that you have and bought the field wherein this pearl is, you will think it no hard market; for if you be in Him, all His is yours. Let us then be glad and rejoice in the salvation of our Lord; for faith had never yet cause to have wet cheeks, and hanging down brows, or to droop or die. None have right to joy but we; for joy is sown for us, and an ill summer or harvest will not spoil the crop. He hath made all His promises good to me, and hath filled up all the blanks with His own hand. I would not exchange my bonds [imprisoned in Aberdeen] with the joy of this whole world.
Samuel Rutherford (1600-1661)

My God, the spring of all my joys, the life of my delights,
The glory of my brightest days, and comfort of my nights!

The opening heavens around me shine, with beams of sacred bliss,
If Jesus shows His mercy mine, and whispers I am His.

In darkest shades, if Thou appear, my dawning is begun;
Thou art my soul's bright morning star, and Thou my rising sun.
Isaac Watts (1674-1748)

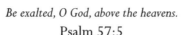

Be exalted, O God, above the heavens.
Psalm 57:5

One God! one Majesty! There is no God but Thee!
Unbounded, unexpended Unity! Unfathomable Sea!
All life is out of Thee, and Thy life is Thy blissful Unity.

Frederick W. Faber (1814-1863)

Your Father in heaven is perfect: perfect in sight, perfect in power, perfect in greatness, perfect in foreknowledge, perfect in goodness, perfect in justice, perfect in loving-kindness: not circumscribed in any space, but the Creator of all space, existing in all, and circumscribed by none. *Heaven is His throne*, but higher is He that sitteth thereon: *and earth is His footstool*, but His power reacheth unto things under the earth.

Cyril of Jerusalem (315-386)

How great is God! How small am I!
A mote in the illimitable sky,
Amidst the glory deep, and wide, and high
O Heaven's unclouded sun.
There to forget myself forever more;
Lost, swallowed up in Love's immensity,
The sea that knows no sounding and no shore,
God only there, not I.

Gerhard Tersteegen (1697-1769)

The one Lord of all is God. For that Sublimity cannot possibly have any compeer, since He alone possesses all power. He cannot be seen, He is too bright for vision; nor comprehended, He is too pure for our discernment; nor estimated, He is too great for our perception. What temple can God have, whose temple is the whole world? He must be dedicated in our mind; in our breast He must be consecrated.

Cyprian of Carthage (200-258)

For what is your life? Why, it is but a mist, which appears for a short time and dissaperars.
James 4:14 (Weymouth)

Life is a *tear*, a scene of varied and multiplied trials: "Born to trouble" is the world's cradle inscription. Life is a *period*, it has a definite length, it also has an end. Life is a *prospect*, looking beyond the bounds of time over into the bosom of eternity and forward to the bar of God. Life is a *want*, alike in its beginning, continuance and end; it is ever needy, as an infant for its mother's arms, or as a vine stretching forth its tendrils for something by which to climb or lean. And how all-happy is that soul that finds the true source of strength, and passes through all the wilderness of this world, and comes up out of it at last *leaning upon her beloved.*

J.C. Hall (1574-1656)

Brief life is here our portion, brief sorrow, short-lived care;
The life that knows no ending, the tearless life, is there.
There grief is turned to pleasure, such pleasure as below
No human voice can utter, no human heart can know.
The morning shall awaken, the shadows shall decay,
And each true-hearted servant shall shine as doth the day.
There God, our King and Portion, in fullness of His grace,
We then shall see for ever, and worship face to face.

Bernard of Cluny (c.1150)

O Lord, let me not henceforth desire health or life except to spend them for you, with you and in you. You alone know what is good for me; do therefore what seems best to you. Give to me or take from me; conform my will to yours; and grant that with humble and perfect submission and in holy confidence I may receive the orders of your eternal providence, and may equally adore all that comes to me from you. Amen.

Blaise Pascal (1623- 1662)

January 20th

For everyone who asks receives.

Matthew 7:8

Our Lord is here instructing beginners in the prayer life. He is teaching the ABC of prayer. And the worst thing which could happen to beginners would be to teach them that they would receive everything for which they asked. Real love, such as God's, gives not what is wanted but what is best. We ought to be just as grateful to the God who does not give us according to *our* will as we are to the God who does give us according to *His* will.... Christ does not here say anything about asking according to the will of God, or that if we abide in Him, we shall ask *whatsoever* we will and it shall be given. All this is true. But it is not the truth for beginners, because a child whose receiving was conditioned upon always asking according to the will of its father or mother, would soon become discouraged. Often God's will is a mystery, and often we come to God not knowing that will. *Everyone that asks receives* – SOMETHING. He is teaching that all prayer brings blessing. In the profoundest sense there is no unanswered prayer. *Everyone who asks receives* – GOOD THINGS. *How much more shall your Father which is in heaven give good things to them that ask Him?* God has a store of general blessings which He gives to all who pray, even where they may not get the special thing for which they asked.

James H. McConkey (n.d.)

I thank thee, Lord, Thou wert too wise to heed
My feeble prayers, and answer as I sought,
Since these rich gifts Thy bounty has bestowed
Have brought me more than I had asked or thought.
Giver of good, so answer each request
With Thine own giving, better than my best.

Annie Johnson Flint (1862-1932)

January 21ˢᵗ

There is a place near Me where you may stand on a rock.
When My glory passes by, I will put you in a cleft in the rock
and cover you with My hand until I have passed by.

Exodus 33:21, 22

There was infinite tenderness in the Lord's proposal that Moses should stand in the cleft of the rock, lest the burning splendour should overpower him. Does not God draw nigh the soul still, and speak in similar words? When bereavement befalls us, and the light of our eyes is removed and a shadow falls over all the world, may we not hear Him saying, *Behold, there is a place near Me. I have put you in this cleft of the rock, and am covering you with My hand.* When our heart is disappointed in human affection, and it appears as though all faith in our fellows is shattered; when we find that the deposit that we placed in the bank of human love is forfeited, and when our soul prefers death to life, again we hear that strong and tender voice saying: *Behold, there is a place near Me.* When we are threatened with the loss of our early faith, and no longer believe with the unquestioning simplicity of our childhood; when imperious questions arise and demand answer, again the Father draws near and says, *My child, you cannot understand, but come nearer to Me; there is a place by Me.* And He puts us in the cleft of the rock and covers us with His hand. So we turn to Christ, the Rock of Ages cleft for us. We understand that if we hide in His riven side, where the spear rent Him, we are sheltered forever. We look out upon God from the place which is called Calvary; we stand upon the Rock of the finished work of the Redeemer; we are hidden beneath the pierced hand, and from that vantage-point we are able to see things that prophets and kings desired to see in vain.

C.H. Mackintosh (1820-1896)

He hideth my soul in the cleft of the rock that shadows a dry, thirsty land; He hideth my life in the depths of his love, and covers me there with his hand.

Fanny Crosby (1820-1915)

In returning and rest shall you be saved;
in quietness and confidence shall be your strength.
Isaiah 30:15, 16

Judah is exhorted to forsake its entangling dependence upon Egypt, and to trust wholly in God. They had gone away from Him in their fears. They must come back by their faith. To them the great lesson was trust in God. "Returning and rest" correspond to "quietness and confidence" so that "rest" answers to "quietness" and "returning" to "confidence." Am I sinful? Then trust. Am I bewildered and ignorant? Then trust. Am I anxious and harassed? Then trust. We come back to God by simple *confidence*, not by preparing ourselves, not by our expiation, but only by trusting in Him. The ground of this confidence is laid in our knowledge of Him.

Alexander Maclaren (1826-1910)

Jesus, I am resting, resting in the joy of what Thou art;
I am finding out the greatness of Thy loving heart.

Thou hast bid me gaze upon Thee, and Thy beauty fills my soul,
For by Thy transforming power, Thou hast made me whole.

Simply trusting Thee Lord Jesus, I behold Thee as Thou art!
And Thy love so pure, so changeless, satisfies my heart:

Satisfies its deepest longings, meets, supplies its every need,
Compasseth me round with blessings: Thine is love indeed!

Ever lift Thy face upon me as I work and wait for Thee;
Resting 'neath Thy smile Lord Jesus, earth's dark shadows flee.

Brightness of my Father's glory, Sunshine of my Father's face,
Keep me ever trusting, resting, fill me with Thy grace.

Jean S. Pigott (1845-1882)

January 23rd

⸻ ⸻

Come and see the works of God…. He turned the sea into dry land:
they went through the flood on foot.

Psalm 66:5, 6

Come and see the works of God. Such glorious events as the cleaving of
the Red Sea and the overthrow of Pharaoh are standing wonders,
and throughout all time a voice sounds forth concerning them -- *come
and see.* Even till the close of all things, the marvelous works of God at
the Red Sea will be the subject of meditation and praise, for standing
on the sea of glass mingled with fire, the triumphal armies of heaven
sing the song of Moses the servant of God, and the song of the Lamb.

He turned the sea into dry land. It was no slight miracle to drive
a pathway through such a sea, and to make it fit for the traffic of
a whole nation. He who did this can do anything, and must be God,
the worthy object of adoration. The Christian's inference is that no
obstacle in one's journey heavenward need hinder, for the sea could
not hinder Israel, and even death itself shall be as life; the sea shall be
dry land when God's presence is felt. *They went through the flood on
foot.* Through the river the tribes passed dry-shod, Jordan was afraid
because of them.

C.H. Spurgeon (1834-1892)

A much greater miracle is that we should pass over the bitter sea
of this life and cross the river of mortality that never ceases to run,
and which swallows up and drowns so many, and still come safe
and alive to the land of eternal promise, and there rejoice in God
Himself, beholding Him face to face; and yet this greater miracle is
so accomplished by God, that many pass through this sea as if it were
dry land, and cross this river with dry feet.

Robert Ballermine (1542-1621)

January 24th

His greatness is unsearchable.
Psalm 145:3

Only to sit and think of God, oh what a joy it is!
To think the thought, to breathe the Name
Earth has no higher bliss.

Frederick W. Faber (1814-1863)

Concerning Him, and concerning those things which are of Himself, the human mind cannot worthily conceive what they are, how great they are, and what they are like; nor does the eloquence of human discourse approach the level of His majesty. He is greater than all discourse, nor can He be declared. For what can you fittingly either say or think concerning Him who is greater than all discourses and thoughts? What can you worthily say of Him who is loftier than all sublimity, higher than all height, deeper than all depth, clearer than all light, and brighter than all brightness; more brilliant than all splendour, stronger than all strength, more powerful than all power, more mighty than all might, greater than all majesty, more potent than all potency, and richer than all riches; more wise than wisdom, more benignant than all kindness, better than all goodness, juster than all justice, and more merciful than all clemency? For all kinds of virtues must need be less than Himself, who is both God and Parent of all virtues, so that it may truly be said that nothing can be compared to Him. For He is above all that can be said.

Novatian of Rome (210-280)

We give Thee thanks, Holy Father, for Thy holy name which Thou hast made to tabernacle in our hearts, and for the knowledge and faith and immortality which Thou hast made known unto us through Thy Son Jesus; Thine is the glory for ever and ever.

Didache (c.100)

January 25th

When you pray, say, Our Father.
Luke 11:2

How great is the Lord's indulgence! How great His condescension and goodness towards us! He has wished us to pray in such a way as to call God Father, and to call ourselves children of God, even as Christ is the Son of God – a name which none of us would dare to venture on in prayer, unless He Himself had allowed us thus to pray! We ought then to remember that when we call God *Father*, we need to act as God's children; so that in the measure in which we find pleasure in considering God as a Father, He might also be able to find pleasure in us. Let us converse as temples of God, that it may be plain that God dwells in us.

Cyprian of Carthage (200-258)

In our prayer life we feel ourselves humiliated by our dependence and need; at the same time, it is in prayer that we are lifted into the immediate presence of the great Lord of the world. Prayer is a piece of eternity within time. In prayer we experience the presence of the heavenly goal while we are yet pilgrims here on earth. To pray in faith is to experience in advance what we shall yet see. To be a son means to be a person of prayer. Those who down here on earth enter God's sanctuary will one day enter His heavenly palace. Priesthood and kingship, temple and throne are linked eternally. Sonship and glory belong together.

Erich Sauer (1899-1959)

> Thou bounteous Giver of all good!
> Thou art of all Thy gifts Thyself the crown!
> Give what Thou canst, without Thee
> We are poor; and with Thee rich,
> Take what Thou wilt away.

William Cowper (1731-1800)

January 26th

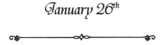

In My Father's house are many mansions... I go to prepare a place for you.
John 14:2

We go to no uncertain home. It is the family mansion, eternally ordained and prepared for the dwelling of the saints. The everlasting love which chose us to salvation, the predestination which appointed us to be sons, provided the home we are eternally to occupy. What a sweet truth is this! After a long journey, we delight to think that we shall find our home all ready for our welcome. Such is our heavenly abode. *For we know that if our earthly house of this tabernacle were dissolved, we have a building of God, a HOUSE not made with hands, eternal in the heavens.* The apostle, too, reminds us that it is *an inheritance incorruptible, and undefiled, and that fades not away, RESERVED in heaven for you.* And did not our blessed Lord declare the same truth when He said, *I go to PREPARE a place for you.* We go, then, to a home all appointed and prepared, all garnished and made ready for our coming. It is even now ready.... When the solemn hour of death has passed, the spirit will find itself ushered into the reception room of heaven, the first of the *many mansions.* There we shall see Jesus who welcomes us home, encircled by the general assembly and church of the first-born, and an innumerable company of angels, waiting to greet our arrival. More eager than all the rest of that blessed throng will be the loved ones from whom we parted on the margin of the river across which they passed to the Celestial City. Oh, what a reception! what greetings! what joy-wishings then! But the Saviour's welcome will be the crowning one of all!

Octavius Winslow (1808-1878)

Face to face! O blissful moment! Face to face – to see and know;
Face to face with my Redeemer, Jesus Christ who loves me so.
Carrie Breck (1855-1934)

January 27th

It is more blessed to give than to receive.

Acts 20:35

Do right, and God's recompense to you will be the power to do more right. Give, and God's reward to you will be the spirit of giving more: blessed spirit, for it is the Spirit of God Himself, whose Life is the blessedness of giving. Love, and God will pay you with the capacity of more love.

F.W. Robertson (1816-1853)

No one is so poor as to have nothing worth giving. Give what you have; to someone it may be better than you dare to think.

H.W. Longfellow (1807-1882)

> Thy neighbor? 'Tis that toiling slave,
> Fetter'd in thought and limb,
> Whose hopes are all beyond the grave?
> Go thou and ransom him.
>
> Thy neighbor? 'Tis that weary man
> Whose years are at the brim,
> Bent down by sickness, care, and pain:
> Go thou and comfort him.
>
> Thy neighbor? 'Tis the fainting poor,
> Whose eyes with want are dim,
> Whom hunger drives from door to door;
> Go thou and cherish him.

James Montgomery (1771-1854)

The love we see God having for us, that same love we extend to everyone else. For when we look at our reflection in the Fountain, the sea of the divine Being, we feel at once compelled to love our neighbors as we love ourselves, because we see that God loves us supremely.

Catherine of Siena (1347-1380)

January 28th

Thanks be unto God, which always causes us to triumph in Christ.
2 Corinthians 2:14

The picture of Joshua's self-surrender is very striking. Standing over against Jericho, perhaps at dead of night, suddenly there stood before him a man with his sword drawn. Nothing daunted, Joshua went to him and said, *Are you for us or for our adversaries?* The answer came that thrilled his soul and laid him on his face before the supernatural presence: *Nay, but as Captain of the host of the Lord am I come. And Joshua fell on his face: What says my Lord unto His servant? And the Captain of the Lord's host said: Loose your shoe from off your foot; for the place where you stand is holy.* Joshua had supposed that he was captain, but henceforth his sword was laid down before the Captain of the Lord's host; and Joshua, with his shoes off his feet, took a servant's place, took his orders from above and followed where the Lord should lead. This is the secret of Christian victory; this is the meaning of that sublime announcement of the Apostle: *Thanks be unto God who always leads us in triumph in Christ Jesus....* We are not the victors but simply the followers of the great Commander. With such a Leader, we must always be victorious. But to have such a Leader we must die to our self-sufficiency and strength. There cannot be two commanders; you and Christ cannot both rule. Christ alone must be known and glorified. Then shall our service abide the testing day; then shall *our light so shine that others see our good works and glorify* – not us, but *our Father in heaven.*

A.B. Simpson (1844-1919)

It is paradoxical that the heart only gains power as it ceases to be free. We must be imprisoned by the mighty power of love before we can be free.

George Matheson (1842-1906)

Be Thou my strong rock, for an house of defence to save me.
Psalm 31:2

Rock of Ages, cleft for me,
Let me hide myself in Thee;
Let the water and the blood,
From Thy riven side which flowed;
Be of sin the double cure,
Cleanse me from its guilt and power.

Not the labours of my hands
Can fulfill Thy law's demands;
Could my zeal no respite know,
Could my tears for ever flow,
All for sin could not atone;
Thou must save, and Thou alone.

Nothing in my hand I bring,
Simply to Thy Cross I cling;
Naked, come to Thee for dress;
Helpless, look to Thee for grace;
Foul, I to the fountain fly;
Wash me, Saviour, or I die.

While I draw this fleeting breath,
When mine eyelids close in death,
When I soar through tracts unknown,
See Thee on Thy judgment throne,
Rock of Ages, cleft for me,
Let me hide myself in Thee.

Augustus Toplady (1740-1778)

Judge and Savior of our race, when we see Thee face to face, grant us
'neath Thy wings a place. Amen.

Isaac Williams (1802-1865)

January 30th

The earth, O Lord, is full of your mercy.
Psalm 119:64

Who could enter a sanctuary, search conscience, look up to heaven, pray or sacrifice, call upon God, or think of the tree of life in the midst of the paradise of God, if there were no mercy. Mercy is in the air which we breathe, the daily light which shines upon us, the gracious rain of God's inheritance; it is the public spring for all the thirsty, the common hospital for all the needy; all the streets of the church are paved with these stones. It is mercy that takes us out of the womb, feeds us in the days of our pilgrimage, furnishes us with spiritual provisions, closes our eyes in peace, and translates us to a secure resting-place. It is the first petitioner's suit, and the first believer's article, the contemplation of Enoch, the confidence of Abraham, the burden of the Prophetic Songs, the glory of the apostles, the plea of the penitent, the ecstasies of the reconciled, the believer's hosanna, the angel's hallelujah. It is the lode-star of the wandering, the ransom of the captive, the antidote of the tempted, the prophet of the living, and the effectual comfort of the dying. There would not be one regenerate saint upon earth, nor one glorified saint in heaven, if it were not for mercy.

G.S. Bowes (1869)

When all Thy mercies, O my God, my rising soul surveys,
Transported with the view I'm lost in wonder, love, and praise.

Through every period of my life Thy goodness I'll pursue;
And after death, in distant worlds, the glorious theme renew.

When nature fails, and day and night divide Thy works no more,
My ever-grateful heart, O Lord, Thy mercy shall adore. Amen.

Joseph Addison (1672-1719)

January 31st

The Lord bless and keep you: the Lord make His face shine upon you
and be gracious unto you: the Lord lift up His countenance upon you
and give you peace.
Numbers 6:24-26

When Jehovah blesses, it is after the manner of His sovereign Almightiness. What an ocean of blessedness is in it! *And keep you...* what safe keeping is that! *The Lord make His face to shine upon you...* what a shine is that! *And be gracious unto you...* what a grace is that! *The Lord lift up His countenance upon you...* oh to be countenanced of God! *And give you peace...* what a peace, *the peace of God which passes all understanding!*

C.H. Spurgeon (1834-1892)

You have been rejoicing in the inexhaustible grace of Jesus: now be *yourself* gracious! You have been in the presence of God, and God is love: now be *yourself* tender-hearted and affectionate! You have enjoyed the radiant fellowship of the Holy Spirit: now be *yourself* companionable and inspiring! If within the house of the Lord, I had been really enjoying the society of that holy Saviour who is Himself the fountain of all grace, surely I must thereafter be *myself* more gracious! If I had gazed upon the Love that will not let me go, surely I must thereafter be *myself* more loving! If I had reveled in the fellowship of the Comforter, surely there can be no soul beneath the stars to whom I can henceforth deny my own sympathy and friendship.

F.W. Boreham (1871-1959)

May the grace of Christ our Saviour, and the Father's boundless love,
with the Holy Spirit's favor, rest upon us from above.
Thus we may abide in union with each other and the Lord,
and possess, in sweet communion, joys which earth cannot afford.
John Newton (1725-1807)

February

February 1st

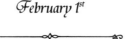

Peace I leave with you; My peace I give unto you.
John 14:27

Peace of heart lies in perfect resignation to God's will. *Martha, Martha, thou art careful and troubled about many things; but one thing is needful.* True simplicity, that calmness which results from submission to whatever God wills, patience and forbearance towards the faults of others, frankness in confessing your faults, accepting reproof, and receiving counsel—these are the graces which will tend to your sanctification.... Leave all in His Hands, and offer all up to Him beforehand. From the moment you give up all self-will, and seek absolutely nothing but what He wills, you will be free from all your restless anxiety and forecasting.... Give yourself up to God, and you will be at rest, and filled with the joys of His Holy Spirit!

François de la Mothe Fénelon (1651-1715)

Here is an assurance that not at holy times and welcome intervals only, not only in the dust of death, but in the dust of life there is prepared for you the peace of God. It is found in Him, cultivated by intercourse with Him. It is *the secret of His presence.* Amidst the circumstances of your life, which are the expression of His will, He can maintain it.

H.C.G. Moule (1841-1920)

Drop Thy still dews of quietness, till all our strivings cease;
Take from our souls the strain and stress,
And let our ordered lives confess
    The beauty of Thy peace.

Breathe through the heats of our desire Thy coolness and Thy balm;
Let sense be dumb, let flesh retire;
Speak through the earthquake, wind and fire,
    O still small voice of calm!

J.G. Whittier (1807-1892)

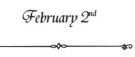

February 2nd

Faith, if it has not works, is dead.
James 2:17

Faith is a divine work in us. It changes us and makes us to be born anew of God; it kills the old Adam and makes altogether different people in heart and spirit and mind and powers, and it brings with it the Holy Spirit. Oh, it is a living, busy, active, mighty thing, this faith; and so it is impossible for it not to do good works incessantly. It does not ask whether there are good works to do, but before the question rises, it has already done them, and is always at the doing of them. Anyone who does not these works is a faithless person.

Faith is a living, daring confidence in God's grace, so sure and certain that we would stake our lives on it a thousand times. This confidence in God's grace, and knowledge of it, makes us bold and happy in dealing with God and all His creatures; and this is the work of the Holy Spirit in faith. Hence a person is ready and glad, without compulsion, to do good to everyone, to serve everyone, to suffer everything, in love and praise to God who has shown this grace; and thus it is impossible to separate works from faith, quite as impossible as to separate heat and light from fires.... Pray God to work faith in you; else you will remain forever without faith, whatever you think or do.

Martin Luther (1483-1546)

It is necessary to do good works, not in order to merit grace thereby, but because of the will of God....The Holy Spirit is received through faith, and hearts are renewed and put on new affections so that they can accomplish good works.

Confession of Augsburg (1530)

Faith is the mother of good will and righteous action.

Ambrose (340-397)

February 3rd

I give unto them eternal life; and they shall never perish,
neither shall any man pluck them out of My hand.
John 10:28

Here is preservation secured. That "never" includes time and eternity, it includes living and dying, it includes the mount and the valley, the tempest and the calm. *In every state secure, kept by the eternal Hand.* If God has given you eternal life, that life comprehends all the future.... You have an existence that will run parallel with the existence of the Deity and eternal life! As long as there is a Christ, there shall be a happy soul, and you shall be that happy soul. As long as there is a God there shall be a beatified existence, and you shall enjoy existence, for Jesus gives you eternal life. Come, mighty angel, plant thy foot upon the sea and upon the land, and swear by Him that liveth that time shall be no more, for even then every Christian shall still live because Christ gives unto them eternal life. We shall be in His hand forever, we shall be in His heart forever, we shall be in His very self forever – one with Him, and none shall pluck us thence.

Charles H. Spurgeon (1834-1892)

Arise, my soul, arise; shake off thy guilty fears;
The bleeding Sacrifice in my behalf appears:
Before the throne my Surety stands,
My name is written on His hands.
My God is reconciled; His pardoning voice I hear:
He owns me for His child; I can no longer fear:
With confidence I now draw nigh,
And "Father, Abba, Father," cry.

Charles Wesley (1707-1788)

Feelings have to do with my fluctuating condition. Faith has to do with Christ's eternally enduring sacrifice.

Anonymous

February 4th

Be careful for nothing; but in everything by prayer and supplication with thanksgiving let your requests be made known unto God.

Philippians 4:6

Do we fail to be anxious for nothing, and to bring *everything by prayer and supplication with thanksgiving* before God? We may bring nine difficulties out of ten to Him, and try to manage the tenth ourselves, and the one little difficulty, like a small leak that runs the vessel dry, is fatal to the whole. Like a small breach in a city wall, it gives entrance to the power of the foe. But if we fulfill the conditions, He is certainly faithful, and instead of our having to keep our hearts and minds – our affections and thoughts – we shall find them kept for us. The peace which we can neither make nor keep will itself, as a garrison, keep and protect us from the cares and worries which strive to enter in vain.

Hudson Taylor (1832-1905)

The peace of God, which passes all understanding, shall keep your hearts and minds through Christ Jesus.

Philippians 4:7

The mind on all such occasions is its own greatest troubler. It is apt to let loose its passions of fear and sorrow, which arouse innumerable perplexing thoughts, until it is carried utterly out of its own power. But in this state a contemplation of the glory of Christ will restore and compose the mind, bring it into a sedate, quiet frame, wherein faith will be able to say to the winds and waves of distempered passions, *Peace, be still,* and they shall obey it.

John Owen (1616-1683)

'Tis what I know of Thee, my Lord and God,
That fills my soul with peace, my lips with song.
Horatius Bonar (1808-1889)

43

Blessed are the people that know the joyful sound: they shall walk,
O Lord, in the light of Thy countenance.
Psalm 89:15

The Psalmist praises God! The circumstances were dark; never in all of Hebrew history had they been blacker and more ominous. The throne of David was gone, the monarchy was in ruins, the surviving kings languished in exile, the people were scattered.... But they that know the *joyful sound* shall be admitted nearer than Moses, so as to see the glory of God's face or brightness of His countenance. The light of God's glory shall not be terrible to them, but easy and sweet, so that they may dwell in it and walk in it; and it shall be to them instead of the light of the sun; for the sun shall no more be their light by day, nor the moon by night, but God shall be their everlasting light.

Jonathan Edwards (1703-1758)

They shall walk in the light of Thy countenance. And what is that holy walking which God's Spirit enables all His people to observe? It is a continued, progressive motion from sin to holiness; from all that is evil to every good word and work. And the self-same *light of God's countenance* in which you, O believer, are enabled to walk, and which at first gave you spiritual feet wherewith to walk, will keep you in a walking and working state to the end of your warfare.

A.M. Toplady (1740-1778)

In John Bunyan's (1628-1688) *Pilgrim's Progress*, as Faithful passed through the Valley of the Shadow of Death, he was not terrorized because he was so happily employed in singing to himself the Psalms.

Sovereign Father, heavenly King, Thee we now presume to sing;
Glad Thine attributes confess, glorious all, and numberless.

Charles Wesley (1707-1788)

The one who is dependable in a very small matter is dependable also in a large deal.
Luke 16:10 (Williams)

It is one of the features of Christian obedience that it consists not simply in certain individual actions, but rather in the temper and frame of mind which leads to those actions.... Obedience is not merely intended for great emergencies, or to attract the gaze and admiration of the multitude; it is meant for everyday life, we are to take up a daily cross. It is intended that in the use of daily prayer and other means of grace, we should exemplify the temper of a "person of God" in those many little things which continually ruffle the temper, excite the pride, tempt the covetousness, and stir up the uncharitableness of our natural dispositions. On these occasions let us continually practice *the soft answer which turns away wrath*; let us strive not be puffed up, nor to behave ourselves unseemly; let us not be laying up treasures for ourselves upon earth; let us not be easily provoked, nor be thinking evil – and be assured that these apparently trifling occurrences will afford the happiest discipline for our souls. They will often require much watchfulness and prayer on our part; we shall not be encouraged in them by the admiration or applause of the world, as when making some splendid sacrifice. And having been faithful in that which is least, we shall be enabled to be faithful also in that which is much....

We should be influenced on all occasions by a desire to do that which is well pleasing in His sight. It will then be the habit of our heart and mind, to seek to obey His commandments in all things; to be faithful in that which is least, in those little everyday occurrences of which the world around us will never be informed, as well as in that which is much, in those splendid actions and great sacrifices.

Francis Fulford (1803-1868)

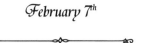

February 7th

Lay up for yourselves treasures in heaven.
Matthew 6:20

There is such a thing as laying up in heaven as truly as there is laying up on earth: if it were not so, our Lord would not have said so. Money spent in the work of God, He marks down in the Book of Remembrance and considers as laid up in heaven. Treasures laid up on earth never can afford spiritual joys. Treasures laid up in heaven bring along with them peace and joy in the Holy Spirit even now; and in the dying hour draw forth thanksgiving that we were permitted and counted worthy to serve the Lord with the means which He was pleased to entrust to us as stewards.

George Müller (1805-1898)

My friends, do not fall prey to the delusions of Mammon. Whatever prospects it may open to you, do not believe the impotent idol. Its golden mountains are but the ocean's foam; its paradises deceptive phantoms. The only really beautifying good upon earth is the peace of God. Follow after this with all your energies; it is worthy of the most serious efforts and endeavours. Sacrificing the peace of God to a carnal dream is the extreme of madness and infernal deception. Though I possessed the whole world, what should I be but a poor, empty, unhappy creature, if I could not console myself with the love of God.

F. W. Krummacher (1796-1869)

Take my silver and my gold; not a mite would I withhold;
Take my intellect and use every power as Thou shalt choose.
Take my hands and let them move at the impulse of Thy love;
Take my feet and let them be swift and beautiful for Thee.
Take my will, and make it Thine – it shall be no longer mine.
Take my heart, it is Thine own; it shall be Thy royal throne.
Frances Havergal (1836-1879)

February 8th

A new commandment I give unto you, that you love one another;
as I have loved you.

John 13:34

A nd yet the commandment to *love your neighbor as yourself is* as old as the Bible, and was enjoined upon the Jewish people almost as soon as they were free from the yoke of the Egyptians. In what sense then is it new? Human selfishness and pride had hidden and buried it.... Jesus unburies the divine jewel, raises it from the grave which human depravity had dug for it, purges it from the thick crust of self-worship with which tradition and self-will had wrapped it round. Then lifting it on high to catch the fullness of divine glory reflected from His own noble and matchless life of love, He commands His disciples to wear the bright and beautiful badge as the distinctive token of their love and loyalty to Himself -- *By this shall all people know that you are my disciples if you have love one to another.*

Richard Hooker (1554-1600)

> Blest be the tie that binds our hearts in Christian love;
> The fellowship of kindred minds is like to that above.
>
> Before our Father's throne we pour our ardent prayers:
> Our fears, our hopes, our aims are one, our comforts and our cares.
>
> We share each other's woes, each other's burdens bear;
> And often for each other flows the sympathizing tear.
>
> One glorious hope revives our courage by the way;
> While each in expectation lives and longs to see the day,
>
> When from all toil and pain and sin we shall be free,
> And perfect love and friendship reign through all eternity.

John Fawcett (1740-1817)

February 9th

This do in remembrance of Me.
1 Corinthians 11: 24

Whatsoever you do, in word or deed, do all in the name of the Lord Jesus.
Colossians 3: 17

One of these commands is taken from the institution of the holiest act of Christ's church; the other command is taken from a series of practical directions to do our work rightly in ordinary life. And yet the two commands are precisely the same.... Every act of our life is to be done from the same motive as that of Holy Communion. *This do in remembrance of Me.* And in like manner, *Whatsoever you do, do all in the name of the Lord Jesus.* Do all for the sake of the character of Him whom you love, giving thanks unto God and the Father by Him.... In Communion it is the *remembrance* of the Lord, in ordinary life it is *in the name of the Lord Jesus.* There is no action of life which is too great to bow to the influence of *This do in remembrance of Me*; and there is no action of life which is too small to be turned into a solemn sacrament.... If you want *to live* in this world, doing the duty of life, knowing the blessings of it, doing your work heartily, remember that the one power whereby you can so act is that all shall be consecrated to Christ and done for His sake! -- to have Jesus Christ for our Lord, to make His will our law, His love our motive, His pattern our example, His glory our end.

Alexander Maclaren (1826-1910)

In Thee all fullness dwelleth, all grace and power divine
The glory that excelleth, O Son of God, is Thine;
We worship Thee, we bless Thee, to Thee, O Christ, we sing;
We praise Thee, and confess Thee our glorious Lord and King.

Frances Havergal (1836-1879)

February 10th

⋯⋯⋯⋯

He shall give you another Comforter, that He may abide with you for ever.
John 14:16

The disciples' fears had gone very deep. Christ was leaving them; they were bewildered. They felt unsheltered, forlorn and terrified. They were but a weak handful. There was a need here for a greater tenderness than He had ever given.

I go unto my Father. This truth had sunk deep into the consciousness of the group already feeling its forlornness, but He continues, *I will not leave you comfortless. I will pray the Father, and He shall give you another Comforter, that He may abide with you forever; even the Spirit of truth.* So, they would lose the sense of losing: Christ's presence would be made real by the Spirit. This was the only thing that saved the disciples from dispersion after the Crucifixion. It was what saved the early church in the times of terrible persecution and harassment... the comfort of the Holy Spirit. Christ's presence was everywhere with them, tender, real, strong.

A Comforter means not only one who administers whispers of consolation in sorrow, but one who, by His presence, makes strong. By reason of the unity of the Godhead, Jesus and the Spirit whom He sends are inseparable, and so indissolubly united that where the Spirit is, there is Christ, and where Christ is, there is the Spirit. Enough for them and enough for us, to know that we have Christ in the Spirit and the Spirit in Christ.

Alexander Maclaren (1826-1910)

> Most tender Spirit! Mighty God!
> Sweet must Thy Presence be,
> If loss of Jesus can be gain,
> So long as we have Thee!
>
> Frederick W. Faber (1814-1863)

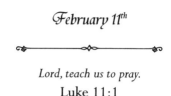

Lord, teach us to pray.
Luke 11:1

Jesus gives us a pattern of prayer. It is addressed to the Father. Our prayers are after the pattern only when they are free, unembarrassed, confident, and utterly frank whispers of a child to its father. Confidence and love should wing the darts which are to reach heaven. "Abba, Father" is the essence of all prayer. Nothing more is needed.

Alexander Maclaren (1826-1910)

> Prayer is the simplest form of speech that infant lips can try;
> Prayer the sublimest strains that reach the Majesty on high.
>
> O Thou by Whom we come to God, the Life, the Truth, the Way,
> The path of prayer Thyself hast trod -- Lord, teach us how to pray!
>
> We perish if we cease from prayer; O grant us power to pray!
> And when to meet Thee we prepare, Lord, meet us by the way.
> James Montgomery (1771-1854)

If you are seeking fine ideas in your prayer and amusing yourself with complicated thoughts, you are making an idol of yourself; you are using time that should be sacred for your own satisfaction. In flattering yourself that you have beautiful sentiments, you are offering a sacrifice to the idol of your own vanity. In prayer let self become nothing, and when we speak of our prayer, let us relate our thoughts humbly; and if there are any thoughts that seem to us fine, let us be distrustful of them, lest they were suggested by vainglory or the devil himself. And because there is always this possibility, whenever we think we have a fine inspiration we must humble ourselves utterly.

Vincent de Paul (1580-1660)

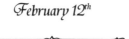

February 12th

Watch and pray lest you enter into temptation.
Mark 14:38

We find Jesus engaging in special prayer when about to enter into temptation. The greatest scene of prayer in His life is undoubtedly Gethsemane. As we enter that garden after Him, we fear almost to look -- it is so sacred and so passes our understanding; and we tremble as we listen to the prayers rising from the ground where He lies. Never were prayers heard like these. We cannot fathom them; yet much may be learned from them. He prayed on this occasion before entering into temptation.... It was the commencement of His final conflict with the powers of wickedness in earth and hell. But He equipped Himself by prayer in the garden beforehand, and so was able to go through all that followed with perfect success. His strength was the strength of prayer. What a contrast was presented on that occasion by the weakness of the disciples! For them also the hour and the power of darkness began at the gate of Gethsemane; but it was an hour of disaster and ignominious defeat. Why? Because they were sleeping when they ought to have been praying. *Watch and pray*, He had said, bending over their prostrate forms, *lest ye enter into temptation*. But they heeded not; and so, when the hour of temptation came, they fell. Alas! their experience has often been ours also. The only armour in which temptation can be successfully met is prayer; and, when the enemy is allowed to come upon us before we have buckled it on, we have not a chance of standing.

James Stalker (1848-1927)

From every stormy wind that blows,
From every swelling tide of woes,
There is a calm, a sure retreat:
'Tis found beneath the mercy seat.

Hugh Stowell (1799-1865)

Let him who boasts, boast of the Lord.
2 Corinthians 10:17 (Moffatt)

This is the true and perfect glorying in God, when we are not lifted up on account of our own righteousness, but know ourselves to be wanting in true righteousness and to be justified by faith alone in Christ. Paul despises his own righteousness, and seeks the righteousness which is through Christ, even that which is from God in faith. Here all pride falls to the ground. Nothing is left for boasting; your whole hope consists in living henceforth the life which is in Christ. You have not known God through righteousness on your part, but God has known you on account of His goodness; you have not apprehended Christ through your virtue, but Christ has apprehended you through His coming.

Basil of Caesarea (329-379)

> To God be the glory, great things He hath done,
> So loved He the world that He gave us His Son.
> Who yielded His life an atonement for sin,
> And opened the Life-gate that all may go in.
>
> O perfect redemption, the purchase of blood,
> To every believer the promise of God;
> The vilest offender who truly believes,
> That moment from Jesus a pardon receives.
>
> Praise the Lord! Praise the Lord! Let the earth hear His voice.
> Praise the Lord! Praise the Lord! Let the people rejoice.
> Oh come to the Father through Jesus the Son,
> And give Him the glory – great things He hath done.
> Fanny Crosby (1820-1915)

Give unto the Lord the glory due unto his name
Psalm 96:8

February 14th

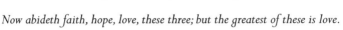

Now abideth faith, hope, love, these three; but the greatest of these is love.
1 Corinthians 13:13

The spectrum of love has nine ingredients: you will observe that all are in relation to me, in relation to life, in relation to the known today and the near tomorrow, and not to the unknown eternity.

PATIENCE – *Love suffers long.*

KINDNESS – *And is kind.*

GENEROSITY – *Love envies not.*

HUMILITY – *Love vaunts not itself, is not puffed up.*

COURTESY – *Does not behave itself unseemly.*

UNSELFISHNESS – *Seeks not her own.*

GOOD TEMPER – *Is not easily provoked.*

GUILELESSNESS – *Thinks no evil.*

SINCERITY – *Rejoiceth not in iniquity, but rejoiceth in truth.*

These nine ingredients make up the supreme gift, the stature of the perfect person. Love is patience. This is the normal attitude of love. Kindness is losing no chance of giving pleasure. Generosity is the grace we need to be fortified with, coupled with humility. Envying is the most despicable of all the unworthy moods which cloud a Christian's soul. Courtesy is love in society, love in relation to etiquette. Unselfishness -- there is no greatness in things; the only greatness is unselfish love. Good temper -- the compatibility of ill temper and high moral character is one of the strangest and saddest problems of ethics. Guilelessness is the great secret of personal influence. Sincerity is the self-restraint which refuses to make capital out of others' faults; the love which delights not in exposing the weaknesses of others, the sincerity of purpose which endeavors to see things as they are, and rejoices to find them better than suspicion feared or calumny denounced.

Henry Drummond (1851-1897)

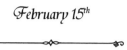

The fruit of the Spirit is love.
Galatians 5:22

There is no heart so dry, so cold, so shut up, as a heart which loves itself alone. There is no heart so tender, open, alive, sweet, lovable and loving, as a heart possessed and filled with the Love of God.

François de la Mothe Fénelon (1651-1715)

The one who does not love believes in vain, even if what they believe is true; they hope in vain, even if what they hope for is generally agreed to pertain to true happiness, unless they believe and hope for this: that they may through prayer obtain the gift of love.... Now this is the true faith of Christ which the Apostle Paul commends: faith that works through love.

Augustine of Hippo (354-430)

Without charity the outward work profits not at all; but whatever is done of charity be it ever so little and despised, becomes wholly fruitful. For God weighs rather the means of the worker than the work that one does. A person does much that loves much. A person does well that serves the community rather than one's own will. Often it seems to be charity, and is rather carnality because natural inclination, self-will, hope of requital, desire of gain, will seldom be away. One that has true and perfect charity seeks oneself in nothing, but only desires in all things that God alone should be glorified. That person also envies none, because they love no private joy; neither will they rejoice in themselves, but wish above all blessings to be made happy in God. To no one do they attribute anything that is good, but refer it all unto God, from whom as Fountain all things flow, and in whom as End all the saints do rest in fruition.

Thomas à Kempis (1380-1471)

February 16th

The fruit of the Spirit is... joy, peace.

Galatians 5:22

Love is the fruitful mother of bright children: joy, peace, longsuffering. These will dwell in our hearts if Love, their mighty mother, be there. If we are without her, we shall be without her children.

Alexander Maclaren (1826-1910)

The fruit of the Spirit is joy in Jesus. Many years ago a martyr wrote in his last letter: Who will believe that which I now state? In a dark hole, I have found cheerfulness; in a place of bitterness and death, I have found rest and the hope of salvation. Where others weep, I have found laughter; where others fear, I have found strength. In a state of misery I have had great pleasures; in a lonely corner, I have had glorious company; in the hardest bonds perfect peace. In all these things Jesus has granted me joy and peace. He is with me.

Biblical Illustrator (1887)

Like a river glorious is God's perfect peace,
Over all victorious is its bright increase;
Perfect, yet it floweth fuller every day,
Perfect, yet it groweth deeper all the way.
    Hidden in the hollow of His blessed hand,
    Never foe can follow, never traitor stand;
    Not a surge of worry, not a shade of care,
    Not a blast of hurry touch the spirit there.
Stayed upon Jehovah, hearts are fully blest –
Finding as He promised, perfect peace and rest.
    Every joy or trial falleth from above,
    Traced upon our dial by the Sun of Love;
    We may trust Him fully all for us to do—
    They who trust Him wholly find Him wholly true.

Frances Havergal (1836-1879)

February 17th

The fruit of the Spirit is… long-suffering, gentleness, goodness.
Galatians 5:22

Long-suffering is a patience. In every station and through every stage of life we are involved in troubles. So necessary is self-possession, that a person without it resembles a ship without a rudder, left to the mercy of the winds, over which the pilot has no command. Patience stands opposed to irritability of temper, undue eagerness of expectation, fretfulness under sufferings, and weariness in well-doing. The Holy Spirit is our Great Teacher, by whose gracious influence we become conformed to the will of God.

Biblical Illustrator (1887)

Gentleness is love in society. It is love in relation to those around it. It is that cordiality of aspect, and that soul of speech, which assures us that kind and earnest hearts may still be met with here below. It is that quiet influence which, like the scented flame of an alabaster lamp, fills many a home with light and warmth, and fragrance altogether…. It is tenderness of feeling. It is warmth of affection. It is promptitude of sympathy. It is love in all its depths and all its delicacy. It is everything included in that matchless grace -- the gentleness of Christ….

Goodness is love in action, with its hand at the plough, with the burden on its back. It is love carrying medicine to the sick and food to the famished. It is love reading the Bible to the blind and explaining the gospel to the felon in his cell. It is love at the Sunday school class, at the hovel door, or sailing far away in the missionary ship. But whatever the task it undertakes, it is still the same – love following His footsteps, *who went about continually doing good.*

J. Hamilton (1814-1867)

February 19th

The fruit of the Spirit is… faith, meekness, temperance.
Galatians 5:22, 23

Our faithfulness is first of all to our God: sincerity in His service, unreserved obedience to His revealed will, and an inflexible adherence to the profession of the gospel. And we must be faithful to others; this requires truth in our words, justice in our actions, steadfastness in our engagements, a conscientious discharge of all our duties. Faithfulness is necessary to the credit of religion and the honour of Christ. It is the Spirit's fruit to be seen in us.

John Thornton (1826)

Meekness describes our attitude of mind and soul to Deity. When the Bible speaks of Moses as being the meekest man, it describes the disposition of his bearing to Deity, not to other people. Furthermore, it is not weakness. *Blessed are the meek, for they shall inherit the earth*, were the words of the Saviour. A person in whose soul is developed the filial fear of God – in whose soul is the inner strength which enables one in the face of all opposition to do right even at the cost of one's life – is a person fitted to possess the earth. Meekness connects us to God, and this is priceless.

Biblical Illustrator (1887)

Temperance is love taking exercise, enduring hardness, seeking to become healthful and athletic, striving for mastery in all things and bringing the body under. It is love with girt loins, dusty feet, and blistered hands. It is love with glowing cheek grown so hardy that it bears all things, believes all things, hopes all things, endures all things.

J. Hamilton (1814-1867)

February 19th

May your hand be ready to help me.
Psalm 119:173

Short Bible prayers are just what we want in days when we are tired or hard-pressed.... There is much comfort in the little prayers of the Gospels. They could not be more little. There was Peter's, *Lord, save me;* the poor mother's, *Lord, help me;* sometimes even less, no prayer at all but only the briefest telling of the trouble, *My servant lies at home sick;* and less than that, a thought and a touch, *She said within herself, If I may but touch....* Again we hear of just a feeling, *They were troubled*, and a cry, *They cried out for fear* – that was all; but it was enough, so tender, so near, is the love of our Lord.

Amy Carmichael (1867-1951)

Prayer is the burden of a sigh, the falling of a tear,
the upward glancing of an eye, when none but God is near.

James Montgomery (1771-1854)

When the mouth prays, people hear; when the heart, God hears.

Joseph Hart (1574-1656)

Dart up thy soul in groans; thy secret groan
    shall pierce His ear, shall pierce His ear alone.
Dart up thy soul in vows; thy secret vow
    shall find Him out, where heaven alone shall know.
Dart up thy soul in sighs; thy whispering sigh
    shall rouse His ears, and fear no listener nigh.
Send up thy groans, thy sighs, thy closet vow:
There's none, there's none shall know, but heaven and thou.
Shoot up the bosom shafts of thy desire,
    feathered with faith, and double-forked with fire,
    and they will hit; fear not, where heaven bids come,
Heaven's never deaf, but when man's heart is dumb.

Francis Quarles (1592-1644)

February 20th

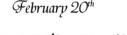

Holy men of God spoke as they were moved by the Holy Spirit.
2 Peter 1: 21

The Bible is the writing of the living God. Each letter was penned with an almighty finger. Each word dropped from the everlasting lips. Albeit that Moses was employed to write his histories with his fiery pen, God guided that pen. David touched his harp and let sweet psalms drop from his fingers; but God moved his hands over the living strings of his golden harp. Solomon sang canticles of love and gave words of consummate wisdom; but God directed his lips and made the preacher eloquent. If I follow the thundering Nahum, when his horses plough the waters; or Habakkuk, when he sees the tents of Cushan in affliction; if I read Malachi, when the earth is burning like an oven; if I turn to the smooth page of John, who tells of love; or the rugged chapters of Peter, who speaks of fire devouring God's enemies; if I turn aside to Jude, who launches forth anathemas upon the foes of God – everywhere I find God speaking. It is God's voice, not ours; the words of the Eternal, the Invisible, the Almighty, the Jehovah of ages. This is God's Bible; and when I see it, I seem to hear a voice springing up from it, saying, "I am the Book of God. Read me. I am God's writing. Study my page, for it was penned by God. Love me, for He is my Author, and you will see Him visible and manifest everywhere."

C.H. Spurgeon (1834-1892)

The Bible! hast thou ever heard
Of such a book? The author, God Himself;
The subject, God and man, salvation, life
And death – eternal life – eternal death --
Dread words! whose meaning has no ends, no bounds!
Most wondrous book; bright candle of the Lord!

Thomas Pollock (1836-1896)

February 21st

Search me, O God… and see if there be any wicked way in me,
and lead me in the way everlasting.

Psalm139:23, 24

Come, O Thou blessed Spirit, Who art the author of all grace and consolation, and represent sin to mine eyes in all its most odious colours, that I may feel a mortal and irreconcilable hatred to it. O represent the majesty and mercy of the blessed God in such a manner that my heart may be alarmed and that it may be melted. Convince me, O Thou blessed Spirit, of sin, of righteousness and of judgment. Show me that I have ruined myself; but that my help is found in God alone through Christ, in whom alone He will extend compassion and help to me. Take of Christ and show me His power to save. Show me His willingness to exert that power. Teach my faith to behold Him as extended on the cross, with open arms, with pierced, bleeding side; and so telling me in the most forcible language what room there is in His very heart for me. May I know what it is to have my whole heart subdued by love; so subdued as to be crucified with Him; as to be dead to sin and dead to the world, but alive unto God through Jesus Christ. In His power and love may I confide. To Him may I without any reserve commit my spirit. His image may I bear. His laws may I observe. His service may I pursue. And may I remain, through time and eternity, a monument of the efficacy of His gospel…. Accomplish in me all the good pleasure of Thy goodness; enrich me, O heavenly Father, with all the graces of Thy Spirit. Form me to the complete image of Thy dear Son; and then, for His sake, come unto me and manifest Thy gracious presence in my soul, till it is ripened for that state of glory for which all these operations are intended to prepare it. Amen.

Philip Doddridge (1702 -1751)

February 22nd

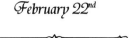

I am the light of the world; he that follows Me shall not walk in darkness,
but shall have the light of life.

John 8:12

Be it our chief pursuit to meditate upon the life of Jesus Christ. The doctrine of Christ excels all doctrines, and whoever has the Spirit would find therein the hidden manna.... Whoever would fully and feelingly understand the words of Christ must endeavour to conform one's whole life to Him. What does it profit you to lecture profoundly on the Trinity, if you are void of humility and thereby displeasing to the Trinity? Truly profound words do not make a person holy and just, but a virtuous life makes one dear to God. I had rather feel compunction than know its definition. If you know the whole Bible to the letter and the sayings of all philosophers, what would all that profit you without the love of God and grace? All is vanity except to love God and to serve Him only.... Vanity it is to seek after perishing riches, and to trust in them. Vanity is it also to solicit honours and climb to high degree. Vanity it is to follow the desires of the flesh and to desire that for which you must afterwards be punished. Vanity it is to covet a long life and neglect a good life. Vanity it is to mind only the present life and not foresee those things which are to come. Vanity it is to set your heart on that which speedily passes away, and not hasten to where everlasting joy abides.

Thomas à Kempis (1380-1471)

May the mind of Christ my Savior live in me from day to day,
by His love and pow'r controlling all I do and say.
May the love of Jesus fill me as the waters fill the sea;
Him exalting, self abasing—this is victory.
May His beauty rest upon me as I seek the lost to win,
and may they forget the channel, seeing only Him.

Kate Wilkinson (1859-1928)

February 23rd

God is to be trusted not to let you be tempted beyond your strength....
1 Corinthians 10:13 (Williams)

What a comfort to know with the utmost certainty that *God is faithful, who will not suffer us to be tempted above that we are able.* He knows what our ability is and cannot be mistaken. In whatever sufferings or temptations we are, our Great Physician never departs from us. He is about our bed and about our path. He observes every symptom of our distress that it may not rise above our strength. And He cannot be mistaken concerning us. He knows the souls and bodies which He has given us. He sees exactly how much we can endure with our present degree of strength. And if this is not sufficient, He can increase strength to whatever degree it pleases Him. Nothing is more certain than that, in consequence of His wisdom, justice, mercy, and faithfulness, He never will, He never can, suffer us to be tempted above the strength which He either has given already or will give as soon as we need it.... Take heed lest you fall into murmuring, "Surely no one's case is like mine; no one was ever tried like *me*." Yea, ten thousand. *There has no temptation taken you* but such as is *common* to humanity; such as you might reasonably expect, if you considered *what you are*: a sinful inhabitant of a mortal body, liable to numberless inward and outward sufferings – and considering *where you are*: in a shattered, disordered world, surrounded by evil. Consider this, and you will not repine at the common lot, the general condition of humanity.... Take heed lest you tempt God by thinking, "This is insupportable; this is too hard; I can never get through it; my burden is heavier than I can bear." Not so; unless something is too hard for God. He will not suffer you to be *tempted above that you are able.* He proportions the burden to your strength. If you want more strength, *ask and it shall be given you.*

John Wesley (1703-1791)

God is to be trusted not to let you be tempted beyond your strength, but when
temptation comes, to make a way out of it so that you can bear up under it.

1 Corinthians 10:13 (Williams)

*H*e *will with the temptation also make a way to escape that we may be able*
to bear it. The word which we render a *way to escape...* literally
means *a way out.* And this, God will either find or make; He that has
all wisdom, as well as all power in heaven and earth, can never be at
a loss how to do.

God is able to deliver *out of* temptation by taking away the very
ground of it. And He is equally able to deliver *in* the temptation;
which, perhaps, is the greatest deliverance of all. Suffering the
occasion to remain as it was, He can take away the bitterness of it;
so that it shall not be a temptation at all, but only an occasion of
thanksgiving. How many proofs of this have the children of God even
in their daily experience! How frequently are they encompassed
with trouble, or visited with pain or sickness! And when they cry
unto the Lord, at some times He takes away the cup from them: He
removes the trouble, or sickness or pain, and it is as though it never
had been. At other times, He does not make any outward change;
outward trouble or pain or sickness continues, but the consolation
of the Holy One so increases as to overbalance them all, and we can
boldly declare: "Labour is rest, when Thou, my God, are here."

Let us receive every trial with calm resignation, and with humble
confidence that He who has all power, all wisdom, all mercy, and all
faithfulness, will support us in every temptation; so that in the end all
things shall work together for good, and we shall happily experience
that all these things were for our profit, that we *might be partakers of*
His holiness.

John Wesley (1703-1791)

Show forth the praises of Him who hath called you
out of darkness into His marvelous light.
1 Peter 2:9

O could I speak the matchless worth,
 O could I sound the glories forth,
Which in my Saviour shine!
I'd sing His glorious righteousness,
And magnify the wondrous grace
Which made salvation mine.

I'd sing the characters He bears,
And all the forms of love He wears,
Exalted on His throne;
In loftiest songs of sweetest praise,
I would to everlasting days
Make all His glories known.

Soon the delightful day will come
When my blest Lord will bring me home,
And I shall see His face;
Then with my Saviour, Brother, Friend,
A blest eternity I'll spend,
Triumphant in His grace.

Samuel Medley (1738-1799)

Justin Martyr (103-166) wanders in search of the highest wisdom, knowledge of God. He tries a stoic, who tells him his search is in vain. He turns to a philosopher, whose mercenary tone quenches any hope of assistance from him. He appeals to a third, who requires the preliminary knowledge of music, astronomy and geometry. He applies to a follower of Plato, under whose guidance he begins to cherish some hope. But in a memorable hour, when earnestly groping after the path, he is met by a nameless old man, who discourses to him about Jesus Christ. Without any more ado, he is at the end of his quest. "Straightway," says Justin, "a flame was kindled in my soul."

Samuel Wilberforce (1805-1873)

February 26th

Seek His face continually.
1 Chronicles 16:11

I have resolved to pray more and to pray always, to pray in all places where quietness invites; in the house, on the highway and on the street; and to know no street or passage in this city that may not witness that I have not forgotten God.

Thomas Browne (1605-1682)

I fell into the habit of talking with God on every occasion. I talk myself asleep at night, and open the morning talking with Him.

Horace Busnell (1802-1876)

It is of great profit to know that it is not necessary to raise one's self to heaven in order to converse with our divine Father and find happiness with Him, nor to elevate our voice so as to be heard; God is so near that He hears the slightest whisper from our lips and the most secret thought. We have no need of wings to go in search of Him; let us enter into the solitude and look within us; it is there that He is. Let us talk with Him in great humility, but also with love, like children talking with their Father, confidently telling Him our troubles and begging Him to help us; and recognising, above all, that we are not worthy to bear the name of His children.

Teresa of Avila (1515-1582)

The greatest thing anyone can do for God and for people is to pray. You can do more than pray after you have prayed, but you cannot do more than pray until you have prayed. Prayer is striking the winning blow... service is gathering up the results.

S. D. Gordon (1859-1936)

Lord, I am blind and helpless, stupid and ignorant. Cause me to hear; cause me to know; teach me to do; lead me. Amen.

Henry Martyn (1781-1812)

February 27th

Behold, I stand at the door and knock: if any one hear My voice and open the door,
I will come in to him, and will sup with him, and he with Me.

Revelation 3:20

After Holman Hunt (1827-1910) painted his famous picture of the thorn-crowned Lord knocking at the door, a friend commented, "Hunt, you have made one mistake here. There is no handle on the door." "No," replied Hunt, "that is not a mistake; that is the door of the human heart, and it must be opened from the inside."

> For in every heart that liveth is that strange, mysterious door—
> There the pierced hand still knocketh,
> And with ever-patient watching... still thy God is waiting there.
> Harriet Beecher Stowe (1812-1896)

God will not go into the house of a person that did not want Him; that would be a mockery. He will not break open your door to walk in; He may send His winds, and storm and lightning to beat your house about your ears, but He will not walk in then. He will come when you want Him. He has been trying all the time to get in, but He will not force His way in. *If anyone will hear My voice and open the door, I will come in and speak with him, and he with Me. I will sit down at his hearth with him, and then he will come up and sit down on My throne.* Oh, the glory of Christ in giving! There is no condescension about Christ, none; the devotion of Christ is the devotion of His Father made visible to us.

George MacDonald (1824-1903)

> O Jesus, Thou art standing outside the fast-closed door,
> In lowly patience waiting to pass the threshold o'er
> O Lord, with shame and sorrow we open now the door;
> dear Saviour, enter, enter, and leave us nevermore. Amen.
> William W. How (1823-1897)

February 28th

Hold fast the form of sound words, which you have heard of me,
in faith and love which is in Christ Jesus.
2 Timothy 1:13

The church, though dispersed throughout the whole world, has received from the apostles and their disciples this faith:

She believes in one God, the Father Almighty, Maker of heaven and earth and the sea, and all things that are in them; and in one Christ Jesus, the Son of God who became incarnate for our salvation; and in the Holy Spirit who proclaimed through the prophets the dispensations of God; the birth from a virgin, the passion, the resurrection from the dead, and the ascension into heaven in the flesh of the beloved Christ Jesus our Lord; and His future manifestation from heaven in the glory of the Father *to gather all things in one*, and to raise up anew all flesh of the whole human race in order that to Christ Jesus, our Lord and God and Saviour and King, according to the will of the invisible Father, *every knee should bow, of things in heaven, and things in earth, and things under the earth, and that every tongue should confess* to Him; and that He should execute just judgment towards all, that He may send *spiritual wickedness* and the angels who transgressed and became apostates, together with the ungodly… into everlasting fire; but may, in the exercise of His grace, confer immortality on the righteous and holy, and those who have kept His commandments and have persevered in His love.

As I have already observed, the church having received this preaching and this faith -- although scattered throughout the whole world, yet as if occupying but one house -- carefully preserves it. She also believes these points just as if she had but one soul, and one and the same heart; and she proclaims them and hands them down with perfect harmony, as if she possessed only one mouth.

Irenaeus of Lyons (130-202)

February 29th

You must all live in harmony, be sympathetic, loving, tenderhearted, humble.
1 Peter 3:8 (Williams)

Reverence is the spirit of the Christian towards God, and sympathy is the spirit towards people. We speak of sympathy as a feeling *for* others, where it is in the fullest sense a feeling *with* others. It is from within – entering into the feelings of another and making them one's own. For the most part, we understand sympathy as a fellowship in suffering. The wonders of Christ's infinite compassion were indeed triumphs of human love rather than of Divine authority, and we discern with something of trembling awe what is meant by *the power of His resurrection and the fellowship of His sufferings*. The service of sympathy does cost us something, but it brings abundant compensation. St Paul told us the secret of his unmatched influence, *I became all things to all people.* He who sways others must be one with them, however far removed by personal gifts. For sympathy is not the communion of like with like, but the power of uniting things different in the embrace of a greater life.

Brooke Westcott (1825-1901)

Gifts from the hand are silver and gold; but the heart gives that which neither silver nor gold can buy. To be full of goodness, cheerfulness, sympathy, helpful hope, causes us to carry blessings of which we are as unconscious as a lamp of its shining.

Henry Ward Beecher (1813-1887)

Teach us the lesson Thou hast taught,
to feel for those Thy blood hath bought,
that every word, and deed and thought,
may work a work for Thee.

Godfrey Thring (1823-1903)

March

March 1st

Ask, and it shall be given you; seek and you shall find;
knock, and it shall be opened unto you.
Matthew 7:7, 8

*A*sk! that you may be filled with the treasures of His love, *seek!* that you may find the rich provision He has laid up for all, *knock!* that door after door in the many mansions of the Father's House may be opened unto you; until at last an entrance is ministered abundantly into the everlasting kingdom, and you go in with the King to the eternal feast.

Alexander Maclaren (1826-1910)

In order to make your prayer profitable and as earnest as you desire, it would be well from the beginning to figure yourself a poor, naked, miserable wretch, perishing of hunger, who knows but one Person of whom you can ask or hope for succour; or a sick person covered with sores and ready to die, unless some pitiful Physician will take you in hand and heal you. These are true representations of our condition before God. Your soul is more bare of heavenly treasure than that poor beggar is of earthly possessions; you need them more urgently, and there is none save God of whom you can ask or expect them. Your soul is infinitely more sin-sick than that sore-stricken patient, and God alone can heal you.... He is able for all this; but remember that He wills only to do when He is asked earnestly, and with real importunity.

François de la Mothe Fénelon (1651-1715)

My soul, ask what thou wilt, thou canst not be too bold; since His own blood for thee He spilt, what else can He withhold?

Anonymous

Let prayer be the key of the morning; and the bolt of the evening. Prayer is not conquering God's reluctance, but taking hold of God's willingness.

Phillips Brooks (1835-1893)

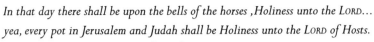

In that day there shall be upon the bells of the horses ,Holiness unto the LORD...
yea, every pot in Jerusalem and Judah shall be Holiness unto the LORD of Hosts.
Zechariah 14:20-21

Long ago a Hebrew prophet had a dream of a good time coming, when the City of God should be built on earth, and humanity should really work with Him and do His will through the whole breadth and reach of their daily lives. All life would be under one roof of God, all of it offered and dedicated to Him, its every-day tasks as well as its sacred corners. Is it not a beautiful and realizable dream, not in some distant heaven but on this very earth? To this end we must ask God to give us a new vision of the essential sacredness of all duty. Every honourable duty, even the humblest, like harnessing a horse or cooking a dinner, has something to do with God, a God-ward side to it, or it is not worth doing. All life is His. And holiness is doing the Will of God in everything.... Till His thirtieth year Jesus lived the life of a village carpenter. And in that humble and secular sphere He served God perfectly! The Carpenter of Nazareth made common things for God! Do not let us think of holiness as a small, narrow thing confined to one corner of life. Holiness is the same word, after all, as *wholesomeness* and *health*, and means the orderly happy working of every department of life. Holiness is a thing so big that it needs all the days of the week to show the different sides of it. It is written on the priest's robe. We all take that for granted. But it can and should be written on the bells of the horses too, on the ledger of the business person, on the tools of the workman, and on the student's books. It should be written on every pleasure we enjoy. And where it cannot be written, we should not be found.

Archibald Alexander (1772-1852)

March 3rd

Love is the fulfilling of the law.
Romans 13:10

We have been accustomed to be told that the greatest thing in the religious world is Faith.... If we have been told that, we may miss the mark. *The greatest of these is love,* says Paul. He was speaking of faith just a moment before and says, *If I have all faith so that I can remove mountains, and have not love, I am nothing.* Then he deliberately contrasts them, *Now abides Faith, Hope and Love,* and without a moment's hesitation the decision falls, *The greatest of these is Love.* But the hand that wrote this, when we meet it first, is stained with blood.

Love is the fulfilling of the law. In those days people were working their passage to heaven by keeping the Ten Commandments, and the hundred and ten other commandments which they had manufactured. Christ said, "I will show you a more simple way." If you do one thing, you will do these hundred and ten things without ever thinking about them. If you love, you will unconsciously fulfill the whole law. *You shall have no other gods before Me;* if people love God, they will not need to be told that. Would they ever dream of taking His name in vain if they loved Him? Would they not be too glad to have one day in seven to dedicate more exclusively to the object of their affection? They could not do anything else but honor their father and mother. You would insult them if you suggested that they should not steal. It would be superfluous to beg them not to bear false witness against their neighbor. You would never dream of urging them not to covet what their neighbors had. In this way, *Love is the fulfilling of the law.*
Henry Drummond (1851-1897)

Love is the very quintessence of the Gospel.
John Bunyan (1628-1688)

March 4th

The Spirit of God has made me, and the breath of the Almighty has given me life.
Job 33:4

We like to have an honorable pedigree. We are proud of a good ancestry, an ancestry whose character was goodness. But we do have an ancestry which goes back beyond nature, beyond maternity, beyond the flesh. We have a pedigree which is older than the mountains, older than the stars, older than the universe. We are come from good stock; we are branches of a high family tree; we are scions of a noble house not made with hands, eternal in the heavens. Nature is the parent of our flesh, but the Divine is the father of our spirits, and the Spirit of God has made us, and the breath of the Almighty has given us life.

George Matheson (1842-1906)

> Lord, what is man that Thou
> So mindful art of him? Or what's the son
> Of man, that Thou the highest heaven didst bow
>   And to our aid didst run?
> Man's but a piece of clay
> That's animated by thy heavenly breath,
> And when that breath Thou tak'st away,
>   We're clay again by death.
> Thou didst Thyself abase,
> And put off all Thy robes of majesty,
> Taking our nature to us Thy grace,
>   To save our life didst die.
> Lo! man is made now even
> With the blest angels, yea, superior far.
> Since Christ sat down at God's right hand in heaven.
>   And God and man one are.
> Thus all thy mercies man inherits
> Though not the least of them he merits.

Thomas Washbourne (1607-1687)

March 5ᵗʰ

Believe on the Lord Jesus Christ, and you shall be saved, and your house.
Acts 16:31

For if you will believe that the Lord Jesus is the Christ and that God has raised Him up from the dead, you shall be saved and shall be translated into Paradise. Wherefore, since He conducted the thief into Paradise, doubt not whether it be possible; for He, who in a single hour saved the believing thief on that holy Golgotha, will also save you, provided you believe.

Cyril of Jerusalem (315-386)

> My faith has found a resting place, not in device or creed:
> I trust the Ever-living One, His wounds for me shall plead.
> Enough for me that Jesus saves, this ends my fear and doubt;
> A sinful soul I come to Him, He'll never cast me out.
>
> My heart is leaning on the Word, the written Word of God:
> Salvation by my Savior's name, salvation thru His blood.
> I need no other argument, I need no other plea;
> It is enough that Jesus died, and that He died for me.

Lidie H. Edmunds (1851-1920)

I believe that Jesus Christ, very God, born of the Father in eternity, and also very man, born of the Virgin Mary, is my Lord; He has redeemed me, a lost and damned person, and has won and delivered me from all sins, from death and from the power of the devil, not with gold and silver, but with His holy and precious blood and with His innocent passion and death; so that I might be His own and might live under Him in His kingdom, and serve Him in everlasting righteousness, innocence and blessing, just as He rose from the dead, and lives and reigns in all eternity. This is a faithful saying.

Luther's Short Catechism (1529)

For none of us lives to himself.
Romans 14:7

Of all the good things in this world, the best are good people. The influence which goes out from the life of a good person is one of the most subtle and pervasive things in the world. People can weigh the moon, but they cannot weigh the influence of a good person. They can tell the distance of one star from another, but they cannot tell how far the influence of a good person's life will reach nor how long it will last.

Calvin Cutler (1791-1844)

There are no neutral characters. We are either the sower that sows and corrupts, or the light that splendidly illuminates and the salt that silently operates; but being dead or alive, every person speaks.

Thomas Chalmers (1780-1847)

It is in this life alone we can learn lessons of patience and self-denial; for there are no sick-beds to watch by, no sufferers to comfort, in the mansions of the Father's House.

George MacDonald (1824-1903)

Does the Lord Jesus Christ make you gentle and loving, faithful and unselfish, at home? The New Testament Christian is 'sweet at home.' Before we think of the evangelization of that neglected street, we remember that our duty within the walls of home is the Lord's first will for us, that we may glorify God there. No activities out of doors can compensate for the failure to manifest indoors the Lord Jesus Christ.

H.C.G. Moule (1841-1920)

The healing of the world is in its nameless saints. Each separate star seems nothing, but a myriad scattered stars break up the night, and make it beautiful.

Elizabeth Browning (1806-1861)

———◦◦———

Trust in the Lord with all your heart; and lean not unto your own understanding.
Proverbs 3:5

God who is able and willing to *take unto* Himself is no less able and willing to *keep for Himself*. Our willing offering has been made by His enabling grace. With the deepest consciousness that He has indeed taken our lives to be His very own, the need of His active and actual keeping of them in every detail and at every moment is most fully realized. Whatever we did really trust Him to keep, He has kept, and the un-kept things were never really entrusted. Sometimes we are led to trust in our trust. If Christ's keeping depends upon our trusting, and our continuing to trust depends upon ourselves, we are in no better or safer position than before. *This is the work of God that you believe in Him who He has sent.* And no less must it be the work of God that we go on believing, and that we go on trusting. Cease the effort and drop the burden, and entrust your *trust* to Him.

Frances Havergal (1836-1879)

> When over dizzy heights we go, one soft hand blinds our eyes,
> The other leads us safe and slow, Oh, love of God most wise!
> Nothing before, nothing behind; the steps of faith
> Fall on the seeming void, and find the rock beneath.
> J.G. Whittier (1807-1892)

Beware of despairing about yourself; you are commanded to put your trust in God and not in yourself.

Augustine of Hippo (354-430)

Sweet it is that our hope should rest in Him who is never shaken; should abide in Him who never changes; should bind us to Him who can hold us fast to Himself, who alone is the full contentment of the soul. "In Him is our being," the One who is love.

E.B. Pusey (1800-1882)

March 8th

Lord, I have called daily upon You, I have stretched out my hands unto You.
Psalm 88:9

Prayer is communication between God and us whereby we expound to Him our desires, joys and sighs, in a word, all the thoughts of our hearts. Every time we invoke the Lord, we must diligently strive to descend to the depth of our hearts and from there seek Him, and not only with the tongue.... If true prayer is nothing else than the pure affection of our hearts when we approach God, we must dismiss all thought of our own glory, all fancy of our own dignity and all self-confidence.... Knowledge of our misery must not bar our access to God, since prayer has not been instituted to raise us arrogantly before God nor to extol our dignity, but to confess with sighs our calamities, just as children expound with familiarity their complaints to their fathers. Such a sentiment should stimulate us to pray more.... By request we disclose before God our hearts' desires. By thanksgiving we acknowledge His benefits toward us.

John Calvin (1509-1564)

All my ways of expressing prayer are imperfect. In God's book, a look toward heaven or an uplifting of the eyes is set down as prayer: *In the morning will I direct my prayer unto You, and will look up* (Ps. 5:3). What is prayer but a pouring out of the soul to God? Faith will find another outlet if one be stopped. Feeling breaks out in looks when voice is lacking, just as smoke pours out of the windows when the door is shut. Dying Stephen looked up to heaven by the window of the soul to give notice that a poor friend was on his way, and that was prayer enough. If I were ready to sink into hell, I should wish no more than to send one longing look to heaven.

Samuel Rutherford (1600-1661)

March 9th

But when the Comforter is come... He will bear witness of Me.
John 15:26

There is no separate Gospel of the Holy Spirit. The plan of God is not to teach us about Christ as a first lesson, and then as a more advanced lesson, to lead us on into truth about the Holy Spirit apart from Christ. We do indeed need teaching about the blessed Spirit. But the more we learn about Him the more surely we shall learn this from Him, that His chosen and beloved work is just this -- to glorify the Lord Jesus Christ. He sheds an illuminating glory upon a heart, a face, an embrace – the beloved Jesus Christ, our Lord.

H.C.G. Moule (1841-1920)

> Come, Holy Spirit, heavenly Dove, with all Thy quickening powers;
> Come, shed abroad a Saviour's love, and that shall kindle ours.
>
> In vain we tune our formal songs, in vain we strive to rise;
> Hosannas languish on our tongues, and our devotion dies.
>
> And shall we then for ever live at this poor dying rate?
> Our love so faint, so cold to Thee, and Thine to us so great!
>
> Come, Holy Spirit, heavenly Dove, with all Thy quickening powers,
> Kindle a flame of sacred love in these cold hearts of ours.
> Isaac Watts (1674-1748)

All our knowledge, sense and sight lie in deepest darkness shrouded, till Thy Spirit breaks our night, with the beams of truth unclouded.
T. Clausnitzer (1618-1684)

Most tender spirit! Mighty God! Sweet must Thy prescence be, If loss of Jesus can be gain, so long as we have Thee!
Frederick W. Faber (1814-1863)

Forbear and forgive each other in any case of complaint.
Colossians 3:13 (Moffatt)

Eschew controversy as you would the entrance to hell itself. Let them have it their way. Let them talk. Let them write. Let them correct you. Let them judge and condemn you. You have not enough of the divine nature in you to be a controversialist. *He was oppressed and He was afflicted, yet He opened not His mouth. Who when He was reviled, reviled not again.*

Alexander Whyte (1836-1921)

Lord, heal me of this lust of mine of always vindicating myself.

Augustine of Hippo (354-430)

There was a day when I *died*. Died to George Müller, his opinions, preferences, tastes and will; died to the world, its approval or censure; died to the approval or blame even of my brethren or friends; and since then I have studied only to show myself approved unto God.

George Müller (1805-1898)

Turn your eyes unto yourself, and beware that you judge not the deeds of others. In judging others a person labors in vain, often errs and easily sins; but in judging and examining ourselves, we always labour fruitfully,

Thomas à Kempis (1380-1471)

Grant, O Lord, that my heart may neither desire nor seek anything but what is necessary for the fulfillment of Thy holy will. May health or sickness, riches or poverty, honors or contempt, humiliations, leave my soul in that state of perfect detachment to which I desire to attain – for Thy greater honor and Thy greater glory. Amen.

Ignatius Loyola (1491-1556)

He is my shield and the horn of my salvation, my high tower and my refuge.
2 Samuel 22:3

God is a perpetual refuge and security to His people. His providence is not confined to one generation; it is not one age only that tastes of His bounty and compassion. His eye never yet slept, nor has He suffered the little ship of His church to be swallowed up, though it has been tossed upon the waves. He has always been a haven to preserve us, a house to secure us; He has always had compassions to pity us and power to protect us; He has had a face to shine, when the world has had an angry countenance to frown. He brought Enoch home by an extraordinary translation from a brutish world; and when He was resolved to reckon with humanity for their brutish lives, He lodged Noah, the phoenix of the world, in an ark, and kept him alive as a spark in the midst of many waters. In all generations He is a dwelling-place to secure His people here or entertain them above. His providence is not wearied nor His care fainting; He never wanted will to relieve us, for *He has been our refuge,* nor ever can want power to support us, for *He is a God from everlasting to everlasting.* The church never wanted for a pilot to steer her and a rock to shelter her.

Stephen Charnock (1628-1680)

O worship the King, all glorious above;
O gratefully sing His power and His love;
Our Shield and Defender, the Ancient of Days,
Pavilioned in splendour, and girded with praise.

Frail children of dust, and feeble as frail,
In Thee do we trust, nor find Thee to fail:
Thy mercies how tender, how firm to the end,
Our Maker, Defender, Redeemer, and Friend.

Robert Grant (1785-1838)

I am the vine, you are the branches… without Me you can do nothing.
John 15:5

Christ Jesus said, "I, the living One who have so completely given Myself to you, am the Vine. You cannot trust Me too much. I am full of divine life and power." Christians, you are the branches of the Lord Jesus Christ. If there is in your heart the consciousness – "I am not a strong, healthy, fruit-bearing branch, I am not closely linked with Jesus, I am not living in Him as I should be" – then listen to His saying: "*I am the Vine*, I will receive you, I will draw you to Myself, I will bless you, I will strengthen you, I will fill you with My Spirit. I, the Vine, have taken you to be My branches, I have given Myself utterly to you; give yourselves utterly to Me. I have surrendered Myself as God absolutely to you, I became man and died for you that I might be entirely yours. Come and surrender yourselves entirely to be Mine."

What shall our answer be? Oh, let it be a prayer from the depths of our heart, that the living Vine shall so link each of us to Himself that we shall go away with our hearts singing: "He is my Vine and I am His branch – I want nothing more – now I have the everlasting Vine." Then when you are alone with Him, worship and adore Him, praise and trust Him, love Him and wait for His love. *You are my Vine, and I am your branch.* It is enough, my soul is satisfied. Glory to His blessed name!

Andrew Murray (1828-1917)

Take my life and let it be consecrated, Lord to Thee:
Take my moments and my days, let them flow in ceaseless praise.
Take my love, my God, I pour at Thy feet its treasures store;
Take myself and I will be, ever, only, all for Thee.

Frances Havergal (1836-1879)

March 13th

And forgive us our sins.
Luke 11:4

In this petition we come to the first sad note in the Lord's prayer. The first three petitions, angels and saints in heaven could offer. The fourth could have been used in Eden, for in innocence our first parents received their daily bread from God. But the fifth is only for sinners of our fallen race. It is a cry out of the depths; a cry which every mortal needs to make. Not to make it is to stay in one's sins. The path of penitence is the only path that leads toward the gates of heaven.

The word "and" in this petition is important. We need food and we pray to our Father, asking Him to give us what we need day by day. But though the wants of our body are supplied most abundantly, we should still perish for ever if that were all we received from heaven. God's most bountiful gifts are not enough; with these we must obtain also God's mercy. The prayer which pleads, "Father, give," must cry also, "Father, forgive." It is an essential link which binds together as in one the two petitions, "Give us this day our daily bread, *and* forgive us our debts." We must never rend them apart, but must always offer them in the same breath.

J.R. Miller (1840-1912)

Nothing more helps us forward in a good course than the frequent recognition of our sins.

John Chrysostom (347-407)

For a good confession three things are necessary: an examination of conscience, sorrow, and a determination to avoid sin.

Alphonsus Luguori (1696-1787)

Dear dying Lamb, thy precious blood shall never lose its power, till all the ransomed church of God be saved, to sin no more.

William Cowper (1731-1800)

March 14th

You shine as lights in the world.
Philippians 2:15

Give unbelievers the chance of believing through you. Consider yourselves employed by God; your lives the form of language in which He addresses them. Be mild when they are angry, humble when they are haughty; to their blasphemy oppose prayer without ceasing; to their inconsistency, a steadfast adherence to your faith.

Ignatius of Antioch (50-107)

Christians are the autograph letters of our Lord and bear His signature. The writing is clear, for we are manifestly declared to be *the epistle of Christ*. This document is a public one. Believers are the library for the world; they are Christian literature; each saint is a volume to expound the grace of God, known and read by everybody.

C.H. Spurgeon (1834-1892)

The Gospel of Christ is a revelation. It is not enough that it is a message of your lips; it must be the message of your life. The message will have power only as it is a lived message.

S.D. Gordon (1859-1936)

I would postpone heaven for many years, to have my fill of Jesus in this life, and to have occasion to offer Christ to my people, and to woo many people to Christ.

Samuel Rutherford (1600-1661)

Lord, speak to me, that I may speak in living echoes of Thy tone; as Thou hast sought, so let me seek Thy erring children lost and lone. O fill me with Thy fullness, Lord, until my very heart o'erflow in kindling thought and glowing word, Thy love to tell, Thy praise to show.

Frances Havergal (1836-1879)

March 15th

Now the God of hope fill you with all joy and peace in believing, that you may
abound in hope through the power of the Holy Spirit.

Romans 15:13

The God of hope fill you... in believing. Paul does not tell us what or whom we are to believe in. He takes that for granted, and his thought is fastened not on the object but on the act of faith. And he wishes to drive home to us that the attitude of trust is the necessary prerequisite condition of God's being able to fill a person's soul.... The best, the highest, the truly divine gifts which He is yearning to give to us all, cannot be given except there be consent, trust and desire for them. There must be a person's faith before there can be God's filling.

The God of hope fill you... through the power of the Holy Spirit. Surely He that made my spirit can touch my spirit; surely He who fills all things according to their capacity can Himself enter into and fill the spirit which is opened to Him by simple faith. He comes directly to, and speaks in, and moves upon, and moulds and blesses, the waiting heart.

The God of hope fill you... in believing, that you may abound in hope. Just as there was no need to say in whom it was that the Christian was to believe, so there is no room to define what it is that the Christian has a right to hope for. For one's hope is intended to cover all the future, the next moment, or tomorrow, or the dimmest distance where time has ceased to be and eternity stands unmoved.

Alexander Maclaren (1826-1910)

> The Lord has promised good to me, His word my hope secures;
> He will my shield and portion be, as long as life endures.
> Yea, when this flesh and heart shall fail, and mortal life shall cease,
> I shall possess within the veil, a life of joy and peace.
>
> John Newton (1715-1807)

March 16th

Praying always with all prayer and supplication in the Spirit.
Ephesians 6:18

We are to pray with all kinds of prayer *in the Spirit*. The Spirit suggests the substance of our prayers. The Spirit reveals the love and helpfulness of God, and so encourages us to present our many and deep needs to Him. The Spirit so identifies Himself with our case that He makes intercession for us. In other words, God's own heart pleads for us.

M .R. Vincent (1834-1922)

If you would endure with patience the adversities and miseries of this life, *Be a person of prayer.*
If you would acquire strength and courage to vanquish the temptations of the enemy, *Be a person of prayer.*
If you would know the wiles of Satan and defend yourself against his snares, *Be a person of prayer.*
If you would live with a happy heart, and pass lightly along the road of penance and sacrifice, *Be a person of prayer.*
If you would drive away vain thoughts and cares which worry the soul like flies, *Be a person of prayer.*
If you would nourish the soul with the sap of devotion and have it always filled with good thoughts and desires, *Be a person of prayer.*
Finally, if you would uproot from your soul all vices, and plant virtues in their place, *Be a person of prayer.*
For herein does a person receive the unction and grace of the Holy Spirit, who teaches all things.

Bonaventura (1221-1274)

Come Holy Spirit, heav'nly Dove, with all Thy quick'ning pow'rs;
Kindle a flame of sacred love in these cold hearts of ours.

Isaac Watts (1674-1748)

Be careful for nothing; but in everything by prayer and supplication with thanksgiving let your requests be made known to God.

Philippians 4:6

When Patrick (389-461) arrived in Ireland to begin his missionary career, he feared persecution from the king at Tara, and composed this striking prayer:

> At Tara today, may
> the strength of God pilot me, the power of God preserve me;
> the wisdom of God instruct me, the eye of God watch over me,
> the ear of God hear me, the Word of God give me sweet talk,
> the hand of God defend me, the way of God guide me.
>
> Christ be with me, Christ within me, Christ behind me,
> Christ before me, Christ under me, Christ over me,
> Christ on my right hand, Christ on my left hand,
> Christ on this side, Christ on that side, Christ at my back.
>
> Christ be in the heart of everyone to whom I speak,
> Christ in the mouth of every person who speaks to me,
> Christ in the eye of every person who looks upon me,
> Christ in the ear of every one who hears me at Tara today.

Live, and pray, and hope, and wait patiently, and do not despond; the promise stands invincible, that He will never leave us nor forsake us.

John Owen (1616-1683)

> No profit canst thou gain by self-consuming care;
> To Him commend they cause, His ear
> Attends the softest prayer.
> Thy everlasting truth, Father, Thy ceaseless love
> Sees all Thy children's wants, and knows
> What best for each will prove.
> Amen

Paul Gerhardt (1606-1676)

March 18th

———◇———

God forbid that I should glory, save in the cross of our Lord Jesus Christ.
Galatians 6:14

W̲hen I survey the wondrous Cross
    On which the Prince of glory died.
My richest gain I count but loss,
And pour contempt on all my pride.

Forbid it, Lord, that I should boast,
Save in the death of Christ my God;
All the vain things that charm me most
I sacrifice them to His blood.

See from His head, His hands, His feet,
Sorrow and love flow mingled down!
Did e'er such love and sorrow meet,
Or thorns compose so rich a crown?

Were the whole realm of nature mine,
That were a present far too small;
Love so amazing, so divine,
Demands my soul, my life, my all.

Isaac Watts (1674-1748)

In the cross is salvation, in the cross is life, in the cross is protection from enemies, in the cross is infusion of heavenly sweetness, in the cross is strength of mind, in the cross is joy of spirit, in the cross is the sum of virtue, in the cross is perfection of holiness: there is no health of soul nor hope of everlasting life, but in the cross. Take your cross therefore and follow Jesus and you shall go into life everlasting.

Thomas à Kempis (1379-1471)

God has made Him to be sin for us, who knew no sin; that we might be made the righteousness of God in Him.
2 Corinthians 5:21

Christ was a substitute for all who believe on Him as their Saviour. It was when He hung on the cross that He became the substitute and not during His life. *The Lord has laid on him the iniquity of us all. He suffered the just for the unjust.* He willingly took the place of the guilty sinner and bore the judgment of sin, that the sinner who believes on Him might not only be pardoned and cleared of guilt and its judgment, but become the righteousness of God in Him.

James H. Todd (1805-1869)

> Alas! and did my Saviour bleed? And did my Sovereign die?
> Would He devote that sacred head for sinners such as I?
>
> Was it for sins that I have done, He groaned upon the Tree?
> Amazing pity! Grace unknown! And love beyond degree!
>
> Well might the sun in darkness hide, and shut his glories in,
> When Christ, the mighty Maker, died for man the creature's sin.
>
> Thus might I hide my blushing face while His dear Cross appears;
> Dissolve my heart in thankfulness, and melt mine eyes to tears.
>
> But drops of grief can ne'er repay the debt of love I owe;
> Here, Lord, I give myself away – 'Tis all that I can do.
>
> Isaac Watts (1674-1748)

To see yourself a sinner is the start of salvation.

Augustine of Hippo (354-430)

It is only the heart broken with godly sorrow that sends forth a true confession.

Nathanael Hardy (1618-1670)

March 20ᵗʰ

Go to the village... and you will find a colt tethered on which no one ever
has sat.... If anyone asks, "Why are you untethering it?"
this is what you will say, "The Lord needs it."
Luke 19:30, 31 (Moffatt)

This statement is the fulfillment of a little, specific, minute, detailed prophecy -- *behold, your King comes unto you; He is just and having salvation; lowly and riding upon a donkey, and upon a colt the foal of a donkey....* That Christ should go into Jerusalem upon a donkey! This is not decorative talk, not mere flowery prophecy or incidental foretelling. What then? If God be careful of such crumbs of prophecy, such little detailed lines of prediction, what of the life of His children? Will He count the hairs upon your head and let the head itself be bruised? Is He careful about birds in the air and careless about lives redeemed by the blood of His Son?

The Lord has need of it. The Lord has a claim on all we possess: our souls, our bodies, our tongues, our time, our talents, our memories, our money, our influence, our beloved relatives. Whenever He has need of anything, we must let it go. We must learn to yield it up to Him as cheerfully as the owner yielded up his colt.

Joseph Parker (1830-1902)

Lord, let me have no will of my own, nor consider my true happiness as depending in the smallest degree on anything that can befall me outwardly, but as consisting altogether in conformity to Thy will. Amen.

Henry Martyn (1781-1812)

The smallest things become great when God requires them of us. They are only small as regards themselves; but they forthwith become great when done for Him, when they lead to Him, and serve to unite with Him eternally.

François de la Mothe Fénelon (1651-1715)

The great mass of people who had come up for the festival heard that Jesus was entering Jerusalem, and taking palm-branches they went out to meet Him, shouting, Hosanna!

John 12:12, 13 (Moffatt)

The expected arrival of the Prophet of Galilee was looked forward to with intense curiosity. Thus a great multitude was prepared to welcome the Deliverer who had raised the dead. And Jesus came, not upon a war-horse, but on an animal which was the symbol of peace. It was a procession of very lowly pomp. But the multitudes spread out their garments to tapestry His path, tearing down branches to scatter before Him. In a burst of enthusiasm they broke out into a shout, *Hosanna to the Son of David! Blessed is the King of Israel that cometh in the name of the Lord!* Then the city of Jerusalem burst into full view, the city of ten thousand memories for Him.... Who can enter into the mighty rush of divine compassion which, at that spectacle, shook the Saviour's soul? As He gazed on the city, there was no exultation in the heart of its true King. He had dropped silent tears at the grave of Lazarus; here He wept aloud.... All the pity that was within Him overmastered His human spirit, and He not only wept, but broke into a lamentation for the city. This had been a strange Messianic triumph!

F. W. Farrar (1831-1903)

> All glory, laud, and honour to Thee, Redeemer, King,
> To whom the lips of children made sweet hosannas ring!
> Thou art the King of Israel, Thou David's royal Son,
> Who in the Lord's Name comest, the Kind and Blessed One.
> To Thee before Thy passion they sang their hymns of praise;
> To Thee now high exalted our melody we raise.
> Though didst accept their praises; accept the prayers we bring,
> Who in all good delightest, Thou good and gracious King.
>
> Theodulph of Orleans (760- 821)

He riseth from supper and laid aside His garments; and took a towel and girded Himself... and began to wash the disciples' feet and to wipe them with the towel.
John 13: 4, 5

O great and significant symbol! O powerful exposition of the words *I came not to be ministered unto but to minister!* O important testimony to that which is of value in His kingdom, and that which is not! O impressive condemnation of all selfishness and self-exaltation! O deeply affecting commendation of humility and self-denial as the characteristics of His children.... This work of condescension proceeds in silence until the turn comes to Simon Peter who cannot comprehend how anything so unseemly should take place. The glory of the Lord and the worthlessness of the creature contrast too strongly. But however commendable may have been such a feeling, it was nevertheless improper. What would have become of us had He not condescended to the depth of that depravity in which He found us? *If I wash you not, you have no part with me.* Yes, He must wash us, for His teaching and setting us an example are not sufficient. He who is not washed in the blood of Christ has no part with Him. He continues, *He that is washed need not wash except his feet....* In the progress of the life of faith, unguarded moments occur in which the person again sins in one way or another. One incautiously thinks, speaks or does that which is improper, and is again guilty of unfaithfulness. The person's walk is polluted; the feet, with which one comes in contact with the earth, are defiled.

F. W. Krummacher (1796-1869)

I am bound to serve all and to minister the balm-bearing words of my Lord.

Francis of Assisi (1181-1226)

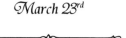

I have finished the work which Thou gavest Me to do.
John 17:4

So collected is our Lord in His own purpose, so at home amidst the certainties of the future, that He affirms, *I have finished the work that You gave Me to do.* Only eighteen hours more, and in literal act and moment, it is to become true. It was His appointed place; and how beautifully silent He was about the time of His leaving till the time came; and then how His heart seemed to bound with delight towards His Father as He exclaimed, *Father, the hour is come! I have finished the work... and now, O Father, glorify Thou Me. Now I am no more in the world; now I come to Thee.*

Gray & Adams Commentary (1951)

Was the work of the Master indeed done? Was not the heaviest task yet to come? He has not yet met the dread hour of death. Why did He say that His work was done? It was because He knew that when the will is given, the battle is ended. He who willed to die has already triumphed over death. The cup which our Father gives us to drink is a cup for the will. It is easy for the lips to drain it when once the heart has accepted it. Not on the heights of Calvary, but in the shadows of Gethsemane is the cup presented; the act is easy after the choice. The real battlefield is in the silence of the spirit. Conquer there, and you are crowned.

Biblical Illustrator (1887)

> My will is not my own till Thou hast made it thine;
> If it would reach a monarch's throne, it must its own resign;
> It only stands unbent, amid the clashing strife,
> When on Thy bosom it has lean't and found in Thee its life.

George Matheson (1842-1906)

Simon, Simon, behold, Satan has desired to have you.... But I have prayed for you that your faith fail not.

Luke 22:31, 32

The Lord Jesus is proceeding to the lonely garden, but the thought of His approaching sufferings retires into the background. That which affects Him more deeply is His love for and care of His flock. Turning to Simon Peter He says, *Satan has desired to have you.* Satan was challenging Peter, and had laid claim to him. After uttering the appalling warning, Jesus looks kindly at His disciples, and encouraging them, tells Simon that He has prayed for him.

F. W. Krummacher (1796-1869)

Jesus is the intercessor for tempted souls. He is the confident and victorious Antagonist of whatsoever mysterious, malignant power may lie beyond the confines of sense. The tenderest of His words, the most pleading and urgent of His petitions, the mightiest gifts of His grace, are given to the weakest, the neediest, the men and women in most sorrow and stress and peril; they who want Him most always have Him nearest. The thicker the darkness, the brighter His light; the drearier our lives, the richer His presence; the more solitary we are, the larger the gifts of His companionship. Our need is the measure of His prayer.... If we look only at Peter's denial, we must admit that his faith did fail. If we look at the whole of the future life of the Apostle, we answer, "No." Eclipse is not extinction; the momentary untruthfulness to one's deepest convictions is not the annihilation of these convictions. Christ's prayer is never in vain.

Alexander Maclaren (1826-1910)

In the hour of trial, Jesus plead for me,
Lest, by base denial, I depart from Thee;
When Thou seest me waver, with a look recall;
Nor for fear or favor, suffer me to fall,

James Montgomery (1771-1854)

Then comes Jesus unto a place called Gethsemane, and says unto the disciples, Sit here while I go and pray yonder. And He... began to be sorrowful and very heavy. Then says He unto them, My soul is exceeding sorrowful, even unto death.... And He went a little farther and fell on His face, and prayed, O my Father, if it be possible, let this cup pass from Me; nevertheless not as I will, but as Thou wilt.

Matthew 26:36-39

We may reverently and adoringly listen to what the Evangelist tells us of the unspeakable hour. Notice the *exceeding sorrow* of the *Man of Sorrows*. Somewhere on the western foot of Olivet lay the garden, named from an oil-press in it, which was to be the scene of the holiest and sorest sorrow. Truly it was 'an oil-press', in which 'the good olive' was crushed by the grip of unparalleled agony, and yielded precious oil which has been poured into many a wound since then.... A storm of agitation and bewilderment broke His calm, and forced from His patient lips the unutterably pathetic cry, *My soul is exceeding sorrowful* -- compassed about with sorrow -- *even unto death.* What lay before Him was not merely death, but the death which was to atone for the world's sin, and in which the whole weight of sin's consequences was concentrated. *The Lord has placed on Him the iniquities of us all,* that is the one sufficient explanation of this infinitely solemn and tender scene.

Alexander Maclaren (1826-1910)

It was alone the Savior prayed in dark Gethsemane;
Alone He drained the bitter cup and suffered there for me.
Can you reject such matchless love? Can you His claim disown?
Come, give your all in gratitude, nor leave Him thus alone.
B.H. Price (n.d.)

He 'came forth' from God, He 'came down' among people, He 'became poor' for our sakes, He 'emptied himself' of the dignities and splendour of deity

D.M. McIntyre (1859-1938)

March 26th

And being in agony He prayed more earnestly: and His sweat was as it were great drops of blood falling down to the ground.
Luke 22:44

The eternal Father's only and supremely beloved Son appears before Him in a position which might melt the flinty rock to pity; but compassion seems a stranger with the Father. There is neither voice, nor response, nor attention, as if the Eternal had no longer a heart for Him who lay in His bosom before the foundation of the world. The cup of horror does not pass from the trembling sufferer; on the contrary, its contents become every moment more bitter. Louder sound the cries of the agonizing Savior; more urgent becomes His prayer; but the Lofty One is silent and heaven seems barred as with a thousand bolts. A holy angel at length approaches; but why an angel only, instead of the immediate and consoling vision of the Father? Does it not seem like irony that a creature should be sent to strengthen the Creator? But let us contemplate this mysterious conflict in Gethsemane a little more closely. Scarcely had Jesus, with His three disciples, penetrated a few paces into the garden, when *He began to be very sorrowful and very heavy.* Something unheard of before now came over Him. *He began to be sore amazed. He wrestled with death.* It was in the horrors of this state that our Surety felt Himself placed -- a mysterious entering into those horrors laid hold of the Holy One so overpoweringly. He entered into much closer contact with *the last enemy.* He emptied the cup of its terrors.

W .F. Krummacher (1796-1869)

My sins, my sins, My Saviour! Their guilt I never knew...
Till with Thee in the garden I heard Thy pleading pray'r
And saw the sweat-drops bloody that told Thy sorrow there.
John S.B. Monsell (1811-1875)

O my Father, if it be possible, let this cup pass from me; nevertheless, not as I will but as Thou wilt.

Matthew 26:39

We enter Gethsemane with a holy hush over our spirit and with awe in our eyes. There is the Kidron brook and the grove of gnarled and knotty olive trees. The moon above is at its full and its brightness makes these shadowed recesses the darker. Here is a group of men lying on the ground, apparently asleep. Over yonder among the trees, a smaller group reclines motionless. And, look, farther in is that lone figure, never more alone, save on the morrow. It is impossible for humanity with sin grained into its fibre to understand the horror with which a sinless one thinks of actual contact with sin. As Jesus enters the grove that night it comes in upon His spirit with terrific intensity that He is actually coming into contact with sin. In some way all too deep for definition He is to be *made sin*. An indescribable horror, a chill of terror, a frenzy of fright seizes Him. And yonder alone among the trees the agony is upon Him as He prays, *If it be possible, let this cup pass.* The strain of spirit almost snaps the life-thread. And angels come with sympathetic strengthening -- with what awe must they have ministered! Even after their ministering, some of His blood slips out there under the trees. And then a changed petition! *Since this cup may not pass, Thy—will—be—done!*

S.D. Gordon (1859-1936)

O Light! O love! O very God, I dare no longer gaze
Upon Thy wondrous attributes, and their mysterious ways.

O Spirit, beautiful and dread! My heart is fit to break
With love of all Thy tenderness for us poor sinners' sake.

Frederick W. Faber (1814-1863)

*March 28*th

Rise up, let us go; lo, he that betrayeth Me is at hand.
Mark 14:42

From whence resounds this courageous and resolute call? From the same lips out of which the cry of distress had only just before ascended to heaven, *If it be possible, let this cup pass from Me!* But now, behold the glorious Conqueror! He emerges from the horrible conflict in Gethsemane as if steeled both in body and soul. His whole bearing breathes self-possession and sublime composure. Aware of who it was that presented the cup to Him in Gethsemane, He willingly emptied it, and knows henceforth that the terrors which may be in reserve are indispensable conditions for completing His great mediatorial work. The divine Sufferer prepares to enter upon the thorny path of bodily affliction. Scarcely had the Saviour risen from the ground when a new cause of alarm awaits Him: a murderous band, armed with swords, staves and spears. We see the priests, the Pharisees, the scribes, the servants of the high priest, and the multitude.

W.F. Krummacher (1796-1869)

Unresisting, uncomplaining, holy, harmless, calm;
Driven, beaten, led to slaughter, God's unblemished Lamb —
Bind me in eternal fetters, lead me, Thine alone;
Silent when contempt and hatred mark me for Thine own.
Gerhard Tersteegen (1697-1769)

Lord, You know what is best; let this be done or that be done as You please. Give what You will, as much as You will, when You will. Do with me as You know best. I am in Your hand; turn me about whichever way You will. Behold, I am Your servant, ready to obey in all things. Not for myself do I desire to live, but for You – would that I could do this worthily and perfectly!

Thomas à Kempis (1380-1471)

March 29th

And they laid their hands on Him and took Him....
Then all the disciples forsook Him and fled.
Mark 14:46, 50

Jesus bound! Can we trust our eyes? Omnipotence in fetters, the Creator bound by the creature! The Lord of the world as the captive of His mortal subjects! How much easier would it have been for Him to have burst those bonds than Manoah's son of old! However, He rends them not, but yields Himself as one who is powerless and overcome. His passive deportment must have had a great and sublime intention, and such was really the case.

F. W. Krummacher (1796-1869)

Then the disciples forsook him and fled. What folly was this, for fear of death to flee from Him whom they themselves knew to be the *Fountain of Life*? It was a part of Christ's suffering to be deserted. There was a mystery in this. Christ, as a sacrifice for sins, stood abandoned.... In this He was made a curse for us, being left as one separated to evil. He had not the assistance of any other in working out our salvation. *He trod the wine-press alone.* Jesus was now alone in the power of His enemies.

Matthew Henry (1662-1714)

> Forsake the Christ thou sawest transfigured, Him
> Who trod the sea and brought the dead to life,
> What should wring this from thee?
> Even a torchlight and a noise,
> The sudden Roman faces, violent hands,
> And fear of what the rulers might do! Just that,
> And it is written, 'I forsook and fled.'
> That was my trial, and it ended thus.
>
> Robert Browning (1812-1889)

He is despised and rejected of men
Isaiah 53:3

Put up your sword into the sheath: the cup which my Father hath given Me,
shall I not drink it?
John 18:11

As Jesus was being bound He said to Peter, *the cup which my Father gives Me, shall I not drink it?* In the cup was the entire curse of the invincible law, all the horrors of conscious guilt, all the terrors of Satan's fiercest temptations, and all the sufferings which can befall body and soul. It contained the dreadful ingredients of abandonment by God, and a bloody death to which the curse was attached – all to be endured while surrounded by the powers of darkness. Here we learn what is implied in the words *Who spared not His own Son. Christ has redeemed us from the curse of the law, being made a curse for us. God made Him to be sin for us, who knew no sin.* All that humanity has heaped up to themselves against the day of God's holy and righteous wrath -- their forgetfulness of God, their selfish conduct, their disobedience, pride, worldly-mindedness, and deceit -- are all united and mingled in the cup, and ferment together into a horrible potion. *Shall I not drink this cup?* asks the Savior. "Yes," we reply. "Empty it, beloved Immanuel! We will kiss Thy feet and offer up ourselves upon Thy holy altar!" He has emptied it, and not a drop remains for His people. The satisfaction He rendered was complete, the reconciliation effected. *There is now no condemnation to them who are in Christ Jesus.* The curse no longer falls upon them. *The chastisement of our peace lay upon Him; and by His stripes we are healed, a*nd nothing remains for us but to sing Hallelujah!

W.F. Krummacher (1796-1869)

My sin – oh, the bliss of this glorious tho't –
My sin not in part, but the whole,
Is nailed to the cross and I bear it no more,
Praise the Lord, Praise the Lord, O my soul.

H.W. Spafford (1828-1888)

March 31st

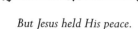

But Jesus held His peace.
Matthew 26:63

He is marched off to the spacious hall of audience where the council of the rulers, with the high priest as its president, are gathered together with representatives from the priesthood, the elders and rulers of the synagogues, the doctors of the law. During this judicial period *Jesus held His peace*. He was also led before Herod and Pilate and *He answered not a word* to the things He was accused. Before these tribunals the Saviour of humanity stands bound... but we must see beyond. The Lord does not stand at the bar as a Holy One, but as the Representative of sinners. Our catalogue of crimes is displayed before Him, as if they were His own. He is laid in the scales of justice with our transgressions, for they are imputed to Him. He stood there in our place... and *He held His peace*. His holding His peace is the reflection of a more mysterious silence before another and higher One than any human tribunal; and regarded from this point of view, it may be considered as a silence of confession and assent. His silence enables us to speak, and gives us power and liberty to lift up our heads boldly against every accusation, while trusting in the justification wrought out for us by the Redeemer.

F. W. Krummacher (1796-1869)

> Silent midst the false accusers, Thou the Witness true;
> Proud, false lips revile and sentence Him they never knew.
> I, the guilty one, acquitted by Thy lips divine;
> Thine the curse and condemnation, life and glory mine.
>
> Gerhard Tersteegen (1697-1769)

Through grace you are saved, not through works but by the will of God through Jesus Christ. Wherefore, having girt up your loins, serve God in fear and truth.

Polycarp of Smyrna (69-155)

April

April 1ˢᵗ

And when they were come to the place, which is called Calvary, there they crucified Him, and the malefactors, one on the right hand and the other on the left.

Luke 23:33

There stands the mysterious cross -- a rock against which the very waves of the curse break. He who so mercifully engaged this judgment against Himself hangs yonder in profound darkness.... Though rejected by heaven and earth, yet He forms the connecting link between them both, and the Mediator of their eternal and renewed amity. His bleeding arms are extended wide; He stretches them out to every sinner. His hands point to the east and west, for He shall gather His children from the ends of the earth. The top of the cross is directed toward the sky; far above the world will its effects extend. Its foot is fixed in the earth; the cross becomes a wondrous tree from which we reap the fruit of eternal reconciliation. O, nothing more is requisite than that God should grant us penitential tears, and then by means of the Holy Spirit show us the Saviour suffering on the cross. For our justification in His sight, nothing more is requisite than that, in the consciousness of our utter helplessness, we lay hold on the horns of that altar which is sprinkled with the blood that *speaketh better things than that of Abel.*

W.F. Krummacher (1796-1869)

> Depth of mercy! can there be
> Mercy still reserved for me?
> Can my God His wrath forbear?
> Me, the chief of sinners spare?
> Still for me the Saviour stands,
> Shows His wounds, and spreads His hands;
> God is love! I know, I feel;
> Jesus weeps, and loves me still.

Charles Wesley (1707-1788)

April 2nd

He saved others; Himself He cannot save.
Matthew 27:42

Because He saves others, Himself He will not, and in a real sense, *He cannot save.* It was His own will and no outward necessity that fastened Him to the cross; and that will was kept immoveable by His love. He Himself fixed the iron chain which bound Him. He Himself made the '*cannot.*' It was His love that made it impossible that He should relinquish the task. Though there were outward powers that seemed to knit Him there, and though to the eye of sense the taunt of the priests might be true – *Himself He cannot save* – the inmost truth of that cross is, *No one takes My life from Me, I lay it down of Myself.* It was not high priests, Pilate, soldiers, nails, that fastened Jesus to the cross. He was bound there by the cords of love, and by the hands of His own infinitely merciful purpose.

Alexander Maclaren (1826-1910)

When scorn and hate, and bitter envious pride,
Hurled all their darts against the Crucified,
Found they no fault but this in Him, so tried?
    "He saved others!"
Those hands, thousands their healing touches knew;
On withered limbs they fell like heavenly dew:
The dead have felt them, and have lived anew;
    "He saved others!"
So many fettered hearts Thy touch hath freed,
Physician! And Thy wound unstaunched must bleed;
Hast Thou no balm for this Thy sorest need?
    "He saved others!"
Lord! and one sign from Thee could rend the sky,
One word from Thee and low those mockers lie;
Thou makest no movement, utterest no cry,
    And savest us.

Anonymous

April 3ʳᵈ

From the sixth hour there was darkness over all the land unto the ninth hour.
Matthew 27:45

The death of our Lord is a profound mystery, and it is impossible for us to understand all that it stands for. There are depths in it we shall never fathom, heights we shall never scale.... This much is clear, that in the person of the Man Jesus Christ the eternal God reconciled the world unto Himself, not imputing their trespasses unto them, because He took them on Himself; not exacting a ransom, because He gave His own blood as a ransom for all; not allowing us to be involved in the ultimate results of sin, because by His obedience He undid the results of human perversity, and made possible for us a new standing in grace and righteousness, through His accepted work on our behalf.

Always and everywhere we must make it clear that God was in Christ and that it was *by the eternal Spirit* that Christ offered Himself without spot to God. The whole Trinity was present at Calvary, doing what Jesus did. His pity was the pity of God; His sacrifice was the sacrifice of God; His sufficient oblation was the gift of God; His travail of soul was the travail of Divine nature. When God set forth a propitiation, it was Himself taking on the brunt and burden of a world's sin.

F.B. Meyer (1847-1929)

Amazing scene! well might the sun, abashed,
Hide its bright face in darkness! well might earth
Shake to her centre! well the rending rocks
Speak out their wonder; and convulsions tear
The universal frame! O love Divine!
O miracle of love! O love of God!
How vast, how wondrous, passing human thought!

E. Young (1681-1755)

April 4th

When Jesus received the vinegar, He said "It is finished,"
and bowed His head and gave up the ghost.
John 19:30

What was finished? ALL THINGS. There is no deficit, nothing that we can add. He finished the task given Him from before the foundation of the world.... His was a life of purpose, and that purpose had been accomplished: a life with a plan, and the plan had been perfected: a life with an aim, and the aim had been attained: a life with a task, and the task had been completed.

J.C. Macaulay (1941)

All the types, promises and prophecies were now fully accomplished in Him. The whole book, from the first to the last, in both the law and the prophets, was finished in Him. There is not a single jewel of promise from the first emerald which fell on the threshold of Eden, to the last sapphire stone of Malachi, which was not set in the breastplate of the true High Priest. There is not a type, from the red heifer downward to the turtle-dove, from the hyssop upwards to Solomon's temple itself, which was not fulfilled in Him; not a prophecy, whether spoken on Chebar's bank or on the shores of Jordan; and not a dream of wise men, whether they had received it in Babylon, Samaria or Judea, which was not now fully wrought out in Christ Jesus.

C.H. Spurgeon (1834-1892)

> Man of Sorrows, what a name, For the Son of God who came
> Ruined sinners to reclaim! Hallelujah! What a Savior!
> Guilty, vile, and helpless, we: Spotless Lamb of God was He:
> Full atonement! Can it be? Hallelujah! What a Savior!
> Lifted up was He to die, "It is finished," was His cry;
> Now in heav'n exalted high: Hallelujah! What a Saviour!
> P.P. Bliss (1836-1876)

Now in the place where He was crucified there was a garden... and in the garden was a new sepulchre... there they laid Jesus.

John 19:41, 42

Perhaps if they had had time, they would have carried Him to Bethany and buried Him among friends. He had more right to have been buried in the chief of the sepulchres of the sons of David than any of the kings of Judah. But *the sepulchre was nigh at hand and the sabbath drew on....* In the Garden of Eden death and the grave first received their power, and now in a garden they are conquered, disarmed and triumphed over. In a garden Christ began His passion, and from a garden He would begin His exaltation.

Matthew Henry (1662-1714)

> Low in the grave He lay, Jesus my Savior!
> Waiting the coming day, Jesus my Lord!
> Vainly they watch His bed, Jesus my Savior!
> Vainly they seal the dead, Jesus my Lord!
>
> Death cannot keep his prey, Jesus my Savior!
> He tore the bars away, Jesus my Lord!
>
> Up from the grave He arose,
> With a mighty triumph o'er His foes;
> He arose a Victor from the dark domain,
> And He lives forever with His saints to reign;
> He arose! Hallelujah! Christ arose!

Robert Lowry (1826-1899)

It is in this grave that the bottom of the grave was knocked out. It is off this grave that we gather the flowers to adorn our mourning garment after our dead. This is a grave which reconciles us to our graves.

Gray & Adams Commentary (1951)

April 6th

On the first day of the week, very early in the morning while it was still dark, Mary of Magdala went to the tomb, and she saw that the stone had been removed from the tomb.
John 20:1 (Williams)

Welcome, happy morning!' Age to age shall say:
  'Hell to-day is vanquished, heaven is won to-day.'
Lo! The dead is living, God for evermore:
Him, their true Creator, all His works adore.
Venantius Fortunatus (530-609)

This is the most celebrated tomb in all the ages. Catacombs of Egypt, tomb of Napoleon, Taj Mahal of India -- nothing compares with it. At the door of this mausoleum a fight took place which decided the question for all graveyards and cemeteries. That day the grave received such a shattering it can never be rebuilt. The King of Terrors retired before the King of Grace. The Lord is risen!
T. DeWitt Talmage (1832-1902)

Crown Him with many crowns, the Lamb upon His throne;
Hark! how the heavenly anthem drowns all music but its own!
Awake, my soul, and sing of Him who died for thee!
And hail Him as thy matchless King thro' all eternity.

Crown Him the Lord of love; behold His hands and side—
Those wounds, yet visible above, in beauty glorified!
No angel in the sky can fully bear that sight,
but downward bends His wondering eye at mysteries so bright.

Crown Him the Lord of life, Who triumphed o'er the grave,
And rose victorious in the strife for those He came to save.
His glories now we sing, Who died and rose on high,
Who died eternal life to bring, and lives that death may die.
Matthew Bridges (1800-1894)

April 7th

He is risen, as He said.
Matthew 28:6

Christ the Lord is risen today, *Hallelujah!*
Sons of men and angels say: *Hallelujah!*
Raise your joys and triumphs high; *Hallelujah!*
Sing, ye heavens, and earth, reply: *Hallelujah!*

Love's redeeming work is done, fought the fight, the battle won;
Lo! our Sun's eclipse is o'er; Lo! He sets in blood no more.

Vain the stone, the watch, the seal; Christ hath burst the gates of hell:
Death in vain forbids Him rise; Christ hath opened Paradise.

Lives again our glorious King; Where, O death, is now thy sting?
Once He died, our souls to save; Where thy victory, O grave?

Soar we now where Christ has led, following our exalted Head;
Made like Him, like Him we rise; Ours the Cross, the grave, the skies.

Hail, the Lord of earth and heaven! Praise to Thee by both be given;
Thee we greet triumphant now; Hail, the Resurrection Thou.
Charles Wesley (1707-1788)

Jesus gave to the whole world forever, while time shall be, the most astounding, clear-cut and soul-stirring promise the race ever had. Other teachers had hoped that there might be a life after death. Other leaders had looked forward to the possibility of learning more about another world when they left this one. But this Teacher, who was the Prophet from the other world, was the first to state with assurance that those who believed in Him and accepted His message were utterly immune to death.
Harry Rimmer (1890-1952)

April 8th

I have seen the Lord.
John 20:18

To Mary of Magdala was this glorious honour. From her impassioned soul not even the white-robed visions and angel-voices could expel the anguish which she experienced in the one haunting thought, *They have taken away my Lord out of the sepulchre, and I know not where they have laid Him.* With her whole heart absorbed in this thought she turned away -- and lo! Jesus Himself standing beside her. There was something spiritual in the risen and glorified body and she did not recognize Him. She fancied it must be the gardener but then Jesus said, *Mary!* That one word at once penetrated her heart. Turning toward Him and trying to clasp His feet, she cried *Rabboni! Oh, my Master!* Then He gave her the message, *Go to My brethren and say to them, I am ascending to my Father and your Father, and My God and your God.* Awe-struck, she hastened to obey and all future ages have thrilled to that first utterance, *I have seen the Lord.*

F. W. Farrar (1831-1903)

He appeared first to Mary Magdalene, out of whom He had cast seven devils. It was not to Peter, nor to James, nor to John that He gave that favour and unparalleled honour. It was to her who loved Him best, and had the best reason to love Him best. Let this lesson be always taught that no depth of sin, and no possession of devils even, shall separate us from the love of Christ. That repentance and love will outlive and overcome everything.... Only repent deep enough and love as Mary loved and He will appear to you also, and will call you by name. And He will employ you in His service even more and better than He honoured and employed Mary Magdalene on the morning of His Resurrection.

Alexander Whyte (1836-1921)

April 9th

The Lord has risen indeed, and has appeared to Simon.
Luke 24:34

The four Gospels are full of Peter. Our Lord speaks oftener to him than to any other of His disciples: sometimes in blame and sometimes in praise. No disciple is so pointedly reproved by our Lord, and no disciple ever ventures to reprove his Master but Peter. No other disciple so boldly confessed and outspokenly acknowledged and encouraged our Lord; and no one ever intruded, interfered and tempted Him as Peter repeatedly did. No disciple speaks so often and so much.... The worst disease of the human heart is coldness. With all his faults, and Peter was full of them, a cold heart was not one of them. All his faults lay in the heat of his heart.... But by degrees, and under the teaching, the example and the training of his Master, Peter's too-hot heart was gradually brought under control till it became the seat of a deep, pure, deathless love and adoration for Jesus Christ.

Alexander Whyte (1836-1921)

Does a dead person prick the consciences of people so that they throw all their traditions to the winds and bow down before the teaching of Christ? If Christ is now dead, how is it that He makes the living to cease from their activities -- the adulterer from adulteries, the murderer from murdering, the unjust from avarice -- and makes the profane and godless devout? This is the work of One who lives, not of one dead; and more than that, it is the work of God. We are agreed that a dead person can do nothing; yet the Savior works mightily every day, drawing people to faith, persuading them to virtue, teaching them about immortality, quickening their thirst for heavenly things, revealing the knowledge of the Father, inspiring strength in the face of death, manifesting Himself to each and displacing the irreligion of idols.

Athanacius of Alexandria (296-373)

April 10th

Look at my hands, put your finger here; and put your hand here into my side;
be no more unbelieving.
John 20:27 (Moffatt)

O sons and daughters, let us sing!
The King of heaven, the glorious King.
O'er death today rose triumphing. *Hallelujah!*

That night the apostles met in fear;
Amidst them came their Lord most dear,
And said, 'My peace be on all here.' *Hallelujah!*

When Thomas first the tidings heard,
He doubted if it were their Lord,
Until He came and spake the word. *Hallelujah!*

'My pierced side, O Thomas, see;
Behold My hands, My feet,' said He,
'Not faithless but believing be.' *Hallelujah!*

No longer Thomas then denied;
He saw the feet, the hands, the side;
'Thou art my Lord and God,' he cried. *Hallelujah!*

How blest are they who have not seen,
And yet whose faith hath constant been,
For they eternal life shall win. *Hallelujah!*

Jean Tisserand (?-1494)

The hands and feet of Jesus still carry the marks of the old ignominy and grief.... But I am thankful for the blessed stigmata. They are the certificates of my redemption.

F.B. Meyer (1847-1929)

They are before the throne of God and serve Him day and night in His temple.
Revelation 7:15

If there is to be service yonder, here is the exercising ground, where we are to cultivate the capacities and acquire the habitudes which there will find ampler scope and larger field. I do not know what we are here in this world for at all, unless it is to apprentice us for heaven. I do not know that there is anything that a person has to do in this life which is worth doing unless it be as training for doing something yonder.... Beyond the grave there lies fields for nobler work for which we are being trained here.

Alexander Maclaren (1826-1910)

God has a will to be done not in earth only, but also in heaven; they are not dismissed from the King's business who are called from the camp to the Court, from being common soldiers to be Privy Councilors.

Abraham Cheare (1668)

If He appoint us here to bear His cross, and draw in His yoke, and serve at His altar, this shall be afterwards neither shame nor grief to us, while the meanest office in God's service will entitle us to a dwelling in the house of the Lord all the days of our life.

Matthew Henry (1662-1732)

> All must be earnest in a world like ours.
> Not many lives, but only one have we,
>   One, only one;
> How sacred should that one life ever be—
>   That narrow span!
> Day after day filled up with blessed toil,
> Hour after hour still bringing in new spoil.
>
> Horatius Bonar (1808-1889)

April 12th

They continued with one accord in prayer and supplication.
Acts 1:14

They were *waiting for the promise.* It is on Thursday, probably in the evening, that the disciples return to Jerusalem. Did they expect to receive the promise that very night? We do not know; but we do know that there opened a new era in the intercourse of humanity with heaven. As they began to pray, they would find their conceptions of the Majesty on high changed! The glory of the Father now encompassed a human form! The exalted Master *has entered for us within the veil! He makes intercession for us!* Which of the twelve says to the others, *Let us ask the Father in His name?* The angels had often sung together over the prayer of repenting sinners. Now for the first time, they hear prayers authorized and accredited by the name of the Only-begotten of the Father. That name had now been set *above every name*, and as it echoes through the host on high, *things in heaven bow.* What must have been that moment for the saints in Paradise who had seen the Saviour afar off, but never knew the joy of praying directly in His name! Father Abraham had *rejoiced to see His day.* What would be his gladness now? What would be *the things touching* the *King* that David would sing in that wonderful moment? Oh the joy of that first hour of praying in the name of Christ!

Biblical Illustrator (1887)

Lord Jesus, teach us to pray. Help us learn how. You know both ends of prayer: the praying end down here and the answering end up yonder. We would be good scholars in your school, punctual in attendance, keeping the door shut, the Book open, and the knee bent. In Jesus' Name. Amen.

S.D. Gordon (1859-1936)

By Him all things consist.
Colossians 1:17

God's work of providence is "most holy, wise and powerful, preserving and governing all His creatures and all their actions." It has no Sabbath. No night suspends it, and from its labors God never rests. Our world is but an outlying corner of creation; bearing, perhaps, as small a proportion of the great universe as a single grain bears to all the sands of the sea-shore, or one small quivering leaf to the foliage of a boundless forest. Yet even within this earth's narrow limits, how vast the work of Providence!

By Jesus Christ all things consist. In the hands once nailed to the cross, is the sceptre of universal empire. Those blessed arms that once were thrown around a mother's neck, now tenderly enfold every child of God. On them hangs the weight of worlds. Great is the mystery of godliness! By Him the angels keep their holiness and the stars their orbits; the tides roll along the deep and the seasons through the year; kings reign and princes decree justice; the church of God is held together, riding out at anchor the rudest storms; and by Him, until the last of His elect are plucked from the wreck and His purposes of mercy are all accomplished, this guilty world is kept from sinking under a growing load of sins.

By Him all things consist; and on raising our eyes to Jesus exalted -- crowned, enthroned, with the government on His shoulder -- our minds revert by way of contrast to Calvary, to the doleful day when He sank beneath the weight, and expired amid the agonies of His cross. If He, who now bears the weight of worlds, once staggered under the burden of our sins, oh! what an incalculable, mysterious load of guilt must there be in sin! It bent the back that bears with ease the burden of ten thousand worlds.

Thomas Guthrie (1803-1873)

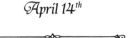

April 14th

There is now no condemnation to those who are in Christ Jesus.
Romans 8:1

When you take your stand by faith at Calvary's Cross you are standing where the fire has been. Judgement cannot ever reach you there. The law put my Substitute to death on that Cross, and therefore it has nothing to say to me. My relationship towards it has been changed by His death.

H.A. Ironside (1876-1951)

Jesus, Thy blood and righteousness
My beauty are, my glorious dress;
'Midst flaming worlds, in these arrayed,
With joy shall I lift up my head.

Bold shall I stand in Thy great day;
For who aught to my charge shall lay?
Fully absolved through these I am—
From sin and fear, from guilt and shame.

Lord, I believe Thy precious blood,
Which at the mercy seat of God
Forever doth for sinners plead,
For me, e'en for my soul, was shed.

Lord, I believe were sinners more
Than sands upon the ocean shore,
Thou hast for all a ransom paid,
For all a full atonement made.

Nicolaus von Zinzendorf (1700-1760)

Peace is that great calm which comes over the conscience when it sees the atonement sufficient and the Saviour willing.

J. Hamilton (1814-1867)

April 15th

Before the mountains were brought forth, or ever Thou had formed the... world, even from everlasting to everlasting, Thou art God.

Psalm 90:2

No age can heap its outward years on Thee;
Dear God! Thou art, Thyself, Thine own eternity.

Frederick W. Faber (1815-1863)

God is eternal. Though years are ascribed to Him, they cannot be numbered since there is no proportion between the duration of God and the years of humans. *The number of His years cannot be searched out.* The number of the drops of rain which have fallen in all parts of the earth since the creation of the world, if subtracted from the number of the years of God, would be a mere nothing.... His duration is infinite, without measure. It might always be said of Him, *He was*; and it may always be said of Him, *He will be*; there is no time when He began, no time when He shall cease. God always is what He was, and always will be what He is.

Stephen Charnock (1628-1680)

Only to sit and think of God
        Oh what a joy it is!
To think the thought, to breathe the Name;
        Earth has no higher bliss.

Father of Jesus, love's reward!
        What rapture it will be!
Prostrate before Thy throne to lie,
        And gaze and gaze on Thee!

Frederick W. Faber (1814-1863)

It is only things spiritual and Divine which are not affected by the mutations of time.

Jerome (340-420)

April 16th

I pray… that you may be able to comprehend with all saints what is the breadth, and length, and depth, and height; and to know the love of Christ, which passes knowledge.
Ephesians 3:18, 19

It is a wonder that He should seek the like of us. But love overlooks fecklessness; for if it had not been so, Christ would never have made so fair and blessed a bargain with us as is the covenant of grace. His love has neither brim nor bottom; His love is like Himself, it passes all natural understanding. I go to fathom it with my arms, but it is as if a child would take the globe of sea and land in her two short arms.

Samuel Rutherford (1600-1661)

> Thou hidden love of God, whose height
> Whose depth unfathomed, no one knows,
> I see from far Thy bounteous light,
> Only I sigh for Thy repose;
> My heart is pained, nor can it be
> At rest till it finds rest in Thee.
>
> Is there a thing beneath the sun
> That strives with Thee my heart to share?
> Ah! Tear it thence, and reign alone,
> The Lord of every motion there;
> Then shall my heart from earth be free,
> When it hath found repose in Thee. Amen.

Gerhard Tersteegen (1697-1769)

Nothing can separate you from God's love, absolutely nothing. God is enough for time, God is enough for eternity. God is enough!

Hannah Pearsall Smith (1832-1911)

For the love of God is broader than the measure of our mind; and the heart of the Eternal is most wonderfully kind.

Frederick Faber (1814-1863)

April 17th

Her sins, which are many, are forgiven; for she loved much: but to whom little is forgiven, the same loves little.

Luke 7:47

A poor woman, discovering that Jesus was supping in the house of the Pharisee, made her way there among the throng of other visitants, carrying with her an alabaster box of spikenard. As she stood humbly behind Him and listened to His words, she began to weep and her tears dropped upon His unsandalled feet.... Sinking down upon her knees, she began with her long hair to wipe the feet which had been wetted with her tears, and then to cover them with kisses, and at last, breaking the alabaster vase, to bathe them with the precious and fragrant nard. Simon the Pharisee looked on with icy disapproval. The appeal to pity of that broken-hearted mourner did not move him. He did not utter what was in his heart but his frigid demeanor showed all that was passing in his heart. Our Lord heard his thoughts and after a short story said, *Her many sins have been forgiven — for she loved much. But he who has been forgiven little loves little.*

F. W. Farrar (1831-1903)

Truly the gift of God is to love God. He has given the gift that He may be loved, He who loves when He is not loved. We were loved when we pleased Him not, that there might spring up in us that which should please Him.

Council of Orange (529)

He who is in Himself Infinite Love, ought to be the only object of love.

Bonaventura (1221-1274)

O Lord our God, grant us grace to desire you with our whole heart, that so desiring we may seek and find you, and so finding you, may love you, and loving you, may hate those sins from which you have redeemed us. Amen.

Anselm (1033-1109)

April 18th

And when they began to sing and to praise, the LORD set ambushments
against the children of Ammon, Moab, and mount Seir,
which were come against Judah; and they were smitten.
2 Chronicles 20:22

Never was an army drawn out to the field of battle as Jehoshaphat's
army. His soldiers were prepared for war, but he took care
that faith should be their armour. He bade them *believe on the Lord
God....* That is true courage which faith inspires; nor will anything
contribute more to the establishing of the heart in shaking times than
a firm belief in the power, mercy and promise of God. *He appointed
singers unto the Lord to praise the beauty of His holiness, as they went out
before the army: Praise the LORD, for His mercy endures forever.* They met
the enemy host armed with song and needed no other weapon. These
singers had nothing else to do but to praise God, to praise His holiness
which is His beauty, to praise Him as they did in the temple with that
ancient and good doxology which eternity itself will not wear threadbare, *Praise the Lord, for His mercy endureth forever.* Jehoshaphat intended
to express his firm reliance upon the word of God, to animate his
soldiers, to confound the enemy, to engage God on their side; for
praise pleases God better than all burnt offering and sacrifice.

Matthew Henry (1662-1714)

When Columba, the Irish missionary to Scotland began his work in
521, he faced opposition from the Druids. At a crucial point, when
he was granted an interview with the reluctant King Brude, the
Druids were there to disrupt. But Columba was undaunted. When
he couldn't be heard for the tumult he just raised his voice and sang
his message. That voice disarmed his enemies and opened Scotland to
him and his message.

Biblical Illustrator (1887)

April 19th

Greater love has no man than this, that a man lay down his life for his friends.
John 15:13

Christ's love is unparalleled in its greatness. It is beyond all human calculation. No human power could have subdued our depravity, no human mercy could have removed our guilt, and no human arm could have rescued us.

Christ's love is unparalleled in the magnitude of His sacrifice. He threw aside His original glory. Human conception is inadequate to the greatness of this sacrifice as He condescended to be made one of us. Then He sustained our sorrows, infirmities and sins. Then we see His love in the depth of His humiliation. He stooped to the lowest grade of society; was charged with the lowest of human delinquency, thus bearing the reproach of His people. But though He died, He lives again; His love was stronger than death.

Biblical Illustrator (1887)

O the deep, deep love of Jesus! Love of every love the best;
'Tis an ocean vast of blessing, 'Tis a haven sweet of rest.
O the deep, deep love of Jesus! 'Tis a heaven of heaven to me;
And it lifts me up to glory, for it lifts me up to Thee.

Samuel T. Francis (1834-1925)

Lift up thine heart unto God with a meek stirring of love; and mean Himself and none of His goods.... This is the work of the soul that most pleases God.

Cloud of Unknowing (14th century)

Love divine, all loves excelling, joy of heaven to earth come down;
Fix in us Thy humble dwelling; all Thy faithful mercies crown.
Jesus, Thou art all compassion; pure, unbounded love Thou art;
Visit us with Thy salvation; enter every trembling heart.

Charles Wesley (1707-1788)

April 20th

Whom do men say that I the Son of Man am?
Matthew 16:13 (Williams)

The crowd that had surged so tumultuously about Him followed at a distance. Only His disciples were near as He stood apart in solitary prayer. And when the prayer was over, He asked them.... *Whom do people say that I the Son of Man am?* The answer was a sad one. The Apostles would not speak anything but the words of soberness and truth, and they made the disheartening admission that the Messiah had not been recognized by the world which He came to save. They could only repeat the idle guesses of the people. Some said that He was John the Baptist; some, who may have heard the sterner denunciations, caught in those mighty utterances the thunder tones of a new Elijah; others who had listened to His accents of tenderness, saw in Him the plaintive soul of Jeremiah; others regarded Him as only "a Prophet." None dreamt of who He was. The light had shone in the darkness, and the darkness comprehended it not.

Son of Man was the first title Jesus adopted by which He described Himself -- the representative of every child in the great human family of God. He was the *Son of Man*, meek and lowly in heart, that His disciples could learn at first to recognize before they gradually came to see in Him the *Son of God*. He was the One who wept over Jerusalem and mourned at the grave of Lazarus, who had a mother and a friend, who disdained none, who pitied all, who humbled Himself to death, even the death of the cross, whose divine excellence we cannot indeed attain because He is God, but whose example we can imitate because He was very Man.

F.W. Farrar (1831-1903)

Lord, in ceaseless contemplation fix my thankful heart on Thee! Till I taste Thy full salvation, and Thy unveiled glory see. Amen.
William W. Shirley (1725-1785)

April 21st

But whom say you that I am?
Matthew 16:15

And the answer came, as from everlasting it had been written in the book of destiny that it should come; and Peter had the immortal honour of giving utterance for them all. *THOU ART THE CHRIST, THE SON OF THE LIVING GOD!* The apostles had made former confessions, but this answer was the clearest and fullest of all. It showed that at last the great mystery was revealed which had been hidden from the ages and the generations. The disciples at last had not only recognized in Jesus of Nazareth the promised Messiah of their nation, but it had been revealed to them by the special grace of God that that Messiah was not only what the Jews expected -- a Prince, and a Ruler, and a Son of David -- but was more than this, even the Son of the living God. With what awful solemnity did the Saviour ratify that great confession, *Blessed are you, Simon, son of Jonas: for flesh and blood has not revealed it unto you, but my Father which is in heaven.*

It was His will that the light of revelation should dawn gradually on the minds of His children; that it should spring more from the truths He spoke and the life He lived, than from the wonders which He wrought; that it should be conveyed not in thunder-crashes of supernatural majesty or visions of unutterable glory, but through the quiet medium of a sinless and self-sacrificing course. It was in the Son of Man that they were to recognize the Son of God.

F. W. Farrar (1831-1903)

I take my conception of Christ as He is painted on dead paper, and to me is interpreted the glory, the sweetness, the patience, the love, the joy-inspiring nature of God; and I do not hesitate to say, "Christ is my God."

H. W. Beecher (1813-1887)

Father, it is my will that these... behold my glory which Thou has given Me.
John 17: 24 (Moffatt)

The hearts of believers are like the needle touched by that loadstone, which cannot rest until it comes to the point where it is directed. For being once touched by the love of Christ, they will ever be in motion and restless until they come to Him and behold His glory.... Beholding the glory of Christ is one of the greatest privileges that believers are capable of in this world or in that which is to come. By this they are first gradually conformed to it and then fixed in the eternal enjoyment of it. For here in this life, beholding His glory, they are *transformed into the likeness of Christ*; and hereafter they shall be *forever like unto Him* because *they shall see Him as He is*. On this our present comforts and future blessedness depend. This is the life and reward of our souls.

John Owen (1616-1683)

Not what I am, O Lord, but what Thou art!
That, that alone, can be my soul's true rest;
Thy love, not mine, bids fear and doubt depart,
And stills the tempest of my tossing heart.

'Tis what I know of Thee, my Lord and God,
That fills my soul with peace, my lips with song:
Thou art my health, my joy, my staff, and rod;
Leaning on Thee, in weakness I am strong.

More of Thyself, oh, show me hour by hour;
More of Thy glory, O my God and Lord;
More of Thyself in all Thy grace and power;
More of Thy love and truth, Incarnate Word.

Horatius Bonar (1808-1889)

April 23rd

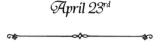

Thy will be done; on earth as it is in heaven.
Matthew 6:10

Oh God, what do I see in the course of the stars, in the order of the seasons, but Thy will which they accomplish? Let it also be fulfilled in my soul. Jesus said, in speaking of His heavenly Father, *For I always do those things that please Him.* May we learn how far we can follow this example, He whose life was devotion to the will of God. May we be united to Him in this spirit; may we no longer follow our own inclinations, but may we not only pray, and teach and suffer, but eat, drink and converse -- do all things -- with reference to His will. Then will our lives be a continual self-sacrifice and an incessant prayer. Every day is a feast day to those who endeavor to live only in the will of God.

François de la Mothe Fénelon (1651-1715)

The only thing in the world worth living for is to find out the will of God and do it.

Temple Gardner (1873-1928)

The world will never be right till the mind of God is the measure of things, and the will of God the law of things. In that Kingdom of Heaven nothing else is acknowledged, and till that kingdom come the mind and will of God must, with those who look for the kingdom, override every other feeling, thinking and judging.

George Macdonald (1824-1903)

Grant that I may e'er endeavor Thy good pleasure to fulfill,
In me, through me, with me ever, Lord, accomplish Thou Thy will.
Ludamilie Elizabeth (1687)

Yours, you made me; Yours, you saved me; Yours, you endured me; Yours, you called me; Yours, you awaited me; Yours, I did not stray; *What do you want of me?*

Teresa of Avila (1515-1582)

———◆———◆◆———◆◆———

Let the fields rejoice, and all that is therein.
I Chronicles 16:32

All creatures of our God and King,
Lift up your voice and with us sing
   Hallelujah, Hallelujah!
Thou burning sun and golden beam,
Thou silver moon with softer gleam,
   O praise Him, O praise Him,
   Hallelujah, Hallelujah, Hallelujah!

Thou rushing wind that art so strong,
Ye clouds that sail in heaven along,
   O praise Him, Hallelujah!
Thou rising morn, in praise rejoice,
Ye lights of evening, find a voice.

Thou flowing water, pure and clear,
Make music for thy Lord to hear,
   Hallelujah, Hallelujah!
Thou fire so masterful and bright,
Thou givest man both warmth and light.

Dear mother earth, who day by day
Unfoldest blessing on our way,
   O praise, Him, Hallelujah!
The flowers and fruits that in thee grow,
Let them His glory also show.

And all ye ones of tender heart,
Forgiving others, take your part,
   O sing ye, Hallelujah!
Ye who long pain and sorrow bear,
Praise God and on Him cast your care.

Let all things their Creator bless,
And worship Him in humbleness,
   O praise Him, Hallelujah!
Praise, praise the Father, praise the Son,
And praise the Spirit, Three in One.
   O praise Him, O praise Him,
   Hallelujah, Hallelujah, Hallelujah! Amen.
       Francis of Assisi (1182-1226)

Make me to know my transgression and my sin.
Job 13:23

Oh how I fear Thee, living God! With deepest, tenderest fears,
and worship Thee with trembling hope, and penitential tears.
Frederick W, Faber (1815-1863)

God's holiness wakens our sense of sinfulness and drives us to confession. This is evident in the prayers of Lancelot Andrews (1555-1626) who worked on the King James translation of the Bible and was chaplain to three monarchs: "O Lover of humanity, very tenderly pitiful, Father of mercies, rich in mercy toward all that call upon Thee: I have sinned against heaven and before Thee, neither am I worthy to be called a son, neither am I worthy to be made an hired servant, no, not the lowest of them. But I repent, alas, I repent; help Thou mine impenitence; be merciful to me a sinner. Where sin abounded let grace much more abound; overcome our evil with Thy good; let Thy mercy rejoice against Thy justice in our sins. Thou that takest away the sins of the world, take away my sins. Thou that didst come to redeem that which was lost, suffer not those to be lost which have been redeemed of Thee. I have deserved death; but even now I appeal from the seat of Thy justice to the throne of Thy grace. Amen."

> O Wind of God, come bend us, break us,
> till humbly we confess our need;
> then in Thy tenderness remake us,
> revive, restore, for this we plead.
> Bessie P. Head (1850-1919)

Repentance unto life is a saving grace, whereby a sinner, out of a true sense of sin and apprehension of the mercy of God in Christ, doth, with grief and hatred of sin, turn from it unto God, with full purpose of, and endeavour after, new obedience.

Westminster Shorter Catechism (1647)

April 26ᵗʰ

Christ also loved the church, and gave Himself for it.
Ephesians 5:25

The church of Christ is God's elect, His saints and beloved, who have washed their clothes in the blood of the Lamb; who are born of God and driven by the Spirit of Christ; who are in Christ and He in them; who hear and believe His Word; who in their weakness obey His commandments, follow in His footsteps with all patience and humility; who hate evil and love the good; who earnestly desire to apprehend Christ as they are apprehended of Him. For all who are in Christ are new creatures, flesh of His flesh, bone of His bone, and members of His body.

Menno Simons (1496-1561)

The Church's one foundation is Jesus Christ her Lord;
She is His new creation by water and the word:
From heaven He came and sought her to be His holy bride;
With His own blood He bought her, and for her life He died.

Elect from every nation, yet one o'er all the earth,
Her charter of salvation one Lord, one faith, one birth,
One holy Name she blesses, partakes one holy food,
And to one hope she presses with every grace endued.

Mid toil and tribulation and tumult of her war,
She waits the consummation of peace for evermore;
Till with the vision glorious her longing eyes are blest,
And the great Church victorious shall be the Church at rest.

Yet she on earth hath union with God the Three in One,
And mystic sweet communion with those whose rest in won.
O happy ones and holy! Lord, give us grace that we,
Like them, the meek and lowly, on high may dwell with Thee.

Samuel Stone (1839-1900)

April 27th

The Son of Man is come to seek and to save that which was lost.
Luke 19:10

I fled Him, down the nights and down the days:
I fled Him, down the arches of the years;
I fled Him, down the labyrinthine ways
Of my own mind; and in the midst of tears
    I hid from Him...
From those strong Feet that followed, followed after.
Francis Thompson (1859-1907)

He is doing all He can to make you know Him.... I believe that if disappointment, pain, sorrow, and fear, anything, will make you turn to God, you shall have it.... For God is in earnest. There is an old Turkish proverb that says: "God has feet of wool, but hands of iron." You may not hear Him coming after you, but you will know it when He has hold of you.
George MacDonald (1824-1903)

Is not this wonderful? People have to run away from the love of God if they are ever without it. They must get somewhere – I know not where. Some strange call of their own invention must be found by those who would escape the love of God; for God's hands are stretched out, and they drip with riches of mercies.
H. W. Webb-Peploe (1816-1880)

I thought His love would weaken
As more, and more He knew me;
But it burneth like a beacon,
And its light and heat go through me;
And I ever hear Him say
As He goes along the way,
    Wandering souls, O do come near Me
    My sheep should never fear Me,
    I am the Shepherd true.
Frederick W. Faber (1814-1863)

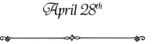

April 28th

Having loved His own which were in the world, He loved them unto the end.
John 13:1

Does it not seem as if John's heart beats audibly through this passage? That which so powerfully affects his heart is the fact that the Lord Jesus, although He was clearly conscious that His hour of return to the bosom of the Father was near at hand, and was soon to re-ascend the throne of divine Majesty – yet He did not forget His followers, but still retained so much room for these pilgrims in His affectionate solicitude and recollection. And yet how much sorrow of heart had these very disciples occasioned Him. O comprehend this depth of fidelity and compassion! He associated with sinners that He might bear them eternally on His heart. Those whom His Father had given Him were more the objects of His affection than the holy angels around the throne of God, and His love to them increased as the end drew near. If a feeling of heavenly rapture thrilled through the apostle John at such a thought, let our hearts vibrate in like manner! Whatever may befall us, His love continues the same.

F.W. Krummacher (1796-1869)

Be His name honoured and loved. He has neither cast out my prayer nor me. His mercy and my cries still meet each other. Blessed be God!

C.H. Spurgeon (1834-1892)

> Through the love of God our Saviour,
>   All will be well;
> Free and changeless is His favour,
>   All, all is well:
> Precious is the blood that healed us,
> Strong the hand stretched out to shield us,
>   All must be well.

Mary Peters (1813-1856)

Men ought always to pray, and not to faint.
Luke 18:1

A family without prayer is like a house without a roof – exposed to every wind that blows and every storm that rages. Prayer will compel one to leave off sinning, or sinning will make one leave off praying. Do you profess to love any one for whom you have never prayed? Rhetoric cannot pray, with all its words; but Faith can pray, even when she has no words. In prayer it is better to have a heart without words than words without a heart. Pray, not only in the name of Christ, but in the faith of Christ. The gift of prayer may have praise from people, but the grace of prayer has power with God.

Gray & Adams Commentary (1951)

> More things are wrought by prayer
> Than the world dreams of. Wherefore let thy voice
> Rise like a fountain for me night and day.
> For what are men better than sheep or goats,
> That nourish a blind life within the brain,
> If knowing God, they lift no hands of prayer
> Both for themselves and those who call them friends?
> For so the whole round earth is every way
> Bound by gold chains about the feet of God.
>
> Alfred Tennyson (1809-1892)

The prayers of holy people appease God's wrath, drive away temptations, resist and overcome the devil, procure the ministry and service of angels, cure sickness and obtain pardon.... Prayer can obtain everything; can open the windows of heaven and shut the gates of hell, can detain an angel till he leave a blessing; can arrest the sun in its course, and send the winds upon our errands.

Jeremy Taylor (1613-1667)

April 30th

For all the promises of God in Him are "Yea," and in Him "Amen,"
unto the glory of God by us.
2 Corinthians 1:20

"Yes" and "Amen" are nearly synonymous and point to the same thing – that Christ is the confirmation and seal of God's promises. It is a poor compliment to God for us to come to His affirmations with a hesitating "Amen." Be certain of the certain things; for it is an insult to the certainty of the revelation when there is hesitation in the believer.... The truths which He confirms are so inextricably intertwined with Himself that you cannot get them and put Him away. Christ's relation to Christ's gospel is not the relation of other teachers to their words, where you can separate them.... Live near Jesus Christ, holding fast by His hand, so you may lift up your joyful "Amen" to every one of God's "yeas"; and when the Voice from Heaven says "Yea!" our choral shout may go up, *"Amen! Thou art the faithful and true witness."*

Alexander Maclaren (1826-1910)

Prayer must be based upon promise, but thank God His promises are always broader than our prayers! No fear of building inverted pyramids here, for Jesus Christ is the foundation and all the promises of God in Him are 'yea' and 'amen,' unto the glory of God by us.

Francis Havergal (1836-1879)

What should our anchor of hope be made of? Go and get a whole number of *Thus saith the Lord's* and weld them together, for the only anchor that is worth anything is that anchor of hope, the very material of which is *"God has said."*

Gray & Adams Commentary (1951)

> Standing on the promises of Christ the Lord,
> Bound to Him eternally by love's strong cord,
> Overcoming daily with the Spirit's sword,
> Standing on the promises of God.

Russell Kelso Carter (1849-1926)

May

May 1ˢᵗ

*I AM THAT I AM; this shall you say to the children of Israel,
I AM has sent me unto you.*
Exodus 3:14

His eternity is evident by the name God gives Himself. This is the name whereby He is distinguished from all creatures; *I Am* is His proper name. That this description is in the present tense shows that His essence knows no past nor future; if it were *He was*, it would intimate He is not now what He once was; if it were *He will be*, it would intimate He is not yet what He will be.... *I Am* speaks the want of no blessedness, and it speaks the want of no duration; He is the Eternal—I am always and immutably the same. The eternity of God is opposed to the volubility of time, which is extended into past, present and to come. Our time is but a small drop, as a sand to all the atoms and small particles of which the world is made; but God is an unbounded sea of being. "I Am that I Am," an infinite life... to which nothing can be added, nothing can be detracted; there is nothing superior to Him which can detract from Him; nothing desirable that can be added to Him.... He fills an eternal duration. He always was and He always will be, having all being in Himself, and He is the fountain of all being to everything else.

Stephen Charnock (1628-1680)

> Ocean, wide-flowing Ocean, Thou, of uncreated Love;
> I tremble as within my soul I feel Thy waters move.
> Thou art a sea without a shore; awful, immense Thou art;
> A sea which can contract itself within my narrow heart
> Frederick William Faber (1814-1863)

What is our chief end? Our chief end is to glorify God and enjoy Him for ever.

Shorter Catechism (1648)

I know that my Redeemer lives, and that He shall stand at the latter day upon the earth, and after my skin has thus been destroyed, yet from my flesh shall I see God.
Job 19:25, 26

*I*f we die, shall we live again? (Job 14:14). Who has not asked this question in suspense, in hope or in fear? We know we must all die; know that those who are dearest to us must die; can our eyes penetrate beyond the veil which death lets fall? Is there any answer in the heart of humanity to Job's questions? The natural inclination of people everywhere is to believe, not in extinction, but in survival. The ideas attached to the word may be vague, but they exercise a real influence upon lives. The Old Testament saints, in the sublime hours of their faith had a sense of their eternal security with God: *Thou shalt guide me with Thy counsel, and afterward receive me unto glory. Thou wilt show me the path of life* -- across that pathless gulf; *in Thy presence is fullness of joy; in Thy right hand there are pleasures forevermore.* In the New Testament the faith in immortality has new features. It has become a faith in the Resurrection. Only one life has ever won the victory over death: only one kind of life can ever win it -- that kind which *is* in Him, which He shares with all whom faith makes one with Him.

James Denny (1856-1917)

Where are all the atoms of the flesh which corrosion has eaten away? In what furrow or bowel of the earth lie all the ashes of a body burned a thousand years since? God knows in what cabinet every seed pearl lies and in what part of the world every grain of every person's dust lies, and in the twinkling of an eye that body that was scattered over all the elements shall sit down at the right hand of God in a glorious resurrection.

John Donne (1571-1631)

They turned back and tempted God and limited the Holy One of Israel.
Psalm 78:41

Here is an awful charge... they limited *God*. They limited the *Almighty*. They limited the *Infinite*. They limited *The Holy One* – the solitary, awful, self-contained Being whose essence is eternity and power; whose self-existence is declared by the amazing marvels of nature; whose life is essential being. They limited *Him – The One* in whose being all being was swallowed up and absorbed; *The One* before whose glance mountains and hills fled away and were not found; *The One* from everlasting, God, *high over all, blessed for evermore.* The One to whom all the nations were as the drop of a bucket, and who took up the isles as a very little thing, Him they limited. *They limited Him.* They had beheld the marvels of His holiness and power in Egypt and in the Red Sea; they had heard of the God of Abraham, Isaac and Jacob; they had heard of Him who had spoken to their Captain in the bush burning with fire; they beheld His pillar of fire and cloud; they knew themselves divinely selected and chosen -- and He who chose, they *limited!*

E. Paxton Hood (1820-1885)

They limited Him. This was Israel's sin, and has it not been ours? We must not limit His wisdom, for it is infinite; we must not limit His power, for it is omnipotent; we must not limit His mercy, for it is high as heaven and deep as hell; we must not limit Him to time, for He will display His sovereignty; He will not be tied to walk by our rules, or be bound to keep our time, but will perform His word, honour our faith, and *reward them that diligently seek Him.*

James Smith (1802-1862)

Lord, I believe; help my unbelief.

Mark 9:24

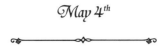

God proves His love for us by this, that Christ died for us when we were still sinners.
Romans 5:8 (Moffatt)

All are offenders against God and breakers of His commandments; no one by their own words and deeds, be they ever so good, can be justified and made righteous before God: everyone is constrained to seek for another righteousness.... There are three things which must go together in our justification: on God's part, His great mercy and grace; on Christ's part, the satisfaction of God's justice; and on our part, true and lively faith in the merits of Jesus Christ. So in our justification there is not only God's mercy and grace, but also His justice in paying our ransom and fulfilling of the law. The grace of God doth not shut out the justice of God, but only shuts out the justice of our works. Because we were not able of ourselves to pay any part toward our ransom, it pleased our heavenly Father in His infinite mercy, without any of our deserving, to prepare for us Christ's body and blood; whereby our ransom might be fully paid, the law fulfilled, and His justice fully satisfied. Christ is now the righteousness of all them that truly do believe in Him. He paid their ransom by His death. He, for them, fulfilled the law in His life.

First Book of Homilies (1802)

My hope is built on nothing less
Than Jesus' blood and righteousness;
I dare not trust the sweetest frame,
But wholly lean on Jesus' name.
His oath, His covenant, His blood,
Support me in the 'whelming flood;
When all around my soul gives way,
He then is all my hope and stay.
On Christ, the solid Rock, I stand;
All other ground is sinking sand.

E. Mote (1797-1874)

May 5th

Be not conformed to this world: but be transformed by the renewing of your mind,
that you may prove what is that good, and acceptable, and perfect, will of God.
Romans 12:2

God's will does not come to us in the whole but in fragments, and generally in small fragments. It is our business to piece it together, and to live it into one vocation.

Frederick W. Faber (1815-1863)

When Madame Guyon (1648-1717) was banished from her home area in France, she said, "All that I know is that God is infinitely holy, righteous and happy; that all goodness is in Him; and that as to myself, I am a mere nothing. To me every condition seems equal. As God is infinitely wise and happy, all my wisdom and happiness are in His will."

> Thou sweet, beloved will of God,
>   My anchor ground, my fortress hill,
>   My spirit's silent, fair abode,
>   In Thee I hide me and am still.
> O Will, that willest good alone,
>   Lead Thou the way, Thou guidest best:
>   A little child, I follow on,
>   And, trusting, lean upon Thy breast.
> Thy wonderful grand will, my God.
>   With triumph now I make it mine;
>   And faith shall cry a joyous "Yes"
>   To every dear command of Thine.

Gerhard Tersteegen (1697-1769)

O Lord, you know what is best for me. Let this or that be done, as you please. Give what you will, how much you will and when you will. Amen.

Thomas à Kempis (1380-1471)

May 6th

Behold the fowls of the air... your heavenly Father feeds them.
Matthew 6:26

Not a sparrow lights to the ground to pick up a grain of corn, but by the providence of God, which extends itself to the commonest creatures. They are fed without any care or project of their own; *they sow not, neither do they reap nor gather into barns. Are you not better than they?* You are dearer to God, and nearer, though they fly in the open firmament of heaven. He is their Maker and Lord, their Owner and Master; but besides all this, He is your Father, and in His account *you are of more value than many sparrows;* you are His children, His first-born; now He that feeds His birds surely will not starve His babes.... If we were, by faith, as unconcerned about the morrow, we should sing cheerfully, for it is worldly care that mars our mirth and damps our joy, and silences our praise, as much as anything.

Matthew Henry (1662-1714)

If ceaseless then, the fowls of heaven He feeds,
If o'er the fields such laced robes He spreads,
Will He not care for you, ye faithless, say?
Is He unwise? Or are ye less than they?

James Thomson (1700-1748)

Let nothing disturb you; let nothing dismay you; all things pass; God never changes. Patience attains all it strives for. Those who have God find they lack nothing: God alone suffices.

Teresa of Avila (1515-1582)

To God thy way commending, trust Him whose arm of might
The heavenly circles bending, guides every star aright.

Paul Gerhardt (1606-1676)

Cast your bread upon the waters: for you shall find it after many days.
Ecclesiastes 11:1

Securities are all very well; but people do not make their fortunes out of hoarded securities. Such securities may suit those whose circumstances compel them to husband jealously their meagre savings; but the big dividends are made out of the risky speculations.... Solomon, with a well-established reputation for wisdom, urges us to venture fearlessly at times upon these more perilous but profitable ventures, *cast thy bread upon the waters.* A person prefers to cast it upon the land. The land is a fixture. The land does not float away or fly away or fade away. You find it where you left it. It is stable, substantial, secure. Because of its fixity, we trust it. For thousands of years it was the bank of the nations. People hid their treasures in fields. But the waters! They ebb and they flow; they rise and they fall; they suck down into their dark depths the treasures confided to their care and leave no trace upon the surface of the hiding-place in which the booty lies concealed. The waters! *Cast thy bread upon the waters!* The Egyptian farmer can sow that portion of land to the waterline, and he does. It is secure. But there is the section of the farm over which the waters are sluggishly drifting. The flood is there. It shows no sign of withdrawing. By the time the waters recede the season may have passed. So the farmer takes the risk and casts seed upon the waters. It seems an awful waste. But in the summer, when he garners a rich harvest from those lands, he blesses the Eastern sage for the wise words. The only way to keep a thing is to throw it away. The only way to hold your money is to invest it. The only way to ensure remembering a poem is to keep repeating it to others. Seeds which are scattered, fill the plain with gold.

F. W. Boreham (1871-1959)

May 8ᵗʰ

Now unto Him that is able to do exceedingly abundantly above all that we ask or think, according to the power that works in us.

Ephesians 3:20

Nothing can restrain or bound the power of God towards us. No limits are set to His power, for it knows no limits, not even the weakness of our prayers and the imperfection of our knowledge, for He is able to transcend all our demands and all our conceptions.... But alas, if this language is infinitely below the reality which is in God, it is infinitely above the reality which is in us! To pass from Scripture to our experience, seems like a fall from heaven to earth. The Lord teach us how to bring our experience into harmony with His promises.

Adolphe Monod (1802-1886)

The promises which God has made are a full storehouse of all kinds of blessings – they include in them both the upper and lower springs, the mercies of this life and of that which is to come; there is no good thing that can present itself as an object to our thought, of which the promises are not a ground for our faith to believe and our hope to expect.

Gray & Adams Commentary (1951)

God cannot bear with patience that we should limit Him either to the time or manner or means of help. It is insufferable to circumscribe an Infinite wisdom and power. He will work, but when He pleases and how He pleases, and by what instruments He pleases, and if He please without instruments, and if He please by weak and improbable instruments.

Joseph Caryl (1602-1673)

No mortal can with Him compare among the sons of men;
Fairer is He than all the fair who fill the heavenly train.
Samuel Stennett (1727-1795)

The Lord is your keeper; the Lord is your shade upon your right hand.
Psalm 121:5

*T*he Lord is your keeper -- this was the Psalmist's gospel. He preached it to others, and he felt it himself. Just such a one is Jesus, the Shepherd of Israel. He says to the Father, *Those that Thou gave me have I kept, and none of them is lost.* Jehovah alone, the omnipotent and self-existent God, is the Keeper and Preserver of His people.

Ambrose Serle (1815)

> Jehovah is Himself thy keeper true,
>   Thy changeless shade;
> Jehovah thy defence on thy right hand Himself hath made.
>   And there no sun by day shall ever smite;
> No moon shall harm thee in the silent night.
>
> From every evil shall He keep thy soul,
>   From every sin;
> Jehovah shall preserve thy going out, thy coming in.
>   Above thee watching,
> He whom we adore shall keep thee henceforth,
>   yea, forevermore.

John D.S. Campbell (1845-1914)

The same protector of the church is engaged for the preservation of every particular believer; the same wisdom, the same power, the same promises. *He that keeps Israel is your keeper.* The Shepherd of the flock is the Shepherd of every sheep, and will take care that not one shall perish.

Matthew Henry (1662-1714)

Lighten our darkness, Lord, we pray; and in your mercy defend us from all perils and dangers of this night. Amen.

Collect (7th century)

Let us lay aside every weight, and the sin which does so easily beset us.
Hebrews 12:1

*C*ast off the sin that goes round about us, is another rendering. This is the body of sin that remains in our nature. The author speaks of this sin as if it had us clasped in its arms. Original sin has us in fetters as captives; it is a thing we cannot win from -- behind us, pulling us back; before us, standing in our way; at our right hand, hindering us to hear prayer, believe, repent, hope. It is like the wind in the face of a weak traveler that blows him some steps back, when he goes one forward. It is in the mind, darkening the judgment; in the will, throwing it the contrary way. And this sin, as woodbine goes about a tree, wraps about us in every possible way.

Samuel Rutherford (1600-1661)

> He saw me plunged in deep distress, and flew to my relief;
> For me He bore the shameful cross, and carried all my grief.
> Since from His bounty I receive such proofs of love divine,
> Had I a thousand hearts to give, Lord, they should all be thine.
>
> Samuel Stennett (1727-1795)

Canon Wilberforce said that one day, while walking in the Isle of Skye, he saw a golden eagle soaring upward. Presently it began to fall. Wanting to know the reason of its death, he hastily examined it and found in its talons a small weasel, which in its flight had sucked the life blood from the eagle's breast. The same end befalls those who cling to some secret sin; sooner or later it will sap the life blood, and they fall. Let us run towards Jesus that we may grow more like Him. It is one of the virtues of Jesus that He transforms into His own image those who look at Him. He photographs Himself upon all sensitive hearts. Run that you may come nearer to Jesus. Seek after more near fellowship with Him.

C.H. Spurgeon (1834-1892)

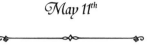

God is able to make all grace abound toward you.
2 Corinthians 9:8

*G*race -- that word is shorthand for the whole sum of the unmerited blessings which come to us through Jesus Christ. It means the unconditioned, undeserved, spontaneous, eternal, stooping, pardoning love of God. The gift from the divine heart, when it comes into our human experience, is like a meteor when it passes into the atmosphere and blazes, showering out a multitude of radiant points of light. The grace is many-sided to us, but one in its source and its character. For at the bottom, that which God in His grace gives to us as His grace is – Himself – or new life through Jesus Christ. This grace is not only many-sided, but abounding. There are no sluices on that great stream so as to regulate its flow, but this fountain is always pouring itself out, and it *abounds*.

God is able. We turn God's ability to give into actual giving by desire, by expectation, by petition, by faithful stewardship. The good gifts of the divine grace will always be proportioned to our work, and to our sufferings, too. If we have strength to do the day's tasks, strength to carry the day's crosses, strength to accept the day's sorrows, and strength to master the day's temptations, that is as much as we need wish to have, even out of the fullness of God.

Alexander Maclaren (1826- 1910)

Grace, 'tis a charming sound, harmonious to my ear;
Heaven with the echo shall resound, and all the earth shall hear.
Grace first contrived a way, to save rebellious man;
And all the steps that grace display, which drew the wondrous plan.
Philip Doddridge (1702-1751)

When God intends great mercy for his people, the first thing he does is set them a-praying.

Matthew Henry (1662-1714)

May 12th

In everything by prayer and supplication with thanksgiving let your requests be made known unto God.

Philippians 4:6

"O God," I said, and that was all. But what are the prayers of the whole universe more than the expression of that one cry?

George MacDonald (1824-1903)

Prayer is the opener of the heart of God, and a means by which the soul, though empty, is filled. By prayer the Christian can open the heart to God as to a friend, and obtain fresh testimony of God's friendship.

John Bunyan (1628-1688)

It is not the arithmetic of our prayers, how many. It is not the rhetoric of our prayers, how eloquent. It is not the geometry of our prayers, how long. It is not the music of our prayers, how sweet. It is not the logic of our prayers, how argumentative. It is not the method of our prayers, how orderly. But, how fervent and how believing are our prayers?

Joseph Hall (1574-1656)

Approach, my soul, the mercy seat, where Jesus answers prayer;
There humbly fall before His feet, for none can perish there.

John Newton (1725-1807)

I can take my telescope and look millions and millions of miles into space, but I can lay it aside and go into my room, shut the door, get down on my knees in earnest prayer and see more of Heaven and get closer to God than I can assisted by all the telescopes and material agencies on earth.

Isaac Newton (1642-1727)

O living Stream; O gracious Rain,
None wait for Thee, and wait in vain.

Gerhard Tersteegen (1697-1769)

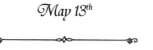

Consecrate yourselves today to the LORD.
Exodus 32:29

Father, I am no longer my own, but yours. Put me to what You will, rank me with whom You will; put me to doing, put me to suffering; let me be employed for You or let me be laid aside for You, exalted for You or brought low for You; let me be full, let me be empty; let me have all things, let me have nothing; I freely and heartily yield all things to Your will and pleasure. Amen.

John Wesley (1703-1791)

I abandon myself forever to Thy arms. Whether gentle or severe, lead me whither Thou wilt. I will not regard the way through which Thou wilt have me pass, but keep my eyes fixed upon Thee, my God, who guides me. My soul finds no rest without the arms and the bosom of this heavenly Providence, my strength and my rampart. I resolve with Thy divine assistance, O my Savior, to follow Thy desires and Thy ordinances, without regarding or examining why Thou does this rather than that; but I will follow Thee according to Thy divine will, without seeking my own inclinations. I am determined to leave all to Thee, taking no part therein save by keeping myself in peace in Thy arms, desiring nothing except as Thou incitest me to desire, to will, to wish. I offer Thee this desire, O my God, beseeching Thee to bless it; I undertake all it includes, relying on Thy goodness, liberality and mercy, with entire confidence in Thee, distrust of myself, and knowledge of my infinite infirmity. Amen.

Jane Frances de Chantal (1572-1641)

Come, pluck up heart, let's neither faint nor fear;
Better, though difficult, the right way to go,
Than wrong, though easy, where the end is woe.

John Bunyan (1628-1688)

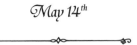

Now unto Him that is able to keep you from falling, and to present you faultless before the presence of His glory with exceeding joy.

Jude 24

This is Jude's doxology to God who *is able,* who *alone is able.* The word that is rendered *from falling* is even more emphatic and carries a larger promise, for it literally means "without stumbling," and stumbling is that which precedes falling. This is the danger implied. When we consider the number, power, malice of our foes, it is wonderful that we can expect victory. It is not surprising that a Christian should fall: we often have to walk in slippery places; we are subject to great weakness; there are many obstacles in our path. To be preserved from the sins of the unbeliever, of the insincere, of the worldly-minded, and of the careless or lukewarm – to be preserved from all these is implied in being *kept from falling.*

Biblical Illustrator (1887)

Faultless is originally applied to the requirement that the sacrificial offerings were to be without blemish. It is then applied more than once to our Lord Himself, as expressive of His perfect, immaculate sinlessness. And it is here applied to the future condition of those who have been kept without stumbling; suggesting at once that they are presented before God at last, stainless as the sacrificial lamb; and that they are conformed to the image of the Lamb of God *without blemish and without spot.* All stains shall melt away and be shaken off as completely as the water of some stagnant pond drops from the white swan plumage, and leaves no stain.

Alexander Maclaren (1826-1910)

O Lord, never suffer us to think that we can stand by ourselves and not need Thee.

John Donne (1571-1631)

May 15th

He is able to save them to the uttermost that come unto God by Him,
seeing He ever lives to make intercession for them.

Hebrews 7:25

He is able to save: to the uttermost ends of the earth; to the uttermost limits of time; to the uttermost period of life; to the uttermost degree of depravity; to the uttermost depth of misery; to the uttermost measure of perfection.

Gray & Adams Commentary (1951)

There is endless salvation in the power of Jesus. Because He never dies, He is endlessly able to save. He is *able to save* from the uttermost of evil to the uttermost of good.... If we were to climb a great hill from which we could see wide fields of spiritual distress and poverty, and if all this represented our experience, yet the Lord is able to spread salvation all round the far-off horizon and encompass all our want. Climb the mountain and look far over this terrible wilderness. As far as ever you can see, or foresee of dreaded need in years to come, so far and much further can the salvation of Jesus reach. As far as with the telescope of apprehension you can spy out trials in life and woes in death, so far is Jesus *able to save* you. The *uttermost* will never be reached by you, but it has long ago been provided for by Him. All that you require He can surely give, since He lives by the power of an endless life to be the fullness of every emptied soul. The Lord Jesus is *able to save* us entirely. He will work out the salvation of the whole person, body, soul and spirit. All that which the first Adam ruined, the second Adam shall restore.... Not a bone, nor a piece of a bone, of a redeemed one shall be left in the hands of the enemy. He is *able to save to the uttermost* from every consequence of the Fall, personal sin and actual death.

C.H. Spurgeon (1834-1892)

Christ… shall reign for ever and ever.
Revelation 11:15

The Lord God omnipotent reigns
Revelation 19:6

Rejoice, the Lord is King; your Lord and King adore;
Rejoice, give thanks and sing and triumph evermore:
Lift up your heart, lift up your voice:
Rejoice; again I say, Rejoice.

Jesus the Saviour reigns, the God of truth and love;
When He had purged our stains, He took His seat above:
Lift up your heart, lift up your voice:
Rejoice; again I say, Rejoice.

His kingdom cannot fail; He rules o'er earth and heaven;
The keys of death and hell are to our Jesus given:
Lift up your heart, lift up your voice:
Rejoice; again I say, Rejoice.

He sits at God's right hand till all His foes submit,
And bow to His command, and fall beneath His feet:
Lift up your heart, lift up your voice:
Rejoice; again I say, Rejoice.

Rejoice in glorious hope; Jesus, the Judge, shall come
And take His servants up to their eternal home:
We soon shall hear the archangel's voice;
The trump of God shall sound, Rejoice.

Charles Wesley (1707-1788)

When that tremendous day shall rise, and all Thine armies shine in robes of victory through the skies, the glory shall be Thine.

Isaac Watts (1674-1748)

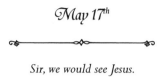

Sir, we would see Jesus.
John 12:21

Only Christ can influence the world; but all that the world sees of Christ is what it sees of you and me. Christ said: *The world sees Me no more, but you see Me.* You see Him, and standing in front of Him, reflect Him, and the world sees the reflection. It cannot see Him. A Christian's usefulness depends solely upon that relationship. Almost everything in Christian experience and character follows from standing before Christ and reflecting His character.... To have lived with Socrates, must have made one wise; with Aristotle, just; with Frances of Assisi, gentle; Savonarola, strong. But to have lived with Christ must have made one like Christ, that is to say "A Christian."

Henry Drummond (1851-1897)

If you seek Jesus in all things, you shall surely find Jesus. But if you seek yourself, you shall also find yourself, but to your own destruction.

Thomas à Kempis (1379-1471)

There is enough in Christ to take up our study and contemplation all our days; and the more we study Christ, the more there will be new wonders still appearing in Him.

John Row (1680)

The name which He bore in His humiliation He bears still in His glory, and is the name which is above every name, at which every knee shall bow.... Through eternity we shall call His name Jesus because He has finally and fully saved us from our sins.

Alexander Maclaren (1826-1910)

Jesus, priceless treasure, source of purest pleasure,
Truest friend to me: ah, how long I've panted
And my heart hath fainted, thirsting, Lord, for Thee.

Johann Franck (1641-1695)

The goodness of God endures continually.
Psalm 52:1

Only God is originally good. All created goodness is a rivulet from this fountain, but Divine goodness has no spring. God has it in and of Himself. All the goodness that is in His creatures is but the flowing of His goodness upon them, and vast as is the number towards whom it flows – angels, glorified spirits, people – there is still less manifested than is left. All creatures are not capable of exhausting its riches. And God is perfectly good, because infinitely good. He is good without indigence, because He has the whole nature of goodness.... As nothing has an absolutely perfect being but God, so nothing has an absolutely perfect goodness but God. And God only is immutably good. Other things may be good by supernatural power, but not in their own nature.... God is so good that He cannot be bad.

Stephen Charnock (1628-1680)

> Yes, God is good; in earth and sky,
> From ocean depths and spreading wood,
> Ten thousand voices seem to cry,
> "God made us all, and God is good."
> And we, in louder notes of praise,
> Should sing for joy that God is good.

John H. Gurney (1802-1862)

When we realize the greatness of God's goodness there will be a greatness of love toward God. When we truly understand the extent of sin which has been pardoned, the depths of misery from which we have been extricated, the heights of glory to which we are to be admitted, then, and not till then, will our hearts burn with love toward God.

Biblical Illustrator (1887)

His goodness is meant to lead you to repentance.

Romans 2:4 (Williams)

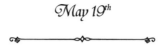

Come unto me, all you that labour and are heavy laden, and I will give you rest.
Matthew 11:28

I have read in Plato and Cicero many sayings that are very wise and beautiful, but I have never read in either of them such words as *Come unto me all you that labour and are heavy laden, and I will give you rest*. Lo, I have viewed the world over in which Thou has set me. I have tried how this and that thing will fit my spirit and the design of my creation, and can find nothing in which to rest, for nothing here doth itself rest. Lo, I come to Thee, the Eternal Being, the Spring of Life, the Centre of rest, the Fullness of all things.

Augustine of Hippo (354-430)

> But rest was ordered long before,
> For this the Saviour left the skies,
> The Home beyond the thousand suns—
> He stretches forth His hands and cries,
> > "Come, come to Me, ye weary ones!
> > Ye long have laboured, come and rest,
> > Lie still, belovéd, on My breast."
> > > J.S. Kunth (?-1700)

Strengthen me, O God, by the grace of your Holy Spirit. Grant me to be strengthened with might in the inner person, and to empty my heart of all useless care and anguish; not to be drawn away with sundry desires of anything whatever, but to look on all things as passing away, and on myself also no less as about to pass away with them.... O Lord, grant me heavenly wisdom, that I may learn above all things to seek and to find You, above all things to relish and to love You, and to think of all other things as being, what indeed they are, at the disposal of Your wisdom. Amen.

Thomas à Kempis (1379-1471)

Stillness midst the ever-changing, Lord my rest art Thou;
So for me has dawned the morning, God's eternal NOW.
Gerhard Tersteegen (1697-1769)

May 20th

The winter is past, the rain is over and gone; the flowers appear on the earth;
the time of the singing of birds is come.
Song of Solomon 2:11, 12

The things which are seen are types of the things which are not seen. The works of creation are pictures to the children of God of the secret mysteries of grace. The very seasons of the year find their parallel in the little world within us. We have had our winter – dreary howling winter – when the north wind of the law rushed forth against us, when every hope was nipped, when all the seeds of joy lay buried beneath the dark clods of despair, when our soul was fast fettered like a river bound with ice, without waves of joy, or flowing of thanksgiving. Thanks be to God, the soft south wind breathed upon our soul, and at once the waters of desire were set free, the spring of love came on, flowers of hope appeared in our hearts, the trees of faith put forth their young shoots, the time of the singing of birds came in our hearts, and we now have joy and peace in believing.

C.H. Spurgeon (1834-1892)

From dearth to plenty, and from death to life, is Nature's progress when she lectures us in heavenly truth; evincing, as she makes the grand transition, that there lives and works a soul in all things, and that soul is God. The beauties of the wilderness are His, the fairer forms that cultivation glories in are His; He set the bright procession on its way, and marshals all the order of the year.

William Cowper (1731-1800)

Christ is the creator of all and the sustainer of all. *He upholds all things by the word of His power.* In Him all things *consist* or hold together. Nature, with its powers and laws, exists and moves only because Christ's energy throbs through it all.

A. H. Strong (1836-1925)

May 21ˢᵗ

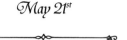

Cause me to hear your loving kindness in the morning.
Psalm 143:8

It is the *voice* of the loving kindness of the Lord that David desires to hear. This voice is the music of heaven, the joyful sound of the gospel, and it makes a jubilee in the Christian's heart. This is the voice that speaks *pardon* through Jesus, the medium of this kindness. *Have mercy upon me, O God, according to Thy loving kindness: according to the multitude of Thy tender mercies blot out my transgressions.* The voice speaks *peace, joy, hope.* With the music of this voice falling upon our ears, the night of hopelessness passes away, and the morning of expectation opens upon us. *The morning* is the season in which David desires to hear the voice of the loving kindness of the Lord. It is well to have a subject like this to occupy our waking thoughts, and to take hold of our first desires. Prayer and praise, reading and meditation, will be sweet with such a subject occupying and influencing our minds.... Waken my ear morning by morning, so that I may enjoy the privilege. And when the morning of eternity shall come, *cause me to hear the voice of Thy loving kindness* welcoming me to its joys.

W. Abbot (1870)

> He saw me ruined by the fall,
> Yet loved me, not withstanding all;
> He saved me from my lost estate,
> His loving kindness, Oh how great!

Samuel Medley (1738-1799)

It may well be said we hear this loving kindness in the morning, since it makes it morning to us when so ever we hear it.

Richard Baker (1568-1645)

Have mercy upon me, O God, according to Thy loving kindness. Amen

Psalm 51:1

May 22nd

O come, let us worship and bow down: let us kneel before the LORD our maker.
Psalm 95:6

The messengers of disaster came to Job, one following hard upon another, like successive shocks of an earthquake, and the ever-recurring close of each woeful tale was, *I only am escaped to tell you.* We almost expect to see Job fall dead, as he is stunned by blow after blow. But no. Greatest of heroes, spectacle for angels to admire, pattern for believers to imitate in the hour of their most adverse fortune, he arose and worshipped.... *Naked came I out of my mother's womb, and naked shall I return thither: the Lord gave, and the Lord has taken away; blessed be the name of the Lord.*

Thomas Guthrie (1803-1873)

> I'll praise Him while He lends me breath;
> And when my voice is lost in death!
> Praise shall employ my nobler powers:
> My days of praise shall be ne'er past,
> While thought and life and being last,
> Or immortality endures.

Isaac Watts (1674-1748)

In all our Maker's grand designs, omnipotence, with wisdom, shines; His works, through all this wondrous frame, declare the glory of His Name.

Thomas Blacklock (1721-1791)

Take, Lord, and receive all my liberty, my memory, my understanding, and my entire will, all that I have and possess. Thou hast given all to me. To Thee, O Lord, I return it all. All is Thine; dispose of it wholly according to Thy will. Give me Thy love and Thy grace, for this is sufficient for me. For with these I am rich enough and desire nothing more. Amen.

Ignatius Loyola (1491-1556)

May 23rd

God forbid that I should glory, save in the cross of our Lord Jesus Christ....
Galatians 6:14

The Cross is not an outrage. It represents justice. Not gross injustice but righteous punishment was His. You must be willing to acknowledge that. This is the only way your own soul can pass into death at Golgotha and through death into life. For if He bore the punishment, you either have no part with Him or else are condemned with Him.... He asks more of you than the sympathy of your feelings. He cannot be satisfied until you have confessed: "*My* chastisement, the chastisement of *my* peace was upon Him."

Abraham Kuyper (1837-1920)

We must preach the sacrifice, the atonement of Christ, without qualification or reserve. We are to preach the same glorious gospel which Paul preached when he uplifted the Cross of Christ as the only hope of a lost and ruined world – Christ the Saviour of sinners!

Biblical Illustrator (1887)

John Williams (1796-1839), martyred in Polynesia, said: "I am resolved never to preach unless salvation through the blood of Christ is its sum and substance. It is a truth worth carrying to the whole world."

> Rejoice, you pure in heart,
> > rejoice, give thanks and sing.
> Your festal banner wave on high,
> > the cross of Christ your King.
> With all the angel choirs,
> > with all the saints on earth,
> Pour out the strains of joy and bliss,
> > true rapture, noblest mirth!

Edward Plumptre (1821-1891)

May 24th

The grace of the Lord Jesus Christ, and the love of God,
and the communion of the Holy Spirit, be with you all.
2 Corinthians 13:14

One God! one Majesty! There is no God but Thee!
Unbounded, unextended Unity!

Awful in unity, O God! we worship Thee,
More simply one, because supremely Three!

Dread, unbeginning One! Single, yet not alone,
Creation hath not set Thee on a higher throne.

Unfathomable Sea! All life is out of Thee,
And Thy life is Thy blissful Unity.

All things that from Thee run, all works that Thou hast done,
Thou didst in honour of Thy being One.

And by Thy being One, ever by that alone,
Couldst Thou do, and doest, what Thou hast done.

We from Thy oneness come, beyond it cannot roam,
And in Thy oneness find our one eternal home.

Blest be Thy Unity! All joys are one to me –
The joy that there can be no other God than Thee!

Frederick W. Faber (1814-1863)

Glory be to the Father, and to the Son, and to the Holy Spirit: as it was in the beginning, is now and ever shall be, world without end. Amen.

Gloria Patri (2nd century)

May 25th

If any one does sin, we have an Advocate with the Father, Jesus Christ the righteous.
1 John 2:1 (Weymouth)

Because we are in this state of God's wrath through original sin, a Mediator was required.... This is the grace of God through Jesus Christ our Lord – that we are reconciled to God through the Mediator and receive the Holy Spirit so that we may be changed from enemies into children of God.

Augustine of Hippo (354-430)

> Now I have found the ground wherein
> Sure my soul's anchor may remain -
> The wounds of Jesus, for my sin
> Before the world's foundation slain;
> Whose mercy shall unshaken stay,
> When heaven and earth are fled away.
> Fixed on this ground will I remain,
> Though my heart fail and flesh decay;
> This anchor shall my soul sustain,
> When earth's foundations melt away;
> Mercy's full power I then shall prove,
> Loved with an everlasting love.

Johann Andreas Rothe (1688-1758)

I am not skilled to understand what God has willed, what God has planned; I only know at His right hand is One who is my Saviour! Yes, living, dying, let me bring my strength, my solace from this spring: that He who lives to be my King once died to be my Saviour!

Dora Greenwell (1821-1882)

This name Jesus is a name of comfort to sinners when they call upon Him, "Jesus, be my Jesus."

Anselm (1033-1109)

May 26th

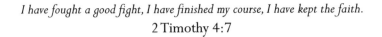

I have fought a good fight, I have finished my course, I have kept the faith.
2 Timothy 4:7

On the evening of May 26, 735, a silence pervaded the Monastery of Jarrow. On a low bed lay an aged priest; his wasted frame and sunken eyes told that death was near; his breathing was slow and labored. Near him sat a young scribe with an open scroll and a pen in his hand. Looking into the face of the dying man he said, "Now, dearest Master, there remains only one chapter, but the exertion is too much for you." "It is easy, my son, take your pen and write quickly." Sentence after sentence was uttered in feeble accents.... "It is finished," said the scribe. "It is finished," repeated the dying man. "Lift up my head; place me in the spot where I have been accustomed to pray." Then clasping his hands, and lifting his eyes heavenward, he exclaimed, "Glory be to the Father, and to the Son, and to the Holy Ghost!" Thus died the venerable Bede (672-735); and thus was completed the first Anglo-Saxon translation of the Gospel of John.

Gray & Adams Commentary (1951)

Polycarp (69-155) was not only instructed by apostles and conversed with many who had seen Christ, but was also appointed bishop of the church in Smyrna. I also saw him in my early youth, for he tarried on earth a very long time. When a very old man, he gloriously and most nobly suffered martyrdom, having always taught the things which he had learned from the apostles, and which the church has handed down, and which alone are true.

Irenaeus of Lyons (130-202)

Who can tell what a day may bring forth? Cause me therefore, gracious God, to live every day as if it were to be my last, for I know not but that it may be such. Cause me to live now as I wish I had done when I come to die. Amen.

Thomas à Kempis (1380-1471)

May 27th

As for God, His way is perfect.
Psalm 18:30

The Psalmist is standing up for God. He commends *His way* – whether it be the way in which we walk with God, personal holiness, or the way wherein God walks with us, the way of His providence and His dispensations. To our corrupt eyes God's way is not always perfect. The way in the wilderness is often crooked. It runs at times seemingly quite contrary to the design of Providence. Often times Providence reads best backwards. But God's way is perfect. It is according to the pattern shown in the Word. It is suited to our need and is ever suited to our time.

Thomas Boston (1678-1732)

Though all acknowledge God to be just, most people are no sooner overtaken by affliction than they quarrel with His severity. Unless their wishes are immediately complied with, they are impatient, and nothing is more common than to hear His justice impeached. As it is everywhere abused by the imputations people cast upon it, here it is very properly vindicated from such ungrateful treatment, and asserted to be constant and unfailing, however loudly the world may disparage it. *The Lord is righteous in all His ways, and holy in all His works.* We fail to give God due honour unless we recognize a constant tenor of righteousness in the whole progress of His operation. Nothing is more difficult in the time of trouble, when God has apparently forsaken us or afflicts us without cause, than to restrain our feelings from breaking out against His judgments. *You are righteous, O God, and just are Your judgments.*

John Calvin (1509-1564)

I plant my feet upon this ground of trust, and silence every fear with – God is just.

William Cowper (1731-1800)

Enter into His gates with thanksgiving, and into His courts with praise.
Psalm 100:4

Here on earth fellowship with God is one of the privileges belonging to the royal nobility of the redeemed. The children of the great King have the right to enter the presence of their heavenly Father. They have the right to approach the throne of grace in prayer.

Erich Sauer (1899-1959)

Come, Thou almighty King, help us Thy Name to sing,
    Help us to praise.
Father all-glorious, o'er all victorious,
Come, and reign over us, Ancient of days.

Come, Thou incarnate Word, gird on Thy mighty sword,
    Our prayer attend;
Come, and Thy people bless, and give Thy word success;
Spirit of holiness, on us descend!

Come, holy Comforter, Thy sacred witness bear
    In this glad hour;
Thou who almighty art, now rule in every heart,
And ne'er from us depart, Spirit of power!

To Thee, great One in Three, eternal praises be,
    Hence evermore;
Thy sovereign majesty may we in glory see,
And to eternity love and adore. Amen.

Whitefield's Leaflet (1757)

Samuel Rutherford (1600-1661) dated his prison letters from "Christ's Palace, Aberdeen."

Call unto Me, and I will answer and show you great and mighty things, which you know not.

Jeremiah 33:3

This good text, all mouldy and chill with the prison in which Jeremiah lay, has a brightness and a beauty about it.... We need to be commanded to attend to the very act which ought to be our greatest happiness, to meet with our God. Art thou sick? Cry unto Me for I am a Great Physician! Does providence trouble thee? Call unto Me! Art thou fearful? Call unto Me! Do thy children vex thee? Are they thankless? Call unto Me! Are thy griefs little yet painful, like prick of thorns? Call unto Me! Is thy burden heavy as though it would make thy back break beneath the load? Call unto Me!

We ought not to tolerate for a minute the ghastly and grievous thought that God will not answer prayer. His nature, as manifested in Christ Jesus, demands it. We misread Calvary if we think that prayer is useless. The saint may expect to discover deeper experience and to know more of the higher spiritual life, by being much in prayer. All believers see Christ; but not all believers put their fingers into the prints of the nails, nor thrust their hand into His side. We have not all the high privilege of John to lean upon Jesus' bosom, nor of Paul to be caught up into the third heaven. It is prevailing prayer that takes Christians to Carmel or that bears them aloft to Pisgah. To grow in experience, there must be much prayer.

C.H. Spurgeon (1834-1892)

The faith that believes that God *will* do what you ask is not born in a hurry; it is not born in the dust of the street or in the noise of the crowd. But faith will have a birthplace and keep growing stronger in every heart that takes quiet time off habitually with God and listens to His voice in His word.

S.D. Gordon (1859-1936)

May 30th

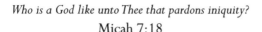

Who is a God like unto Thee that pardons iniquity?
Micah 7:18

When we think on the difference between God's creating a world and God's pardoning a sin – the one done without effort, the other demanding an instrumentality terribly sublime; the one effected by a word, the other wrought out in agony and blood on a quaking earth and beneath a darkened heaven – the one is as nothing beside the other. That God can pardon is at the very summit of what is wonderful.

H. Melville (1837)

> Great God of wonders, all Thy ways
> Are matchless, godlike and divine;
> But the fair glories of Thy grace
> Most godlike and unrivalled shine:
> In wonder lost, with trembling joy,
> We take the pardon of our God,
> Pardon for sins of deepest dye,
> A pardon sealed with Jesus' blood:
> O may this strange, this wondrous grace,
> This matchless miracle of love,
> Fill the wide earth with grateful praise,
> And all the angelic choirs above:
> *Who is a pardoning God like Thee?*
> *Or who has grace so rich and free?*
> Samuel Davies (1723-1761)

Tell me the distance from the east to the west and I will tell you the distance which the pardoned sinner is from sin. It is a casting them into the *depths of the sea*. Not on the shore to be washed back by the incoming waves, but into the *depths*. Into the abysses of some mighty Atlantic, where no storms shall stir them from their graves.

Biblical Illustrator (1887)

Now unto the King eternal, immortal, invisible, the only wise God, be honour and glory for ever and ever.
1 Timothy 1:17

While as yet no star traversed its course, no sun threw its flood of light and energy through space, no systems of stars and suns swept through infinity in mighty curves and uniform relations, there God was; He the eternal without beginning, He who is above the whole course of time, He who in harmony beyond explanation possesses unity and life, the Father, the Son, and the Holy Spirit, the basis of eternity, the Living One, the only God. Three divine Persons and yet one God.

Erich Sauer (1899-1959)

Immortal, invisible, God only wise,
In light inaccessible hid from our eyes,
Most blessed, most glorious, the Ancient of Days,
Almighty, victorious, Thy great Name we praise.

Unresting, unhasting, and silent as light,
Nor wanting, nor wasting, Thou rulest in might;
Thy justice like mountains high soaring above
Thy clouds which are fountains of goodness and love.

To all life Thou givest—to both great and small;
In all life Thou livest, the true life of all;
We blossom and flourish as leaves on the tree,
And wither and perish—but naught changeth Thee.

Great Father of glory, pure Father of light,
Thine angels adore Thee, all veiling their sight.
All laud we would render: O help us to see
'Tis only the splendour of light hideth Thee. Amen.

Walter C. Smith (1824-1908)

June

June 1

By one offering He has perfected forever those who are sanctified.
Hebrews 10:14

That "one offering" offered once for all, was so divine, so holy, so complete, so satisfactory, it has forever perfected the pardon, perfected the justification, perfected the adoption, and will perfect the glory of all the elect of Jehovah. Beloved, is not this enough to check every sigh, quell every fear, annihilate every doubt, and fill you with peace and joy in believing? What shouts of praise to Jesus should burst from every lip as each believer contemplates the sacrifice that has secured eternal salvation! When Titus liberated the imprisoned Greeks, they clustered around his tent, chanting his praises and exclaiming with fervor, "A savior!" Oh, with what deeper emphasis may every child of God, freed from the chains of sin and of death by the liberty with which Christ has made us free, extol the person and chant the praises of that glorious Savior, and exclaim, "Jesus! Jesus! Jesus! He has saved His people from their sins!" Believer, demonstrate your sense of the preciousness of this great sacrifice by bringing to it daily sins, drawing from it hourly comfort, and laying yourself upon it, body, soul, and spirit, a living sacrifice unto God…

If you have fled to Jesus as a poor, empty, believing sinner, there is not a throb of love in His loving heart, nor a drop of blood in His flowing veins, nor a particle of grace in His mediatorial fullness, nor a thought of peace in His divine mind, which is not yours, all yours, inalienably yours, as much yours as if you were its sole possessor! And in proportion as you thus deal with Christ – traveling to Him, living upon and out of Him, dealing as personally with Him as He deals personally with you – He will become growingly precious to your soul…. "Precious Jesus! O how lovely are You to my longing heart. Never, never let me grieve You, never from You let me depart. All in all to me You art."

Octavius Winslow (1808-1878)

June 2

When He had spoken these things, while they beheld, He was taken up:
and a cloud received Him out of their sight.

Acts 1:9

The time had now come when His earthly presence should be taken away from them forever, until He returned in glory to judge the world. He met them in Jerusalem, and as He led them towards Bethany, He bade them wait in this Holy City until they had received the promise of the Spirit. He checked their eager inquiry about the times and seasons, and bade them be His witnesses in all the world. When these farewells were over, He lifted up His hands and blessed them, and even as He blessed them, was parted from them, and as He passed from before their yearning eyes a cloud received Him out of their sight.

Between us and His visible presence – between us and that glorified Redeemer who now sits at the right hand of God – that cloud still rolls. But the eye of faith can pierce it; the incense of true prayer can rise above it; through it the dew of blessing can descend. And if He is gone away, yet He has given us in His Holy Spirit a nearer sense of His presence, a closer infolding in the arms of His tenderness, than we could have enjoyed even if we had lived with Him of old in the home of Nazareth, or sailed with Him in the little boat over the crystal waters of Gennesareth....

It was but for thirty-three years of a short lifetime that He lived on earth; it was but for three broken and troubled years that He preached the Gospel of the Kingdom; but forever, even until all the eons have been closed, and the earth itself, with the heavens that now are, have passed away, shall every one of His true and faithful children find peace and hope and forgiveness in His name, and that name shall be Emmanuel, which is, GOD WITH US.

F. W. Farrar (1831-1903)

June 3

Lift up your heads, O ye gates; even lift them up, ye everlasting doors;
and the King of glory shall come in. Who is this King of glory?
The LORD of hosts, He is the King of glory.
Psalm 24:9, 10

In this Psalm we have an account of the entrance of Christ into heaven. The Lord ascended with a shout; He approached the heavenly portal – the herald in His escort demanded an entrance, *Lift up your heads, O you gates, and be lifted up, you everlasting doors; and the King of glory shall come in.* The celestial watchers within ask, *Who is this King of Glory?* The herald answers, *The Lord strong and mighty, the Lord mighty in battle.* The gates lift up their heads, and the everlasting doors are lifted up. The Prince enters His Father's palace, greeted with the acclamations of heaven, whose inhabitants unite in one shout of joy ineffable. *The Lord of Hosts, He is the King of glory.*

Christmas Evans (1766-1838)

Christ is our life, and our growth in spiritual life is Christ increasing within us. It is impossible to cherish a holy desire, or to conceive a heavenly thought, or to perform a good action, or to conquer a single infirmity, or to battle a solitary temptation apart from Christ. Absence from His beatific presence and distance from His blest abode do not render the Savior less precious to the believing soul.

Octavius Winslow (1808-1878)

When the living presence of Jesus was taken away from His own, it was not that they were to have Him less, but rather in a lovelier way. For when He rose up to heaven, He took with Him all their hearts, and all their minds, and all their love.

Henry Suso (1300-1366)

Lord, Thou hast been our dwelling place in all generations.
Psalm 90:1

O God, our help in ages past, our hope for years to come,
Our shelter from the stormy blast, and our eternal home.

Under the shadow of Thy throne Thy saints have dwelt secure;
Sufficient is Thine arm alone, and our defense is sure.

Before the hills in order stood, or earth received her frame,
From everlasting Thou art God, to endless years the same.

A thousand ages in Thy sight are like an evening gone,
Short as the watch that ends the night before the rising sun.

Time, like an ever-rolling stream, bears all its sons away;
They fly forgotten, as a dream dies at the opening day.

O God, our help in ages past, our hope for years to come,
Be Thou our guard while troubles last, and our eternal home. Amen.

Isaac Watts (1674-1748)

God's eternity is duration without beginning or end; existence without bounds or dimensions; present without past or future. His eternity is youth without infancy or old age, life without birth or death, today without yesterday or to-morrow. Who can know God but God? Who can reveal Him but the Only-begotten? And who can comprehend the fullness of Him who is the beginning and the end, the first and the last?

Stephen Charnock (1628-1680)

If He is my refuge, who can pursue me? If my defense, what temptation shall wound me? If my rock, what storm shall shake me? If my salvation, what melancholy shall deject me? If my glory, what calumny shall defame me?

John Donne (1573-1631)

June 5

Hallowed be Thy name.
Matthew 6:9

It is the greatest name in the universe. Angels cannot bear to see it dishonored, because He is God their Maker and Sovereign; His children cannot, because He is their Father, and they have all the honorable sentiments of children. The Eternal One, the Mighty God, the Everlasting Father – He who is Himself the beginning, and measure, and end of all that exists, and from whom every creature has received all that it is and has – deserves the homage He claims. The Being whose nature, purposes and word are such as His, is worthy of the hallowed exaltation for which His people are taught to pray. This immense and infinite Deity, who is everywhere, and whose being and presence are separated by no distance and confined by no space, is worthy to dwell in the thoughts, have a throne in the heart, be extolled by the lips, and shine forth in the life of creatures who are enfolded in the arms and carried in the bosom of His infinity! This holy Being, the splendor of whose purity dazzles the sun, is worthy to be hallowed by people and all the angels. The all-powerful God well commands the respect of creatures who dwell in tabernacles of clay. He whose watchful eye equally discerns whatever passes in the thickest darkness and in the clearest light, who knows intuitively all that can be known, and who *destroys the wisdom of the wise, and brings to naught the understanding of the prudent,* ought not in vain to look from heaven upon humanity, to see if they respect His intelligence and bow humbly before the dictates of His wisdom. The good and gracious God, who loves the weak and guilty inhabitants of this lower world, who took their nature, and in that nature suffered and died that they might not suffer and die, deserves every expression of grateful homage. Sovereign honors belong to the just God; earth and heaven should resound with *the song of the Lamb.*

Gardiner Spring (1785-1873)

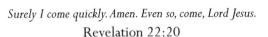

Surely I come quickly. Amen. Even so, come, Lord Jesus.
Revelation 22:20

Come to our full and final salvation. Come, that we the beings whom Thou has made and remade may enjoy the liberty of the glory for which we were destined in Thy love. Come that we may be forever happy, and strong and free, in that wonderful world of the resurrection. Come that we may meet again with exceeding joy the beloved ones who have gone before us, and all Thy saints. But oh, come yet more for Thyself, and for Thy glory, and to take Thy full possession.

H.C.G. Moule (1841-1920)

Come, Thou long-expected Jesus,
        born to set Thy people free;
From our fears and sins release us,
        let us find our rest in Thee.
Israel's strength and consolation,
        hope of all the earth Thou art;
Dear Desire of every nation,
        joy of every longing heart.
By Thine own eternal Spirit
        rule in all our hearts alone;
By Thine all-sufficient merit
        raise us to Thy glorious throne.

Charles Wesley (1707-1788)

Bring us, O Lord God, at the last awakening into the house and gate of heaven, to enter into that gate and dwell in that house where there shall be no darkness nor dazzling, but one equal light; no noise nor silence, but one equal music; no fears nor hopes, but an equal possession; no ends nor beginnings, but one equal eternity, in the habitations of Thy majesty and Thy glory, world without end. Amen.

John Donne (1571-1631)

In whom we have redemption through His blood, even the forgiveness of sins.
Colossians 1:14

As the demand of the law is perfect obedience, so the offer of Christ is perfect forgiveness. Perfect obedience no one has paid or can pay. Perfect forgiveness every one may enjoy, who seeks to be accepted through the righteousness which is of God by faith. The two covenants have this great distinction. One is command; the other is mercy: mercy, which assures us that, although we had transgressed the covenant of command, God had still in store a covenant of mercy; that although we had fallen far short of the obedience which God required, God has not altogether cast off His unworthy servants. Herein was love: not that we loved God, but that He loved us, and while we were yet sinners, hath reconciled us to Himself by the death of His Son.

Richard Hooker (1554-1600)

Though I have, by His grace, loved Him in my youth and feared Him in mine age, and laboured to have a conscience void of offence to Him and to all people; yet, if Thou, O Lord, be extreme to mark what I have done amiss, who can abide it? And, therefore, where I have failed, Lord, show mercy to me; for I plead not my righteousness, but the forgiveness of my unrighteousness, for His merits who died to purchase a pardon for penitent sinners.

Richard Hooker (1554-1600)

On his deathbed, Richard Hooker stated: Dear doctor, God hath heard my daily petitions; for I am at peace with all people, and He is at peace with me: from which blessed assurance I feel that inward joy which this world can neither give nor take from me.

June 8

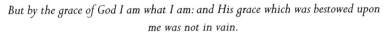

But by the grace of God I am what I am: and His grace which was bestowed upon me was not in vain.

1 Corinthians 15:10

Paul had a vivid remembrance of the mercy that had been shown him. Like a silver refrain, it came back to him in all times of anguish, distress, and virulent opposition.... *I obtained mercy*, he declared. It was as though he never could forget how deeply he had sinned, and how strenuously he had resisted that very grace which he now proclaimed. But perhaps the secret of Paul's success lay most of all in his faculty of extracting power from his weaknesses. He had eminent gifts of character, of energy, of power to command and lead and organize, of thought and speech; but had it not been for the presence of his infirmity, he might never have become the great Apostle to the Gentiles. He might have yielded to self-confidence in his heart-depths, and relied on these extraordinary endowments, instead of casting himself absolutely on the power of God; in consequence of which his life-work was accomplished, not by himself, but by God operating through the frail organism of his mortal body. Had Paul been strong, he might have been an Apollos, a Chrysostom, an Augustine, a Luther, but never Paul. Because he was weak he was strong; because he bore chains he was the great emancipator from chains; because he was poor he succeeded in making so many rich.

F.B. Meyer (1847-1929)

He uses our blundering efforts, if only love and faith be in them, to bless others, to do good, to build up His Kingdom. Christ is saving the world today, not through faultless work of perfect angels, but through the poor, ignorant, flawed, oft-times very tactless, foolish work of disciples who love Him

J.R. Miller (1840-1912)

June 9

*For as the heavens are higher than the earth, so are my ways higher than your ways,
and my thoughts than your thoughts.*

Isaiah 55:9

God moves in a mysterious way His wonders to perform;
He plants his footsteps in the sea, and rides upon the storm.

Ye fearful saints, fresh courage take; the clouds ye so much dread
Are big with mercy, and shall break in blessings on your head.

Judge not the Lord by feeble sense, but trust Him for his grace;
Behind a frowning providence He hides a smiling face.

His purposes will ripen fast, unfolding every hour;
The bud may have a bitter taste, but sweet will be the flower.

Blind unbelief is sure to err, and scan His work in vain;
God is His own interpreter, and He will make it plain.

William Cowper (1731-1800)

Where faith begins, anxiety ends; where anxiety begins, faith ends. As long as we are able to trust in God holding fast in heart, that He is able and willing to help those who rest on the Lord Jesus for salvation, in all matters which are for His glory and their good, the heart remains calm and peaceful. It is only when we practically let go of faith in His power or His love, that we lose our peace and become troubled.

George Müller (1805-1898)

If our circumstances find us in God, we shall find God in all our circumstances.

Anonymous

Nothing is so firm a foundation as past experience of God's faithfulness.

Samuel Rutherford (1600-1661)

June 10

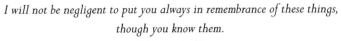

I will not be negligent to put you always in remembrance of these things,
though you know them.
2 Peter 1:12

In John Bunyan's (1628-1688) Pilgrim's Progress, Christiana and the boys arrived at the place where Christian had his battle with Apollyon, and they were anxious to see the exact spot. Greatheart pointed out the place, saying, "Your father had the battle with Apollyon at a place yonder before us, in a narrow passage just beyond Forgetful Green. And indeed that place is the most dangerous place in all these parts. For if at any time the pilgrims meet with any brunt, it is when they forget what favours they have received, and how unworthy they are of them." Moses wrote a whole book on the subject. In the old days people did not consider it essential that a book should bear an attractive title. The book that Moses wrote is called Deuteronomy. If it had been written nowadays, it would have been entitled "The Danger of Forgetful Green." Every chapter urges the importance of not forgetting. Beware lest you forget the Lord which brought you up from the land of Egypt. *Beware lest you forget the day when you came forth out of the land of Egypt. Beware lest you forget that you were a bondman in the land of Egypt. Beware lest you forget all the way which the Lord your God has led you. Beware lest you forget what the Lord your God did unto Pharaoh. Beware lest you forget what the Lord your God did unto Miriam. Beware lest you forget what Amalek did unto you by the way when you came forth out of Egypt. Beware lest you forget how you provoked the Lord your God to anger in the wilderness.* "Beware," he cries, again and again and again, "beware of Forgetful Green."

F. W. Boreham (1871-1959)

The Spirit of God dwelleth in you.
1 Corinthians 3:16

It is certain from the Holy Scriptures that the Spirit of God dwells within us, acts there, prays without ceasing, groans, desires, asks for us what we know not how to ask for ourselves, urges us on, animates us, speaks to us when we are silent, suggests to us all truth, and so unites us to Him that we become one spirit.... We must silence every creature, including self, so that in the deep stillness of the soul we may perceive the ineffable voice of the Bridegroom. We hear well enough that He is speaking and that He is asking for something, but we cannot distinguish what is said, and often we are glad enough that we cannot. The least reserve, the slightest act rooted in self-consideration, the most imperceptible fear of hearing too clearly what God demands interferes with the still small voice.

François de la Mothe Fénelon (1651-1715)

Come down, O Love Divine,
Seek Thou this soul of mine,
And visit it with Thine own ardour glowing;
O Comforter, draw near, within my heart appear,
And kindle it, Thy holy flame bestowing.

O let it freely burn,
Till earthly passions turn
To dust and ashes, in its heat consuming;
And let Thy glorious light shine ever on my sight,
And clothe me round, the while my path illuming.

And so the yearning strong,
With which the soul will long,
Shall far outpass the power of human telling;
For none can guess its grace, till he become the place
Wherein the Holy Spirit makes His dwelling.

Bianco Da Siena (?-1434)

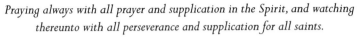

Praying always with all prayer and supplication in the Spirit, and watching thereunto with all perseverance and supplication for all saints.
Ephesians 6:18

Ephesians is a prayer epistle. From praying himself, Paul goes to urging them to pray. The main drive of all their living and warfare seems very clear to Paul, this scarred veteran: *that you may be able to withstand the wiles of the devil.* That is the foe. Large numbers of highly endowed spirit beings, compactly organized, the sovereigns of the present age of moral darkness, are concerned with human beings upon the earth. Paul tells us how the fight is to be won. And his sentence runs unbroken through many verses. Leading up to it he gives the pieces of armour used by the Roman soldier in the action of battle – the loins girt, the breastplate on, the feet shod, the shield, the helmet, the sword.... But when Paul reaches the climax, he puts in the thing with which the fighting is done – "with all prayer praying." Our fighting is praying. Praying is fighting – spirit-fighting. That word *praying* is the climax of this long sentence, and of this whole epistle. This is the sort of action that turns the enemy's flank, and reveals his heels. He cannot stand before persistent knee-work.

This verse is bristling with points. Soldier points all of them, like bayonet points. *With all prayer and supplication* – there is intensity; *always* – at all seasons, day and night, hot and cold, wet and dry; *in the Spirit* – as guided by the Chief; *watching thereunto* – sleepless vigilance; *watching* is ever a fighting word, watch the enemy, watch your own forces; *with all perseverance* – dogged persistence, bulldog tenacity; *and supplication* – intensity again; *for all saints* – the sweep of the action; keep in touch with the whole army. And Paul does not want to be forgotten and adds, *and on my behalf.*

S.D. Gordon (1859-1936)

June 13

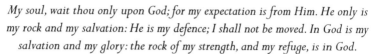

*My soul, wait thou only upon God; for my expectation is from Him. He only is
my rock and my salvation: He is my defence; I shall not be moved. In God is my
salvation and my glory: the rock of my strength, and my refuge, is in God.*
Psalm 62:5-7

In a little bay off Tierra del Fuego, the remains of Allen Gardiner
(1794-1851), the Sailor Martyr, were found in 1851. Near at hand
was a cavern, outside on which were painted, beneath a hand, the
above verses of Psalm 62. On thinking they would have to abandon
this mission, he had written, "We can never do wrong in casting
the Gospel net on any side or in any place. During many a dark and
wearisome night we may appear to have toiled in vain, but it will not
be always so. If we will but wait the appointed time, the promise,
though long delayed, will assuredly come to pass." One of the last
entries in his diary read, "Yet a little while, and through grace we
may join that blessed throng to sing the praises of Christ throughout
eternity. I neither hunger nor thirst, though five days without food!
Marvelous loving-kindness to me, a sinner." During that frightful
period, Gardiner also wrote the following, which shows wondrous
strength:

> Let that sweet word our spirits cheer
> which quelled the tossed disciples' fear:
> > 'Be not afraid!'
> He who could bid the tempest cease
> can keep our souls in perfect peace
> > if on Him stayed.
> And we shall own 'twas good to wait:
> no blessing ever came too late.
>
> Charlotte M. Yonge (1823-1873)

No rude storm, how fierce soe'er it flieth, disturbs the soul that
dwells, O Lord, in Thee.

Harriet Beecher Stowe (1812-1896)

June 14

He that seeketh findeth.
Matthew 7:8

Faith asks, hope seeks, and love knocks. They that seek shall find, shall enjoy, shall grasp, shall know that they have obtained. Hope having asked expects, and therefore seeks for the blessing.... Surely there is no difficulty about seeking. When the woman in the parable lost her money, she lit a candle and sought for it. I do not suppose she had ever been to the university, or qualified as a physician, or that she could have sat on the School Board as a woman of superior sense – but she could seek. Anybody who desires to do so can seek, and for their encouragement the promise is given, they that seek shall find.

C.H. Spurgeon (1834-1892)

God directs and prospers and establishes the ways of those who seek His face in prayer, and who back their prayers by watchful effort.

H.C.G. Moule (1841-1920)

Come, my soul, thy suit prepare,
   Jesus loves to answer prayer;
He Himself has bid thee pray,
   therefore will not say thee nay.
Thou art coming to a King;
   large petitions with thee bring;
For His grace and power are such,
   none can ever ask too much.

John Newton (1725-1807)

Prayer is the pulse of life. By this pulse we can tell what is the condition of the heart. The sin of prayerlessness is a proof that the life of God in the soul is in deadly weakness and sickness.... It is nothing but the sin of prayerlessness which is the cause of the lack of a powerful spiritual life!

Andrew Murray (1828-1917)

Demas hath forsaken me, having loved this present world....
2 Timothy 4:10

A favorite fiction of our childhood was the voyage of Sinbad the Sailor into the Indian Sea. There was the magnetic rock that rose from the surface of the placid waters. Silently Sinbad's vessel was attracted towards it; silently the bolts were drawn out of the ship's side, one by one, through the subtle attraction of that magnetic rock. And when the fated vessel drew so near that every bolt and clamp were unloosed, the whole structure of bulwark, mast and spars tumbled into ruin on the sea, and the sleeping sailors awoke to their drowning agonies. So stands the magnetic rock of worldliness athwart the Christian's path. Its attraction is subtle, silent, slow, but fearfully powerful on every soul that floats within its range. Under its enchanting spell bolt after bolt of good resolution, clamp after clamp of Christian obligation, are steadily drawn out. They cannot hold together under a tempest of trial. They are no longer held together by a Divine principle within. It has been silently drawn out of them by that mighty loadstone of attraction – a sinful, godless, Christ-rejecting world.

Gray & Adams Commentary (1951)

My soul, be on thy guard, ten thousand foes arise;
The hosts of sin are pressing hard to draw thee from the skies.
Ne'er think the victory won, nor lay thine armor down;
The work of faith will not be done, till thou obtain the crown.

George Heath (1750-1822)

O Saviour, I have naught to plead in earth beneath or heaven above, but just my own exceeding need, and Thy exceeding love. Amen.

Jane Crewdson (1809-1863)

June 16

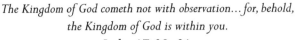

The Kingdom of God cometh not with observation... for, behold,
the Kingdom of God is within you.
Luke 17:20, 21

It is a visible Kingdom, and yet at the same time it is a Kingdom that comes *not with observation*; unseen in its progress, seen in its conclusion; unheard in its onward march, felt in its results. In the life of Christ it was the same. The world was stirred, troubled, uneasy, perplexed. It felt that it was in the presence of a strange power. An undefined, unknown, yet real presence was with it. But it knew Him not. There is in each heart the law of the kingdom's establishment. In the heart, none can ever trace the kingdom's beginnings. It is the receiving of a life, a being, a breath. It is the passing over us of God's hand, the inbreathing of His Spirit. This is its secret history; and this humanity cannot reach. And yet it is a Kingdom. It makes the will a captive, the affections its ministers, and the person its glad vassal. Though it comes without observation yet it is indeed a kingdom.

Samuel Wilberforce (1805-1873)

Turn with your whole heart unto the Lord, and forsake this world, and your soul shall find rest... and you shall feel the Kingdom of God arise within you. For the Kingdom of God is joy and peace in the Holy Spirit; and this is not given to the wicked. Christ will come to you and reveal to you His consolation, provided that you prepare for Him a worthy dwelling-place within you. All His glory and beauty are from within, and there He delights Himself. Many visits He makes to the inner person, soothing it, filling it with peace, and admitting it to an exceedingly wonderful familiarity with Him. Prepare your heart for this Spouse, that He may abide within you.

Thomas à Kempis (1380-1471)

Jesus Christ the same yesterday, and today, and forever.
Hebrews 13:8

The time comes when the actor must leave the public stage; when the reins drop from the leader's grasp; the orator's tongue falters; the workman's stout arm grows feeble; the fire of wit is quenched; and those of understanding pass into a second childhood. But the time shall never come when it can be said of Jesus, *His hand is shortened that it cannot save. The same yesterday, today and forever,* there is nothing He ever did in saving, blessing, sanctifying that He cannot do again. This gives undying value to all the offers, invitations and promises of the Gospel.

Thomas Guthrie (1803-1873)

> All hail the power of Jesus' name!
> Let angels prostrate fall;
> Bring forth the royal diadem,
>   and crown Him Lord of all.
>
> Let ev'ry kindred, ev'ry tribe,
> on this terrestrial ball,
> To Him all majesty ascribe,
>   and crown Him Lord of all.
>
> Oh, that with yonder sacred throng
> we at His feet may fall;
> We'll join the everlasting song,
>   and crown Him Lord of all.

Edward Perronet (1726-1792)

It is finished. He had made an end of sin; He had abolished death, and swallowed it up in victory; He had become the resurrection and the life in perpetuity, throughout all the ages, world without end.

Gray & Adams Commentary (1951)

It pleased the Father that in Him should all fullness dwell.
Colossians 1:19

Transferring divine wealth to our account in heaven, and giving us an unlimited credit there, Jesus says: *Whatsoever you ask in prayer believing, you shall receive.* There is all fullness of mercy of pardon in Him. This pardon is not confined within limits of time, or age, or guilt, or character. Who will not accept of it? Offer a starving person bread, he will take it; offer a poor person money, she will take it; offer a sick person health, he will take it; offer an ambitious person honor, she will take it. Salvation, which is the one thing needful, is the only thing people will not accept. Besides, there is *fullness of grace* in Christ – a constant supply of pardoning and sanctifying grace. We may ask too little, we cannot ask too much; we may go too seldom, we cannot go too often to the throne; for in Jesus *dwelleth all the fullness of the Godhead bodily....* Watch the rise of the sun above the crest of a mountain. It has melted the snows of so many winters, renewed the verdure of so many springs, painted the flowers of so many summers, and ripened the golden harvest of so many autumns, and yet shines as brilliant as ever. Yet what are these but images of the fullness that is in Christ?

Thomas Guthrie (1803-1873)

Father, Thine everlasting grace
 Our scanty thought surpasses far,
Thy heart still melts with tenderness,
 Thine arms of love still open are
Returning sinners to receive,
 That mercy they may taste and live.

Johann Andreas Rothe (1688-1758)

I have set the LORD always before me.
Psalm 16:8

Be Thou my Vision, O Lord of my heart;
Naught be all else to me, save that Thou art,
Thou my best thought, by day or by night,
Waking or sleeping, Thy presence my light.

Be Thou my Wisdom, Thou my true Word;
I ever with Thee, Thou with me, Lord;
Thou my great Father, I Thy true son;
Thou in me dwelling, and I with Thee one.

Be Thou my battle-shield, sword for the fight;
Be Thou my dignity, Thou my delight,
Thou my soul's shelter, Thou my high tower:
Raise Thou me heavenward, O Power of my power.

Riches I heed not, nor man's empty praise,
Thou mine inheritance, now and always:
Thou and Thou only, first in my heart,
High King of heaven, my treasure Thou art.

High King of heaven, after victory won,
May I reach heaven's joys, O bright heaven's Sun!
Heart of my own heart, whatever befall,
Still be my Vision, O Ruler of all.

Ancient Irish hymn

By often thinking of God, the heart will be enticed into desires after Him.

William Gurnall (1617-1679)

Henry Martyn's (1781-1812) last written words from Persia: "I sat in the orchard and thought with sweet comfort and peace of my God, in solitude with my Company, my Friend and Comforter."

June 20

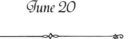

Darkness and light are both alike to Thee.
Psalm 139:12

Though they are both alike to Him, yet He can bring light out of darkness. It was out of the cloud that the deluge came, yet it is upon it that the bow is set! The cloud is a thing of darkness, yet God chooses it for the place where He bends the arch of light! Such is the way of our God. He knows that we need the cloud, and that a bright sky without a speck or shadow would not suit us in our passage to the Kingdom. Therefore He draws the cloud above us, He braids the cloud with sunshine – nay, makes it the object which gleams to our eye with the very fairest hues of heaven. It is not merely light after the darkness has fled away. But it is light in darkness; light beaming out of a ray produced by that darkness! Water from the rock, wells from the sand, light from the very cloud that darkens – life in the very midst of death! This is the marvel, this is the joy. Peace in trouble, gladness in sorrow; nay, peace and gladness produced by the very tribulation itself; peace and gladness which nothing but that tribulation could have produced! Such is the deep love of God; and such is the way in which He makes all things work together for good to us.

Horatius Bonar (1808-1889).

Happy the one who sees a God employed
In the good and ill that chequer life.

William Cowper (1731-1800)

When this world's account is summed up, we shall find that we owe more to grief than we do to joy, and that sorrow has been the veiled angel of God come to teach us some of the deepest lessons which can ever be learnt by human students.

Joseph Parker (1830-1902)

June 21

So mightily grew the Word of God and prevailed.
Acts 19:20

Paul tells us how the beacon-lights of Christianity flashed from Jerusalem to Antioch, to Ephesus, to Troas, to Philippi, to Athens and Corinth, until at last it was kindled in the very palace and Praetorian camp of the Caesars at Imperial Rome. The Light of the World dawned in the little Judean village, brightened in the Galilean hills, and then it seemed to set upon Golgotha amid disastrous eclipse. The book of Acts shows us how, rekindled from its apparent embers, in the brief space of thirty years, it had filled Asia and Greece and Italy with such light as had never shone before on land or sea.

F. W. Farrar (1831-1903)

Paul felt that if he did not preach the gospel he would do violence to his sense of justice. The gospel was not his to keep for himself, *for God so loved the world that He gave* His Son to save it. Like the natural sun in the heavens the incarnate Sun of Righteousness is the property of all. And how could he sin against the law of gratitude? *While we were yet sinners Christ died for us*, measures his sense of obligation to his Saviour; and if this sense is to take a practical form, it could only be by extending to all the knowledge of such a redemption. To believe the gospel and to do nothing for its acceptance among people is a contradiction in terms. *Woe is me if I preach not the gospel*. There was a divine impulse within that he could not resist. The fire that blazed within would have burnt deep scars upon his heart if his mouth had kept silence.

Canon Lidden (1829-1890)

> You servants of God, your Master proclaim,
> And publish abroad His wonderful Name;
> The Name all-victorious of Jesus extol;
> His Kingdom is glorious, and rules over all.

Charles Wesley (1707-1788)

June 22

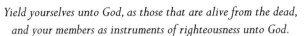

Yield yourselves unto God, as those that are alive from the dead,
and your members as instruments of righteousness unto God.
Romans 6:13

All that we have to do is to maintain this attitude of full surrender, by the grace of the Holy Spirit. Remember that Jesus Christ offered Himself to God, through the Eternal Spirit; and He waits to do as much for you. Ask Him to maintain you in this attitude, and to maintain this attitude in you. Use regularly the means of meditation, private prayer and Bible study. Seek forgiveness for any failure, directly when you are conscious of it; and ask to be restored. Practice the holy habit of the constant recollection of God. Do not be eager to work for God, but let God work through you. Accept everything that happens to you as being permitted, and therefore sent by the will of Him who loves you definitely.

F.B. Meyer (1847-1929)

Consecration may be greatly simplified and may be made intensely practical if we bring it down to a daily matter, attempting to cover no more than the one day, and if we each morning formally give the day to the Lord, to be occupied as He may wish, surrendering all our plans to Him, to be set aside or affirmed by Him as He may choose.

J.R. Miller (1840-1912)

> I take God the Father to be my God;
> I take God the Son to be my Saviour;
> I take the Holy Spirit to be my Sanctifier;
> I take the Word of God to be my rule;
> I take the people of God to be my people;
> And I do hereby dedicate and yield my whole self to the Lord;
> And I do this deliberately, freely, and forever. Amen

Matthew Henry (1662-1714)

June 23

All scripture is given by inspiration of God, and is profitable for doctrine,
for reproof, for correction, for instruction in righteousness.

2 Timothy 3:16

When we pray we speak to God; when we read the Bible God speaks to us.

Aelfric of Canterbury (955-1020)

The authority of the Holy Scripture depends not on the testimony of any person or church, but wholly upon God the author who is Truth.... Our full persuasion and assurance of the infallible truth and divine authority is from the inward work of the Holy Spirit, bearing witness by and with the Word, in our hearts.

Westminster Confession of Faith (1643)

Most wondrous book! Bright candle of the Lord! Star of Eternity! The only star by which the bark of humans can navigate the sea of life, and gain the coast of bliss securely.

R. Pollock (1799-1827)

O Lord, heavenly Father, in whom is the fullness of light and wisdom, enlighten our minds by your Holy Spirit, and give us grace to receive your Word with reverence and humility, without which no one can understand your truth. Amen.

John Calvin (1509-1564)

At the end of his life, David Brainerd (1718-1747) wrote: Oh that dear Book! That lovely Book! I shall soon see it opened! The mysteries that are in it, and the mysteries of God's providence, will be all unfolded! Engraved as in eternal brass the mighty promise shines; nor can the powers of darkness erase those everlasting lines.

The joy of the Lord is your strength.
Nehemiah 8:10

Spiritual joy is not a thing – not a lump of joy, so to speak – stored away in one's heart to be looked at and rejoiced over. Joy is only the gladness that comes from the possession of something good or the knowledge of something pleasant. And the Christian's joy is simply gladness in knowing Christ, and in one's possession of such a God and Saviour. We do not rejoice in our joy, but in the thing that causes our joy. We are to rejoice in the Lord, the God of our salvation; and this joy no person nor devil can take from us, and no earthly sorrows can touch.

Hannah Pearsall Smith (1832-1911)

The devout soul draws strength from godly thankfulness and holy joy, because it knows that God will help those who praise Him and rejoice in Him. If the strength of the Lord is our joy, then the joy of the Lord will be our strength.

Christopher Wordsworth (1807-1885)

> My God, the springs of all my joys,
>   the life of my delights,
> The glory of my brightest days,
>   and comfort of my nights!
>
> The opening heavens around me shine,
>   with beams of sacred bliss,
> If Jesus shows His mercy mine,
>   and whispers I am His.
>
> In darkest shades, if Thou appear,
>   my dawning is begun;
> Thou art my soul's bright morning star,
>   and Thus my rising sun.

Isaac Watts (1674-1748)

Lord, increase our faith.
Luke 17:5

There is nothing like faith to help at a pinch; faith dissolves doubts as the sun drives away the mists. Your time for believing always is. There are times when some graces may be out of use, but there is no time wherein faith can be said to be so. Faith must always be in exercise. Faith is the eye, is the mouth, is the hand, and one of these is in use all the day long. Faith is to see, to receive, to work, or to eat; and a Christian should be seeing, or receiving, or working, or feeding, all the day long. Let it rain, let it blow, let it thunder, let it lighten, a Christian must still believe.

John Bunyan (1628-1688)

The waverings of faith are like the tossings of a ship fast at anchor – where there is still a relying upon God – not like a boat carried by the waves of the sea to be dashed against a rock. If the heart stays on Christ in the midst of these doubtings, it is not an evil heart of unbelief. The indwelling Spirit, Who is in the heart, performs the office of the Comforter against such fears and expels those thick fumes of nature.

Stephen Charnock (1626-1680)

I am trusting Thee, Lord Jesus, trusting only Thee;
Trusting Thee for full salvation, great and Free.
I am trusting Thee to guide me; Thou alone shalt lead,
Every day and hour supplying all my need.
I am trusting Thee, Lord Jesus, never let me fall;
I am trusting Thee forever, and for all.

Frances Havergal (1836-1879)

Through doubt, through faith, through bliss, through stark dismay; through sunshine, wind, or snow, or fog, or shower, draw me to Thee, who art my only day. Amen.

George Macdonald (1824-1903)

In the beginning God created the heaven and the earth.
Genesis 1:1

The Christian believes that the cause of all created things, whether in heaven or on earth, whether visible or invisible, is nothing other than the goodness of the Creator, who is the one and the true God. The Christian believes that nothing exists save God Himself and what comes from Him, and believes that God is triune. By this Trinity, supremely and equally and immutably good, were all things created.... Each single created thing is good, and taken as a whole they are very good, because together they constitute a universe of admirable beauty.

Augustine of Hippo (354-430)

I praised the earth, in beauty seen
With garlands gay, of various green,
I praised the sea, whose ample field
Shone glorious as a silver shield;
And earth, and ocean seem'd to say,
"Our beauties are but for a day."

I praised the sun whose chariot roll'd
In wheels of amber and of gold;
I praised the moon, whose softer eye,
Gleamed sweetly through the summer sky,
And moon and sun in answer said,
"Our days of light are numbered."

O God! O Good beyond compare!
If thus thy meaner works are fair,
If thus thy bounties gild the span
Of ruin'd earth and sinful man,
How glorious must the mansion be,
Where Thy redeemed shall dwell with Thee!

Reginald Heber (1783-1826)

June 27

If thou put the brethren in mind of these things, thou shalt be a good minister of
Christ Jesus, nourished in the words of the faith,
and of the good doctrine which thou has followed.

1 Timothy 4:6 (RV)

I believe in God the Father Almighty,
Maker of heaven and earth;
and in Jesus Christ His only Son our Lord,
Who was conceived by the Holy Spirit,
born of the Virgin Mary,
suffered under Pontius Pilate,
was crucified, dead and buried:
He descended into hell;
the third day he rose again from the dead;
He ascended into heaven,
and sits on the right hand of God the Father Almighty;
from thence He shall come to judge the quick and the dead.
I believe in the Holy Spirit;
the holy catholic church;
the communion of saints;
the forgiveness of sins;
the resurrection of the body;
and the Life everlasting.
Amen

The Apostles' Creed (2nd century)

In physical food you receive no nourishment until you chew and swallow the food. The food may taste good in your mouth as you continue to enjoy its flavor. But it is in swallowing and digesting that it benefits the body. In an act of love, full of respect and confidence in God, swallow the blessed spiritual food He has given to you. It will cause you to become a mature Christian.

Jeanne Marie de la Mothe Guyon (1648-1717)

June 28

Lord, remember me when Thou comest into Thy kingdom.... Today shalt thou be with Me in paradise.
Luke 23:42-43

The thief believes not merely in the holy innocence of Christ. No, in that brow crowned with thorns and covered with blood – in that head laden with insult and with shame – he sees with the eye of faith a royal majesty, the majesty of a king who holds in His pierced hand the keys of paradise: *Lord, remember me when you come into your kingdom.* See here what a true faith means. Faith is the wing of the soul by which she darts her way far above and beyond what is seen, into the regions of the invisible. Faith is the eye of the soul which sees majesty where the eye of the flesh sees only shame; which sees light where the other sees only darkness; which recognizes life where the other perceives only death; and which in Jesus, who to the eye of flesh is nothing more than a condemned malefactor, owns and worships the King of heaven. Such is the eye of faith, and that eye of faith the dying thief possessed. Thus to repent and believe is no vain idea; it is a power of God capable of creating a new person, of which it may with truth be said, *Old things are passed away; behold, all things are become new.* Yes, a child was born there into the kingdom of God – the gloomy cross was his cradle – and the great, wide eternity became the scene of his growth. The spring of the new life which was then poured into his soul shall be throughout eternity a well of living water springing up into everlasting life.

See, all around the tree of shame, attendant angels wait,
To bear to heaven that ransomed soul, returned to God so late.
That through eternal years of bliss, in the light of God on high,
His new-born spirit may expand beneath his Saviour's eye.
August Tholuck (1799-1877)

193

June 29

Looking unto Jesus the author and finisher of our faith.
Hebrews 12:2

To a Christian mind Christ is all; the measure of all things; the standard and the reference. All things centre in Him. The life and death of Christ got by heart, not by rote, must be the rule for every act.

Frederick W. Robertson (1816-1853)

> We would see Jesus – for the shadows lengthen
> Across this little landscape of our life;
> We would see Jesus, our weak faith to strengthen
> For the last weariness, and the final strife.
>
> We would see Jesus – the great Rock Foundation,
> Whereon our feet were set with sovereign grace;
> Not life, nor death, with all their agitation,
> Can thence remove us, if we see His face.

Anna Warner (1820-1915)

The religion of Christ lives and moves and has its being in Christ. The personality of Christ is more closely interwoven with the gospel, and more essential to its influence and propagation, than the founder of any system of philosophy or religion is to the system that bears their name.

David Gracey (1894)

> Thou, O Christ, art all I want;
> More than all in Thee I find;
> Raise the fallen, cheer the faint,
> Heal the sick, and lead the blind.
> Just and holy is Thy Name;
> I am all unrighteousness;
> False and full of sin I am,
> Thou art full of truth and grace.

Charles Wesley (1707-1788)

June 30

For to me to live is Christ, and to die is gain.
Philippians 1:21

After his conversion the whole life of Paul was comprehended in one word: Christ. The prominent peculiarity of his Christianity was that there was so much of Christ in it. He expressed this in the characteristic saying, *To me to live is Christ.* Christ retained an extensive hold on his emotional nature. His was a large heart, and it was all Christ's. We may be shy of speaking of our personal feeling towards the Saviour, and may feel that the conventional terms of affection for Him, which are made use of in the hymns of the Church, transcend our actual experience. Paul, on the contrary, has no hesitation in employing language commonly used to describe the most absorbing passion, when love is filling life with a sweet delirium and making everything easy which has to be done for the sake of its object. Paul's achievements and self-denials were almost more than human, but his own explanation of them was simple: *The love of Christ constrains me.* He had to forego the prizes which to others make life worth living, but what did he care? *I count them but dung*, he says, *that I may win Christ.* He retained one thing: *Who shall separate us from the love of Christ? For I am persuaded that neither death, nor life, nor angels, nor principalities, nor powers, nor things present, nor things to come, nor height, nor depth, nor any other creature, shall be able to separate us from the love of God, which is in Christ Jesus our Lord.* These sound like the fervors of first love; but they are the words of a man at the height of his powers. And in old age he was still the same; Christ was the star of life, and the hope of being with Him annihilated the terrors of death. *I am in a strait betwixt two, having a desire to depart, and to be with Christ, which is far better.*
James Stalker (1848-1927)

July

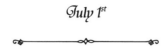

He shall have dominion also from sea to sea,
and from the river unto the ends of the earth.
Psalm 72:8

I do not see the cathedral as yet, when I go into the confused quarry-yard and see there the half-wrought stones, the clumsy blocks. I do not see the picture yet, when I look upon the palette with its blotches and stains of color. I do not see the perfect kingdom of God upon earth, but I see the colors which are to blend in it and the half-chiseled rock out of which it shall be wrought, and I am not going to despond.

Gray & Adams Commentary (1951)

Jesus shall reign where'er the sun
Does his successive journeys run;
His Kingdom stretch from shore to shore,
Till moons shall wax and wane no more.
To Him shall endless prayer be made,
And praises throng to crown His head;
His Name like sweet perfume shall rise
With every morning sacrifice.

Blessings abound where'er He reigns;
The prisoner leaps to lose his chains;
The weary find eternal rest,
And all the sons of want are blest.
Let every creature rise and bring
Peculiar honours to our King;
Angels descend with songs again,
And earth repeat the long Amen.

Isaac Watts (1674-1748)

Shine, light of God! Make broad Thy scope -- to all who sin and suffer -- more and better than we hope. With Heaven's compassion make our longings poor!

J.G. Whittier (1807-1892)

God is love.
1 John 4:8

This single announcement of the beloved disciple is contradicted by so many appearances in the world around us, is met by many a 'no' and many a murmur, and yet is countersigned by Jehovah's handwriting on the tablets of the heart; this shortest of sentences and most summary of gospels, which a breath can utter and which a signet ring can contain, is the truth which, shining bright at the Advent, will overspread the world.... It is a truth on which no one has mused too much, even though they have pondered it all their days; and to which no anthem can do justice, except that which the redeemed from among humanity will sing helped by the golden harps of the seraphim.

J. Hamilton (1814-1867)

To write the love of God above would drain the ocean deep; nor could the scroll contain the whole, though stretched from sky to sky.

Frederick Lehman (1886-1953)

All other mercies are as nothing in comparison to the love of God in giving His Son to be our Saviour; they are all swallowed up in this, as the light of candles when brought into the sunshine.

J. Flavel (1627-1691)

> I rejoice that I cannot but love Him,
>   because He first loved me;
> I would that measureless, changeless
>   my love might be;
> A love unto death and for ever;
>   for, soul, He died for thee.
> Give thanks that for thee He delighted
>   to leave His glory on high;
> For thee to be humbled, forsaken,
>   for thee to die.
> Wilt thou render Him love for His loving?

Mechthild of Hellfde (?-1277)

July 3rd

Who shall separate us from the love of Christ?
Romans 8:35

The only matter about which the Apostle felt any anxiety was whether anything could cut him off from the living, loving Lord. Taking the extreme conditions, he carefully examines them, knowing that they include all between. First he interrogates the extremes of existence, *death and life*; the extremes of created intelligences, *angels and principalities and powers*; the extremes of time, *things present and things to come*; the extremes of space, height and depth; lastly, the extremes of the created universe, *any other creature*. Each of these extremes thus passed in review, and he has eagerly peered into its depths. He is like a man proving every link of the chain on which he is going to swing out over the abyss. Carefully and fervently he has tested all, and is satisfied that none of them can cut him off from the love of God. We strangely misjudge the love of God. We think that our distresses and sufferings, our sins and failures, may make Him love us less, whereas they will draw Him nearer, and make His love exert itself more evidently and tenderly. Oh, blessed love that comes down to us from the heart of Jesus, the essence of the eternal love of God dwelling there and coming through Jesus to us – nothing can ever staunch, nothing exhaust, nothing intercept it! It will not let us go. It leaps the gulf of space untenanted, it bridges time unexhausted. It does not depend on our reciprocation or response. It is not our love that holds God, but God's that holds us. Not our love to Him, but His to us. And since nothing can separate us from the love of God, He will go on loving us for ever, and pouring into us the entire fullness of His life and glory.

F.B. Meyer (1847-1929)

[Nothing]... shall be able to separate us from the love of God, which is in Christ Jesus our Lord.

Romans 8: 39

July 4th

Grieve not the Holy Spirit of God,
whereby you are sealed unto the day of redemption.
Ephesians 4:30

A holy friendship exists between the Holy Spirit and the believer's soul. It is implied in the words *Grieve not the Holy Spirit*. It is only a friend we can grieve.

I will put my Spirit within you, and cause you to walk in my statutes, and you shall keep my judgments and do them (Ezekiel 36:27). And so the Lord Jesus tells us, *I will pray the Father, and He will give you another Comforter, that He may abide with you forever, even the Spirit of truth; whom the world cannot receive, because it sees Him not, neither knows Him.* And accordingly the apostle Paul says, *What! know you not that your body is the temple of the Holy Ghost which is in you, which you have of God?* Can friendship be compared with this?

The Holy Spirit teaches believing souls. *He will guide you into all truth.* The Holy Spirit comes and teaches us *all things.* He bears with our stupidity and opens our hearts to receive the truth in the love of it. This is friendship.

The Holy Spirit teaches us to pray, yea, He prays in us. And He helps our infirmities in this regard by *coming under the burden*, for we know not what we should pray for as we ought. The colour of our life is taken from those among whom we live. How much more an impression does the Spirit make: it is like the mark that the seal makes on wax, and it is to the day of redemption, and cannot be broken, if we are sealed with the Holy Spirit of promise.

Robert Murray M'Cheyne (1813-43)

> Spirit of God, descend upon my heart;
> Wean it from earth; through all its pulses move;
> Stoop to my weakness, mighty as Thou art,
> And make me love Thee as I ought to love.

George Croly (1780-1860)

My heart stands in awe of your word.
Psalm 119:161

There is an awe of the Word that makes us not shy of it, but tender of violating or doing anything contrary to it. This is not the fruit of slavish fear, but of holy love; it is not being afraid of the Word, but delighting in it, as the Word discovers the mind of God to us. This awe is called reverence or godly fear, when we consider whose word it is: the word of the Lord who is our God and has a right to command what He pleases; to whose will and word we have already yielded obedience and devoted ourselves to walk worthy of Him in all well-pleasing; and who can find us out in all our failings, as knowing our very thoughts afar off and having all our ways before Him.

Thomas Manton (1620-1677)

I would advise all that come to the reading or hearing of this Book -- which is the Word of God, the most precious jewel, and most holy relic that remains upon earth -- that you bring with you the fear of God, and that you read with all due reverence, and use your knowledge thereof, not to vain glory of frivolous disputation, but to the honour of God, increase of virtue, and edification of both yourselves and others.

Thomas Cranmer (1489-1555)

Consider and hold fast the Scriptures, which are set and nourished in the root of the Holy Spirit, and are written in the Divine wisdom. The Scripture is a mirror in which we see God. We ought never to tempt Him by curious questions, but reverently adore Him. People often desire to know what is not permitted to know, and so depart from divine obedience; at this the devil greatly rejoices. Often the adversary shoots such arrows into our hearts, that through them we may misconceive God. Happy is the one who does not accept them.

Hildegarde of Rupertsberg (1098-1179)

July 6ᵗʰ

Bless the Lord, O my soul: and all that is within me, bless His holy name.
Psalm 103:1

Through all eternity, to Thee a grateful song I'll raise;
But O eternity's too short to utter all Thy praise.
Joseph Addison (1672-1719)

To bless the Lord is an eminent work, and requires many and able agents to perform it. Therefore, go not alone but take with thee *all that is within thee*; all the forces in thy magazine, whether it be the heart or spirit, whether the will or the affections, whether thy understanding or thy memory; take them all with thee and bless the Lord.

Richard Baker (1568-1645)

Let your conscience bless the Lord by unvarying fidelity. Let your judgment bless Him by decisions in accordance with His word. Let your imagination bless Him by pure and holy musings. Let your affections praise Him by loving whatsoever He loves. Let your desires bless Him by seeking only His glory. Let your memory bless Him by not forgetting any of His benefits. Let your thoughts bless Him by meditating on His excellencies. Let your hope praise Him by longing and looking for the glory that is to be revealed. Let your every sense bless Him by its fealty, your every word by its truth, and your every act by its integrity.

John Stevenson (1842)

Stand up, and bless the Lord,
        ye people of His choice;
Stand up, and bless the Lord,
        your God with heart and soul and voice.
Though high above all praise,
        above all blessing high,
Who would not fear His holy name,
        and praise and magnify?
James Montgomery (1771-1854)

Hatred stirs up strife: but love covers all sins.
Proverbs 10:12

No Christian can yield to the spirit of hatred. When one feels that that spirit is getting the upper hand, one betakes to secret communion with God and fights the awful battle at the Cross.

Joseph Parker (1830-1902)

Souls are made sweet not by taking the acid fluids out, but by putting something in – a great love, a new spirit, the spirit of Christ. Christ, the spirit of Christ, interpenetrating our souls, sweetens, purifies, transforms all. This only can eradicate what is wrong, work a chemical change, renovate and regenerate, and rehabilitate the inner person. Will-power does not change us. Time does not change us – Christ does. Therefore, *Let this mind be in you which was also in Christ Jesus.*

Henry Drummond (1851-1897)

Speak gently! It is better far to rule by love than fear.
Speak gently to the little child! Its love be sure to gain;
Teach it in accents soft and mild: it may not long remain.
Speak gently to the young, for they will have enough to bear –
Pass through this life as best they may, 'tis full of anxious care!
Speak gently to the aged one, grieve not the careworn heart;
The sands of life are nearly run – let each in peace depart!

Speak gently, kindly, to the poor; let no harsh tone be heard;
They have enough they must endure, without an unkind word.
Speak gently to the erring: know they may have toiled in vain;
Perchance unkindness made them so; oh, win them back again!
Speak gently! 'Tis a little thing dropped in the heart's deep well.
The good, the joy, which it may bring, Eternity shall tell.

William Bates (1625-1699)

Then shall they see the Son of man coming in a cloud with power and great glory.
Luke 21:27

What a day will that be when Christ shall come from heaven to set His captives free! It will not be a coming as His first was in poverty and contempt. He will not come to be buffeted, and scorned and crucified again. He will not come to be slighted and neglected by a careless world any more. And yet that first coming, which was a reproach for our sakes, had its glory. If the angels of heaven were the messengers of that first coming and the heavenly host celebrated His nativity in the sublimest strains, saying *Glory to God in the highest and on earth peace, good will*; Oh! with what shoutings will saints and angels at that day proclaim *Glory to God, and peace and good will towards earth*! If the stars of heaven must lead wise men from remote parts of the world to come to worship a child in a manger, how will the glory of His next appearing constrain all the world to acknowledge His sovereignty! If He rode into Jerusalem amidst hosannas, *Blessed be the King that comes in the name of the Lord; peace in heaven, and glory in the highest*, Oh! with what proclamations of blessings, peace and glory will He enter the new Jerusalem! If, when He was in the form of servant, they cried out *What manner of man is this, that even the winds and the sea obey Him?* what will they say when they shall see Him coming in His glory! *Then shall appear the sign of the Son of Man in heaven, and then shall all the tribes of the earth mourn, and they shall see the Son of Man coming in the clouds of heaven with power and great glory.* The promise of His coming and of our deliverance is comfortable. What will it be to see Him with all the glorious attendance of His angels, come in person to deliver us!

Richard Baxter (1615-1691)

Lord, may we day by day prepare to see Thy face, and serve Thee there. Amen.

Thomas Pollock (1836-1896)

Who are you, Lord?...What shall I do, Lord?
Acts 22:8,10

At the moment of conversion these two questions arise naturally upon our lips. As to the first, we can only await the gradual revelation. It will take an eternity to know all that Jesus Christ is and can be to His own. As to the second, we are no less dependent on the Divine revealing hand, indicating the path we are to tread. Often at the beginning of the new life we attempt to forecast the work which we hope to accomplish. We take into account our tastes and aptitudes, our faculties and talents, our birth and circumstances. From these we infer that we shall probably succeed best along a certain line of useful activity. But as the moments lengthen into years, it becomes apparent that the door of opportunity is closing in that direction. It is a bitter disappointment. We refuse to believe that the hindrances to the fulfillment of our cherished hopes can be permanent. We cast ourselves against the closing door, as sea birds on the illumined glass of the lighthouse tower, to fall dazed and bewildered to the ground. And it is only after such a period of disappointment that we come to perceive that God's ways are not as our ways, nor His thoughts as our thoughts. Be not afraid to trust God utterly. As you go down the long corridor you may find that He has preceded you, and locked many doors which you would fain have entered; but be sure that beyond these there is one which He has left unlocked. Open it and enter, and you will find yourself face to face with... opportunity greater than anything you dared to imagine in your sunniest dreams.

F.B. Meyer (1847-1929)

Oh! be my will so swallowed up in Thine, that I may do Thy will in doing mine.

George Matheson (1842-1906)

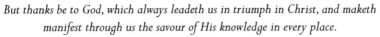

But thanks be to God, which always leadeth us in triumph in Christ, and maketh manifest through us the savour of His knowledge in every place.
2 Corinthians 2:14 (RV)

God makes manifest through the Apostle the sweet savour of the knowledge of Jesus. Wherever he went, people knew Jesus better; the loveliness of the Master's character became more apparent. People became aware of a subtle fragrance poured upon the air, which attracted them to the Man of Nazareth. What an ideal this is for us all, so to live that though we are unable to speak much or occupy a commanding position, yet from our lives a holy savour may spread abroad, which will not be ours, but Christ's! Let us live so near Him, that we may absorb His fragrance; and then go forth to exhale it again in pureness, in knowledge, in longsuffering, in kindness, in the Holy Spirit, in love unfeigned, in the word of truth, and in the power of God....

How marvelously scent awakens memory! In a moment it will waft us back through long years to some old country lane, garden, or orange-grove, summoning to mind people and events associated with it in the happy past. As God watches us from day to day, He should see Jesus, that blessed life which was offered as an offering and a sacrifice to God for a sweet-smelling savour.

F.B. Meyer (1847-1929)

A holy Christian life is made up of a number of small things! Little words, not eloquent sermons; little deeds, not miracles of battle nor one great heroic deed of martyrdom; the little constant sunbeam, not the lightning. The avoidance of little evils, little sins, little inconsistencies make up the beauty of a holy life.

Andrew Bonar (1810-1892)

July 11th

I will pray the Father, and He shall give you another Comforter, that He may abide with you forever.
John 14:16

Jesus went out of this world wrapped in the shroud of human hate, calumny and shame. He left a few disciples to represent Him. But they would have an honourable, potent and divine witness! They would have almighty support in their witness. If we would walk with Jesus, we must have the Holy Spirit to make His presence real to us. If we would know the peace which passes all understanding, it must be breathed upon our hearts by the Holy Spirit. If we would faithfully and effectively witness for our Lord, and turn the shame of His cross into His glory, we must know the leading partnership of the Holy Spirit. If we would see others bow in submission to the truth of sin, righteousness and judgment, we must depend upon the deep, convicting work of the Holy Spirit. If we would come to maturity of knowledge and understanding of the things of the Lord, we must allow the Holy Spirit to illumine our hearts and turn light upon the face of Jesus for us.

J.C. Macaulay (1941)

> O Spirit, beautiful and dread!
> My heart is fit to break
> with love of all Thy tenderness
> for us poor sinners' sake.
> Thy love of Jesus I adore;
> My comfort this shall be,
> that when I serve my dearest Lord,
> that service worships Thee!
>
> Frederick W. Faber (1814-1863)

> Pass me not, O mighty Spirit!
> Draw this lifeless heart to Thee;
> impute to me the Saviour's merits;
> blessing others, oh! bless me, even me.
>
> Elizabeth Codner (1824-1919)

Which hope we have as an anchor of the soul, both sure and stedfast.
Hebrews 6:19

My soul has found the steadfast ground,
    There ever shall my anchor hold –
That ground is in my Saviour Christ,
    Before the world was from of old –
And that sure ground shall be my stay,
    When Heaven and Earth shall pass away.

That ground is Thine Eternal Love,
    Thy Love that through all ages burns –
The open arms of mercy stretched
    To meet the sinner who returns;
The Love that calleth everywhere,
    If we will hear or will forbear.

God willeth not we should be lost,
    He wills to save the sons of men;
For this His Son came down from Heaven,
    For this returned to Heaven again;
For this He standeth at the door,
    He knocketh, waiteth, evermore –

In that deep sea of love I sink
    In perfect peace and endless rest,
And when my sins condemn my soul,
    Cling closer to my Saviour's breast –
For there I find, go when I will,
    Unchanging love and mercy still.

      J.A. Rothe (1688-1758)

Whatever is to be done, whatever is to be declined, whatever is to be chosen, Thou O Lord are my hope. Let others hope in other things, in their knowledge of letters, in their worldly wisdom, in their nobility, in their dignity, in some other vanity; for Thy sake I have made all things loss since Thou, Lord, are my hope. Amen.

      Bernard of Clairvaux (1090-1153)

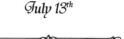

Unto me… is this grace given, that I should preach among the Gentiles
the unsearchable riches of Christ.
Ephesians 3:8

This suggests the figure of a man standing with uplifted hands, in a posture of great amazement, before continuous revelations of immeasurable and unspeakable glory. In whatever way he turns, the splendour confronts him! *According to the riches of His grace -- the riches of His glory -- the exceeding riches of His grace -- O the depth both of the wisdom and knowledge of God!* The riches are unsearchable. These unsearchable riches are not merely the subjects of contemplation, they are objects of appropriation. This ideal wealth is usable. These riches fit themselves into every possible condition of human poverty and need. The ocean of grace flows about the shore of common life, into all its distresses and gaping wants, and it fills every crack and crevice to the full. He stands before sin and proclaims that it can be destroyed. He stands before sorrow and proclaims that sorrow can be transfigured. He stands before the broken relationships and proclaims that they can all be rectified. And all this strength is in *the unsearchable riches of Christ*. Paul finds special delight in proclaiming the all-sufficiency of redeeming grace in its relationship to the worst. He knows that redemption cannot possibly fail. Turn to some of the gloomy catalogues which are found in some of his epistles, long appalling lists of human depravity and need, and see his glowing confidence in the powers of redeeming grace. *Such were some of you*, he declares, *but you are washed*. When Paul wants to bring correcting and enriching forces into human affairs, he seeks the wealthy energy in *the unsearchable riches of Christ*.

J.H. Jowett (1864-1923)

Venture on Him, venture wholly, let no other trust intrude:
None but Jesus can do helpless sinners good

Joseph Hart (1712-1798)

All things were made by Him.
John 1:3

Christ is the Creator and Upholder of the universe. The design of the physical world is simply to reveal God. Nature is the omnipresent Christ manifesting God to creatures. The sunset clouds are painted by His hand; the sun that lights those clouds is itself kindled by the Sun of Righteousness

A.H. Strong (1836-1921)

> Fairest Lord Jesus, ruler of all nature,
>   O Thou of God and man the Son!
> Thee will I worship, Thee will I honor,
>   Thou, my soul's glory, joy, and crown.
> Fair are the meadows, fairer still the woodlands
>   Robed in the blooming garb of spring;
> Jesus is fairer, Jesus is purer,
>   Who makes the woeful heart to sing.
> Fair is the sunshine, fairer still the moonlight,
>   And all the twinkling, starry host;
> Jesus shines brighter, Jesus shines purer
>   Than all the angels heaven can boast.
>
> German hymn (1677)

Augustine (354-430), in his search for God, said: I asked the earth, and it said, "I am not He," and all that is upon it made the same confession. I asked the sun, and the depths, and the creeping things that have life, and they answered, "We are not thy God; look thou above us." I asked the breezes and the gales; and the whole air with its inhabitants said to me, "We are not God." I asked the heaven, the sun, the moon, the stars. "We too are not the God whom thou seekest." And I said to all the creatures that surround the doors of my senses, "You have said to me that you are not He; tell me somewhat of Him." And with a great voice they exclaimed, "He made us."

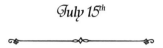

I live by the faith of the Son of God, who loved me, and gave Himself for me.
Galatians 2:20

The Son of God loved me and gave Himself for me. Yes, Himself! What is the Bride's true and central treasure? What calls forth the deepest, brightest, sweetest thrill of love and praise? Not the Bridegroom's priceless gifts, not the role of His resplendent righteousness, not the dowry of unsearchable riches, not the magnificence of the palace home to which He is bringing her, not the glory which she shall share with Him, but Himself! Jesus Christ, who His own self bare our sins in His own body on the tree; this same Jesus, whom having not seen, we love; the Son of God and the Man of Sorrows; my Saviour, my Friend, my Master, my King, my Priest, my Lord and my God – He says, "I also for thee!" What an "I"! What power we feel in it, so different from any human "I," for all His Godhead and all His manhood are concentrated in it; and all for thee! And not only all, but ever for thee! His unchangeableness is the seal upon every attribute; He will be the same Jesus forever. How can mortal mind estimate this enormous promise? How can mortal heart conceive what is enfolded in these words, "I also for thee"? One glimpse of its fullness and glory, and we feel that henceforth it must be, shall be, and by His grace will be our true-hearted, wholehearted cry – Take my self and I will be ever, only, all for Thee!

> Made for Thyself, O God!
> Made for Thy love, Thy service, Thy delight;
> Made to show forth Thy wisdom, grace, and might;
> Made for Thy praise, whom veiled archangels laud;
> O strange and glorious thought, that we may be
>   A joy to Thee!
>
> Frances Havergal (1836-1879)

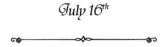

Andrew... first finds his own brother Simon, and says unto him,
We have found the Messiah, which is, being interpreted, the Christ.
John 1:41

No Christian need delay to testify to Christ because one is not a theologian. One may at least do as well as Andrew. Religious truth cannot be horded like money, like a discovery for which a person wishes to take out a patent. It belongs to humanity, and in the first instance to those who stand by providence nearest to its possessors. Andrew found his own brother.

H. Lidden (1829-1890)

The flowers do not require to be sternly told to grow and blossom and make themselves beautiful; let the sun but shine and they will do it out of the gladness of their own hearts. Birds need not an almanac to apprise them that the month of May, the season for open-air concerts, has arrived. And once people have been in the presence of Christ they require no elaborate certificate to empower them to go and tell others of His beauties – the fire burns, and speak they must. Commission or no commission, be not ashamed to tell others that you have found the Saviour.

J.C. Jones (1829-1890)

Jesus, and shall it ever be, a mortal man ashamed of Thee? Ashamed of Thee, whom angels praise, whose glories shine through endless day? Ashamed of Jesus! that dear Friend on whom my hopes of heaven depend! No, when I blush, be this my shame, that I no more revere His name. Ashamed of Jesus! yes, I may, when I've no guilt to wash away; no tear to wipe, no good to crave, no fears to quell, no soul to save. Till then, nor is my boasting vain, till then I boast a Saviour slain: and O may this my glory be, that Christ is not ashamed of me.

Joseph Grigg (1720-1768)

July 17th

Fear not, Abram: I am your shield and your exceeding great reward.
And Abram said, Lord God, what will Thou give me, seeing I go childless...?

Genesis 15:1, 2

I am your exceeding great reward. And Abram said, Lord God. Abram felt that his own short life was too small to hold all the riches God was giving him. How could the great Euphrates be confined within one man's garden plot? God had given Abram everything but a child, and therefore it seemed to him that all this flow of God's love was running into a pool where it could only stand still. And Abram told God his fear in plain words. He told him at eventide when the stars were coming out. *I have no child.* And whilst he was talking the stars came out more and more, all of them – millions of silvery eyes, throng upon throng, glowing overhead, sparkling over the distant hills, glittering in the east, throbbing like hearts on the western horizon. It was in that hour that the Lord said to Abram, *Look up.* And Abram looked; and God said, *Count them.* Abram said, *My Lord, who can count the host?* The Lord said, *So shall your seed be.*

Joseph Parker (1830-1902)

God doth not need either our work or our own gifts: who best bear His mild yoke, they serve Him best; His state is kingly, thousands at His bidding speed and post o'er land and ocean without rest; they also serve who only stand and wait.

John Milton (1608-1674)

My times are in thy hand!
I know not what a day
Or even an hour may bring to me,
But I am safe while trusting Thee,
Though all things pass away;
All weakness, I on Him rely,
Who fixed the earth and spread the starry sky

Anonymous

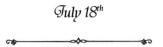

July 18ᵗʰ

And Abram believed in the LORD; and He counted it to him for righteousness.
Genesis 15:6

This is the first time the word *believed* occurs in the Bible. Believed -- what a history opens in this one word! The moment Abram believed, he was truly born again. Paul says of Abram that *against hope he believed in hope*: and that *he staggered not at the promise of God through unbelief.* Abram believed – he nourished and nurtured himself in God; he hid his life and his future in this promise, as a child might hide or nestle in a mother's breast. That is faith. He took the promise as a fulfillment; the word was to him a fact. Thus he was called out of himself, out of his own trust, out of his own resources, and his life was fostered upon God. It was surely a perilous moment. Appearances were against the promise. But Abram staggered not. God's love was set before him like an open door, and Abram went in and became a child at home. Henceforward the stars had new meanings to him as, long before, the rainbow had to Noah. Abram drew himself up by the stars. Every night they spoke to him of his posterity and his greatness. They were henceforward not stars but promises, and oaths, and blessings. What Abram did, we ourselves have to do. He rested on the word of God; he did not wait until the child was born. That would not have been faith. Thus I must believe God; I must throw my whole soul upon Him, and drive all doubt, all fear, from my heart, and take the promise as a fact. See how large a life Abram entered into when he believed! He became a contemporary of all ages, a citizen of all cities the world over and time without end. Life without faith is an earth without a sky.

Joseph Parker (1830-1902)

Our faith is fed by what is plain in Scripture, and tried by what is obscure.

Augustine of Hippo (354-430)

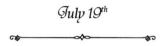

Whosoever will, let them take the water of life freely.
Revelation 22:17

God closes His Bible with a last word of invitation, and that word is *Whosoever will let them take of the water of life freely.* Every persuasion that He has made to the intellect, the heart, the conscience, the memory, the imagination, the self-interests, has been directed toward the will. In almost every battlefield there is some one spot where the issue of the battle is decided. Similarly in every human being there is one element about which the battle of life is fought. It is the will. As goes the will, so goes the person – for time and for eternity. Character is finally a choice, and choice is the determination and expression of the will. Here is one sphere of life where the will is all-decisive. It chooses good or evil, just as it pleases. In the sphere of moral choices, its realm is absolutely sovereign and unquestionable. But when the will acts in the line of God's will, then there is security. Anyone who yields to God yields to Him who is absolutely good and whose kingdom knows no end. We put ourselves into the keeping of the Omnipotent and Eternal when we let God take us to His arms and heart. For us thenceforward the stars will shine, and the rivers flow and the angels sing. Life's harmony will be found.

James G.K. McClure (1899)

Write your blessed Name, O Lord, upon my heart, there to remain so engraved that no prosperity or adversity shall ever move me from your love. Be to me a strong tower of defense, a comforter in tribulation, a deliverer in distress, a very present help in trouble, and a guide to heaven through the many temptations and dangers of life. Amen.

Thomas à Kempis (1380-1471)

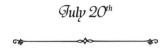

July 20th

Search the scriptures; for in them you think you have eternal life.
John 5:39

I have worked at the Bible, prayed over the Bible, lived by the Bible for more than sixty years, and I tell you there is no book like the Bible. It is a miracle of literature, a perennial spring of wisdom, a wonder book of surprises, a revelation of mystery, an infallible guide of conduct, and an unspeakable source of comfort. Read it for yourself; study it according to its own directions. Live by its principles. Believe its message. Follow its precepts. No person is uneducated who knows the Bible, and no one is wise who is ignorant of its teaching.

Samuel Chadwick (1860-1932)

What do I not owe to the Lord for permitting me to take a part in the translation of His Word? Never did I see such wonders and wisdom and love in His blessed Book as since I have been obliged to study every expression. And it is a delightful reflection that death cannot deprive us of the pleasure of studying its mysteries.

Henry Martyn (1781-1812)

If the reader understands very little of the Word of God, one ought to read it very much; for the Spirit explains the Word by the Word. And if one enjoys the reading of the Word little, that is just the reason why one should read it very much; for the frequent reading of the Scriptures creates a delight in them.

George Müller (1805-1898)

Father of mercies, in Thy Word what endless glory shines!
For ever be Thy Name adored for these celestial lines.
Divine Instructor, gracious Lord, be Thou for ever near;
Teach me to love Thy sacred Word, and view my Saviour there.
Anne Steele (1716-1778)

July 21st

Work out your own salvation with fear and trembling.
For it is God which works in you both to will and to do of His good pleasure.
Philippians 2:12, 13

What a staggering thought is excited by these words! Stay, my soul, and wonder that the Eternal God should stoop to work within my narrow limits. Is it not a marvel indeed that He, whom the heavens cannot contain, should trouble Himself to work on such unpromising material and amidst circumstances so uncongenial? How careful should we be to make Him welcome and to throw no hindrance in His way! Surely we should have holy reverence as we *work out* into daily act and life all that our Father is *working in*.

F.B. Meyer (1847-1929)

The greatest praise to your faith, the greatest honour to Christ, is when faith walks upon fewer legs -- neither feeling, nor joy, nor comfort, nor experience, nor sight -- but only this one: *He is faithful who has promised.* And when we rest upon the Lord, then we take a right grip of the promises. The happiness of the lost and perishing depends on this, to trust Christ and His strength.

Samuel Rutherford (1600-1661)

> Sing, pray, and keep His ways unswerving;
> So do thine own part faithfully,
> And trust His words -- though undeserving,
> Thou yet shalt find it true for thee;
> God never yet forsook in need
> The soul that trusted Him indeed.

George C. Neumark (1621-1681)

We must leave to God all that depends on Him, and think only of being faithful in all that depends upon ourselves.

François de la Mothe Fénelon (1651-1715)

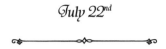

Come unto Me, all you that labour and are heavy laden, and I will give you rest.
Matthew 11:28

Thou hast made us for Thyself, O Lord, and our hearts are restless until they find their rest in Thee.

Augustine of Hippo (354-430)

> I heard the voice of Jesus say, "Come unto Me, and rest;
> Lay down, thou weary one, lay down, thy head upon My breast."
> I came to Jesus as I was — weary, and worn, and sad;
> I found in Him a resting place, and He has made me glad.
> I heard the voice of Jesus say, "Behold, I freely give
> The living water—thirsty one, stoop down, and drink, and live."
> I came to Jesus, and I drank of that life-giving stream;
> My thirst was quenched, my soul revived, and now I live in Him.
> I heard the voice of Jesus say, "I am this dark world's Light:
> Look unto Me, thy morn shall rise, and all thy day be bright."
> I looked to Jesus, and I found in Him my Star, my Sun;
> And in that Light of life I'll walk till traveling days are done.
>
> Horatius Bonar (1808-1889)

To every toiling, heavy-laden sinner, Jesus says, *Come to me and rest.* But there are many heavy-laden believers too. For them this same invitation is meant. Note well the words of Jesus, if you are heavy-laden with your service. It is not, "Go, labor on," as perhaps you imagine. On the contrary, it is stop, turn back, *Come to me and rest.* Never, never did Christ send a heavy laden one to work; never, never did He send a hungry one, a weary one, a sick or sorrowing one, away on any service. For such the Bible only says, Come, come, come.

Hudson Taylor (1832-1905)

Jesus, my strength, my hope, on Thee I cast my case; With humble confidence look up, and know thou hear'st prayer.

Charles Wesley

Praise the Lord, O my soul. While I live I will praise the LORD:
I will sing praises unto my God while I have any being.

Psalm 146:1, 2

O for a heart full of joyful gratitude that we may run, leap and glorify God, even as these Psalms do. *Praise the Lord, O my soul.* He would practise what he preached. He would be the leader of the choir which he had summoned. It is a poor business if we solely exhort others and do not stir up our own soul. It is an evil thing to say, Praise you, and never to add, *Praise, O my soul.* When we praise God let us arouse our innermost self, our central life: we have but one soul, and if it be saved from eternal wrath, it is bound to praise its Saviour. Let me put my soul into the centre of the choir, and then let my better nature excite my whole being to the utmost height of loving praise. O for a well-tuned harp! Nay, rather, O for a sanctified heart. Then if my voice should be of the poorer sort, and somewhat lacking in melody, yet my soul without my voice shall accomplish my resolve to magnify the Lord.

While I live I will praise the Lord. I shall not live here for ever. This mortal life will find a finish in death; but while it lasts I will laud the Lord my God. I cannot tell how long or short my life may be; but every hour of it shall be given to the praises of my God. While I live I'll love; and while I breathe I'll bless. It is but for awhile, and I will not wile that time away in idleness, but consecrate it to the same service which it shall occupy eternally. We cannot be too firm in the holy resolve to praise God, for it is the chief end of our living and being that we should glorify God and enjoy him for ever.

C.H. Spurgeon (1834-1892)

By him therefore let us offer the sacrifice of praise to God continually.

Hebrews 13:15

*He that dwells in the secret place of the most High shall abide
under the shadow of the Almighty.*
Psalm 91:1

What intimate and unrestrained communion does this describe!
-- the Christian in everything making known her heart, with
its needs and wishes, its thoughts and feelings, its doubts and anxieties,
its sorrows and its joys, to God as to a loving, perfect friend. This
Almighty Friend has admitted His chosen ones to His secret place. It
is almost too wonderful to be true. But He himself permits it, desires
it, teaches us that it is communion to which He calls us.

Mary B. Duncan (1825-1865)

It is of great profit for anyone to know that it is not necessary to raise
ourselves to heaven in order to converse with our divine Father and
find happiness with Him, not to elevate our voices so as to be heard;
God is so near that He hears the slightest whisper from our lips and
the most secret thought. We have no need of wings to go in search of
Him; let us enter into the solitude and look within us, it is there that
He is. Let us talk with Him in great humility, but also with love, like
children talking with their father, confidently telling Him our troubles and begging Him to help us.

Teresa of Avila (1515-1582)

Jesus, I am resting, resting in the joy of what Thou art,
I am finding out the greatness of Thy loving heart.
Here I gaze and gaze upon Thee, as Thy beauty fills my soul,
For by Thy transforming image, Thou hast made me whole.
Simply trusting Thee, Lord Jesus, I behold Thee as Thou art,
And Thy love, so pure, so changeless, satisfies my heart,
Satisfies its deepest longing, meets, supplies my every need,
Compasseth me round with blessing: Thine is love indeed.
Jean S. Pigott (1845-1882)

July 25th

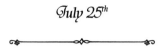

Except I shall see in His hands the print of the nails, and put my finger into the print of the nails, and thrust my hand into His side, I will not believe.

John 20:25

The disciples went to His grave on the morning of the third day in the twilight of hope. When Jesus was restored to them, they at once believed. But fainthearted Thomas, how was it in your soul? After the sun had set, did a glimmer of hope remain for you, or was it altogether night?

Eight days of contentment mingled with longing passed for the believing followers of Christ; but for Thomas they had been comfortless days. Then once more Jesus stood in their midst with the salutation of peace. Now, Thomas, you have what you wanted, put Him to the proof; behold He offers Himself to you. But lo! all his tests are forgotten in the very moment when he could apply them; and the power of faith which had been suppressed, in a moment springs forth. The beloved countenance of the Holy One is there before him again, and upon its features the light of the resurrection morning rests. Is there any need now that he should stretch forth his hands to touch his Lord – does not his heart feel Him nigh? Yes, it is He, it is He! Who else could it be but Him? And falling on his knees, he cries: *My Lord and my God!* This expression shows how strong was the bond which, in spite of his disbelief, still knit him to his Saviour. Doubt had lain upon his heart only as a thin layer of earth. And now that the sun puts forth its might, the hidden seed of faith shoots up with power. He had been drawn by the Father to the Son, and this hour completed his spiritual training. He now goes forth with a legacy from his Saviour, *Blessed are they who have not seen, and yet have believed.* With what power will he preach that truth to others after his own deep experience!

August Tholuck (1799-1877)

July 26th

Let the lives you live be worthy of the gospel of Christ.
Philippians 1:27 (Weymouth)

Christians are distinguished from other people neither by country, nor language, nor the customs which they observe. They neither inhabit cities of their own, nor employ a peculiar form of speech, nor lead a life which is marked out by any singularity. The course of conduct which they follow has not been devised by any speculation of inquisitive men; nor do they proclaim themselves the advocates of merely human doctrines. But, inhabiting Greek as well as barbarian cities, and following the customs of the natives in respect to clothing, food and the rest of their ordinary conduct, they display to us their wonderful and confessedly striking method of life. They dwell in their own countries, but simply as sojourners. As citizens, they share in all things with others, and yet endure all things as if foreigners. Every foreign land is to them as their native country, and every land of their birth as a land of strangers. They marry, as do all others; they beget children, but they do not destroy their offspring. They have a common table, but not a common bed. They are in the flesh, but they do not live after the flesh. They pass their days on earth, but they are citizens of heaven. They obey the prescribed laws, and at the same time surpass the laws by their lives. They love all people, and are persecuted by all. They are put to death, and restored to life. They are poor, yet make many rich; they are in lack of all things, and yet abound in all; they are dishonoured, and yet in their very dishonour are glorified. They are evil spoken of, and yet are justified; they are reviled, and bless; they are insulted, and repay the insult with honour; they do good, yet are punished as evil-doers. When punished, they rejoice as if quickened into life; they are assailed, yet those who hate them are unable to assign any reason for their hatred.

Mathetes (130)

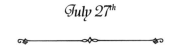

We love Him, because He first loved us.
1 John 4:19

My God, I love Thee; not because I hope for heaven thereby,
Nor yet because who love Thee not are lost eternally.

Thou, O my Jesus, Thou didst me upon the cross embrace;
For me didst bear the nails and spear, and manifold disgrace,

And griefs and torments numberless, and sweat of agony;
Even death itself; and all for one who was Thine enemy.

Then why, most loving Jesus Christ, should I not love Thee well,
Not for the sake of winning heaven, or of escaping hell;

Not with the hope of gaining aught, not seeking a reward;
But as Thyself hast loved me, O ever-loving Lord?

Even so I love Thee, and will love, and in Thy praise will sing,
Solely because Thou art my God, and my eternal King. Amen.

Francis Xavier (1506-1552)

God gives us His own self in Jesus. Jesus comes to live inside us. He doesn't give us things, but Himself.

S.D. Gordon (1859-1936)

God has loved humanity… whom He formed after His own image, to whom He sent His only begotten Son, to whom He has promised a kingdom in heaven, and will give it to those who have loved Him. And when you have attained this knowledge, with what joy do you think you will be filled? How will you love Him who first so loved you? And if you love Him, you will be an imitator of His kindness.

Mathetes (120)

July 28th

That hope we have as an anchor of the soul——an anchor
that can neither break nor drag. It passes in behind the veil,
where Jesus has entered as a forerunner on our behalf.
Hebrews 6:19, 20 (Weymouth)

Keep fast hold of your hope in Christ, and you will be able to hold your ground. Never let go your spiritual anchor and you will successfully resist the strong currents around you. The 'veil' takes us back to the ancient Jewish sanctuary. Although the pious worshippers never entered within that curtain, never saw behind it, yet they knew perfectly what was there; they knew the blessed truth set forth by that mercy-seat, and all their spiritual hope was based upon it. The anchor of their souls entered into that within the veil and took hold of the blood-sprinkled mercy-seat of God. It won't do to ground your soul's anchor in the mere indulgence of an amiable God. The anchor must be fixed in the ground God has provided. It must lay hold on covenant mercy, on the finished work of Christ.

Biblical Illustrator (1887)

From every stormy wind that blows, from every swelling tide of woes,
There is a calm, a sweet retreat; 'tis found beneath the mercy seat.
There is a place where Jesus sheds, the oil of gladness on our heads,
A place than all beside more sweet; it is the blood-stained mercy-seat.
Ah! whither could we flee for aid, when tempted, desolate, dismayed,
Or how the hosts of hell defeat, had suffering saints no mercy-seat?
O let my hands forget their skill, my tongue be silent, cold and still,
This bounding heart forget to beat, if I forget the mercy-seat.
Hugh Stowell (1799-1865)

I commend myself to the infinite mercies of God in the incarnate Son, as my only sufficient hope.

William Gladstone (1809-1898)

Thou knowest my downsitting and mine uprising,
Thou understandest my thoughts afar off.
Psalm 139:2

If the Lord knows our thoughts before their existence, before they can be properly called ours, much more does He know them when they actually spring up in us; He knows the tendency of them; He knows them exactly.

Stephen Charnock (1628-1680)

Not an action is lost or a thought overlooked. No wonder David adds the words, *such knowledge is too wonderful for me; it is high, I cannot attain unto it.* We get used to the thought that God made the sun and sky, the moon and stars which He has ordained, and we bow to the fact that they are the work of His fingers. Let us go further! The *coming in* and *going out* is mentioned several times in Psalm 139 as though it were very important. David was given preservation and wisdom in his *goings out* and his *comings in.*

Lady Hope (1884)

O Lord, in me there lieth nought
     but to Thy search revealed lies;
For when I sit Thou markest it;
     No less Thou notest when I rise;
Yea, closest closet of my thought
     hath open windows to Thine eyes.

Thou walkest with me when I walk,
     when to my bed for rest I go,
I find Thee there, and everywhere;
     Not youngest thought in me doth grow,
no, not one word I cast to talk
     but, yet unuttered, Thou doest know.

Philip Sidney (1554-1586)

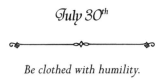

July 30th

Be clothed with humility.
1 Peter 5:5

Let us be of humble mind, laying aside all haughtiness, pride and angry feelings; and let us act according to that which is written, for the Holy Spirit says, *Let not the wise glory in wisdom, neither let the mighty glory in might, neither let the rich glory in riches; but let him that glories glory in the Lord, in diligently seeking Him, and doing righteousness.* Let us especially be mindful of the words of the Lord Jesus teaching us meekness and long-suffering: *Be merciful, that you may obtain mercy; forgive, that you may be forgiven; as you judge, so shall you be judged; as you are kind, so shall kindness be shown to you; with what measure you mete, with the same it shall be measured to you.* By this precept let us establish ourselves that we walk with all humility in obedience to His holy words. *On whom shall I look, but on him that is meek and peaceable, and that trembles at My words?*

Clement of Rome (30-100)

Remember what thou wert before thy birth – nothing; what thou wert for many years after – weakness; what in all thy life – a great sinner; what in all thy excellencies – a mere debtor to God, to thy parents, to the earth, and to all creatures. If we dwell on these, we shall see nothing more reasonable than to be humble, and nothing more foolish than to be proud.

Jeremy Taylor (1613-1667)

Always to think well and highly of others is great wisdom. You should not reckon yourself better than others, lest perhaps in the eyes of God, who knows what is in people, you are considered worse. If there is good in yourself, believe that there is more in others, that you may preserve your humility.

Thomas à Kempis (1380-1471)

As my Father has sent Me, even so send I you.
John 20:21

Our errand in this world is in a small way the same that Christ's errand was. He does not now Himself in person go about doing good; we are to go for Him. The only hands Christ has for doing kindnesses are our hands. The only feet He has to run the errands of love are our feet. The only voice He has to speak cheer to the troubled is our voice. We crave the human touch, the human voice, and human love. Thus it comes that He sends us to represent Him, we are to be hands and face and voice and heart to Him.

J.R. Miller (1840-1912)

> Christ has no body now on earth but yours;
>> yours are the only hands with which He can do His work,
>> yours are the only feet with which He can go about the world,
>> yours are the only eyes through which His compassion
>>> can shine forth upon a troubled world.
> Christ has no body now on earth but yours.

Teresa of Avila (1515-1582)

Beware lest you be like those of the earth, who when they waken in another world, awaken with empty hands because they placed nothing in Christ's Hands, which were stretched out to them in the hands of His poor and needy.

Augustine of Hippo (354-430)

> O Lord! that I could waste my life for others,
>> with no ends of my own;
> that I could pour myself into others,
>> and live for them alone!

Frederick W. Faber (1814-1863)

Oh God, you put into my heart this great desire to devote myself to the sick and sorrowful; I offer it to you. Do with it what is for your service. Amen.

Florence Nightingale (1820-1910)

August

August 1st

---◆---

My presence shall go with you, and I will give you rest.
Exodus 33:14

We should never leave our prayer closets in the morning without having concentrated our thoughts deeply and intensely on the fact of the actual presence of God there with us, encompassing us, and filling the room as literally as it fills heaven itself. It may not lead to any distinct results at first, but as we make repeated efforts to realize the presence of God, it will become increasingly real to us. And as the habit grows upon us when alone in a room... or when pacing the stony street – in the silence of the night, or amid the teeming crowds of daylight – we shall often find ourselves whispering the words, "Thou art near; Thou art here, O Lord."

F.B. Meyer (1847-1929)

The time of business does not with me differ from the time of prayer, and in the noise and clatter of my kitchen, while several persons are at the same time calling for different things, I possess God in as great tranquility as if I were upon my knees at the blessed sacrament.

Brother Lawrence (1605-1691)

May not a single moment of my life be spent outside the light, love and joy of God's presence and not a moment without the entire surrender of my self as a vessel for Him to fill full of His Spirit and His love.

Andrew Murray (1828-1917)

O my God, since Thou art with me, and I must now in obedience to Thy commands apply my mind to these outward things, I beseech Thee to grant me the grace to continue in Thy presence; and to this end do Thou prosper me with Thy assistance, receive all my works, and possess all my affections.... Lord of all pots and pans and things... make me a saint by getting meals and washing up the plates. Amen.

Brother Lawrence (1605-1691)

August 2ⁿᵈ

Search me, O God, and know my heart: try me, and know my thoughts: and see if there be any wicked way in me, and lead me in the way everlasting.

Psalm 139:23, 24

Is there any exercise of the soul which any one of us is found so unsatisfactory, so almost impossible, as self-examination? The heart is so exceedingly complicated and intricate, and it is so very near the eye which is to investigate it. There are chambers receding within a sinner's heart, which no mere human investigation ever will reach. It is the prerogative of God alone to search the human heart.

James Vaughn (1878)

Sometimes the evil may be hidden even in what at a cursory glance would look good. Beneath apparent zeal for the truth may be hidden a judging spirit or a subtle leaning to our own understanding. Beneath apparent Christian faithfulness may be hidden an absence of Christian love. Beneath an apparently rightful care for our affairs may be hidden a great want of trust in God. I believe our blessed Guide, the indwelling Holy Spirit, is always secretly discovering these things to us by continual little checks and pangs of conscience, so that we are left without excuse. But it is very easy to disregard His gentle voice, and insist to ourselves that all is right, causing defeat in most unexpected quarters.

Hannah Pearsall Smith (1832-1911)

Let me know Thee, O Thou who knows me; let me know Thee, as I am known. O Thou strength of my soul, enter into it and prepare it for Thyself that Thou may have and hold it without spot or wrinkle. And from Thee, O Lord, unto whose eyes the depths of my conscience are naked, what in me could be hidden though I were unwilling to confess to Thee? To Thee then, O Lord, am I manifest.

Augustine of Hippo (354-430)

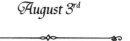

August 3rd

Peace I leave with you, My peace I give unto you...
Let not your heart be troubled, neither let it be afraid.

John 14:27

You may have stood by the side of one of those brawling mountain streams which descend into the sea. Such a stream rushes with its noisy waters down its narrow channel, every pebble rattles in the torrent, every ripple makes a murmur of its own. Suddenly the sound ceases; a deep stillness fills the banks from side to side. Why? It is the broad sweep of the advancing tide of the ocean that has checked the stream and occupied the whole space of its narrow channel with its own strong, silent, overwhelming waters. Even so it is with all the little cares, difficulties and distractions that make up the noise and clatter of the stream of our daily life. They go on increasing and increasing; they engross our whole attention till they are suddenly met and absorbed by some thought or object greater than themselves, advancing from a wider, deeper, stronger sphere. From a thousand heights the streams of human life are forever rushing down; but there is another stream advancing into each of those channels, a tide from that wider and trackless ocean; and deep indeed is the peace which those tides may bring with them wherever their force extends. The very measure of the greatness of the idea of God and of the things of God is the depth of the peace which that idea is able to impart.

Dean Stanley (1815-1881)

How precious are Thy thoughts of peace,
O God, to me! how great the sum!
New every morn, they never cease;
They were, they are, and yet shall come,
In number and in compass more
Than ocean's sands on ocean's shore.

James Montgomery (1771-1854)

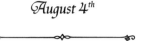

Speak, Lord, for your servant hears.
1 Samuel 3:9

The person who serves God best is the one who is less intent on hearing from God what one wills to hear, than on shaping one's will according to what one hears from God.

Augustine of Hippo (354-430)

Master, speak, Thy servant heareth,
waiting for Thy gracious word,
longing for Thy voice that cheereth;
Master, let it now be heard.
I am listening, Lord, for Thee:
what hast Thou to say to me?

Speak to me by name, O Master,
let me know it is to me;
speak, that I may follow faster,
with a step more firm and free,
where the Shepherd leads the flock
in the shadow of the rock.

Master, speak: and make me ready
when Thy voice is truly heard,
with obedience glad and steady
still to follow every word.
I am listening, Lord, for Thee;
Master, speak, O speak to me!

Frances Havergal (1836-1879)

Wherefore callest thou Him "our Lord"? Because He hath redeemed us, both soul and body, from all our sins, not with silver or gold but with His precious blood, and has delivered us from all the power of the devil; and thus has made us His own property.

Heidelberg Confession (1563)

August 5th

And a vision appeared to Paul in the night; there stood a man of Macedonia,
and prayed him, saying, Come over into Macedonia and help us.

Acts 16:9

The book of Acts is careful to point out how each fresh step in the extension of the Church's work was directed and commanded by Jesus Christ Himself. Paul had no doubt that what he saw was a vision from Christ, and not a mere dream. The next step was to be quite sure of what the vision meant. Wisely, he does not make up his mind himself, but calls in the three men who were with him. Timothy, Silas, and Luke come together to understand what the vision meant. The Holy Spirit had already forbidden them to speak the Word in one region and checked and hindered them when they endeavoured to go into another. *He that follows Me shall not walk in darkness, but shall have the light of life.* Careful consideration is a preliminary to all good Christian work. And if you can, talk to some Timothy and Silas and Luke about your course, and do not be above taking advice. When they had assuredly gathered that the Lord had called them, immediately they endeavored to go into Macedonia. For us, too, the fields are white, the labourers are few, the Lord of the harvest is imperative, the sun is hurrying to the west, and the sickles will have to be laid down before long.

In deepest truth, there is always a calm voyage for the person whose eyes are open to discern, and whose hands are swift to fulfill the commandments of their Father in heaven. For them all winds blow to their port; for them all things work together for good. Careful study of providences, of hindrances and stimuli, careful setting of our lives side by side with the Master's, and a swift delight in doing the will of the Lord, will secure for us a prosperous voyage, till all storms are hushed; so He bringeth them to their desired haven.

Alexander Maclaren (1826-1910)

I am the way, and the truth, and the life; no one comes unto the Father but by me.
John 14:6

We have no wings to soar to the high privilege of communing with a holy God. Access to God as the Hearer of prayer is the effect only of that great work of redeeming mercy in which the second person of the ever-blessed and adorable Trinity came to seek and save those which were lost, and advance them to the privileges of children. We have nothing of our own to plead; yet in His name may our prayers go up as incense, and the lifting up of our hands as an acceptable sacrifice. Humbling as the consideration is, we have not a rag of righteousness left us, in which we may appear before the throne. The worthiness is not in us. Christ's name, Christ's sacrifice, Christ's righteousness, Christ's work, Christ's entire mediation as the interceding High Priest, form the centre and channel of all God's communications with apostate humanity, and the medium of their access to God. *For through Him we have access by one Spirit unto the Father.* It is not possible for a sinner to find any other way of access.... As sinners, we can have nothing to do with God except through Christ. We have freedom of access only in that way which He has consecrated by His blood. We have no other. He is the altar whence the hallowed incense arises which is expressive of the purity and ardor of a true devotion. Prayer, therefore, is an unspeakable privilege. For a creature to be allowed to draw nigh to the Holy God, and express all the desires of one's heart, in the name of Jesus, and plead the full merits of Him in whom the Eternal Father is well pleased, is indeed the privilege of sons. Here the Father of mercies meets His offending creature with the smile of reconciliation; and here the creature, with a heart sprinkled from an evil conscience, meets its offended, but gracious and reconciled Father.

Gardiner Spring (1785-1873)

August 7th

I poured out my complaint before Him.
Psalm 142:2

Before God we may speak out our minds fully; be very particular in secret prayer, as to sins, wants and mercies. Be not ashamed to open out all thy necessities. Before God we may name the persons that afflict, affront or trouble us. A great reason why we reap so little benefit in prayer is because we rest too much in generals.

Samuel Lee (1625-1691)

Accustom yourself to talking with God, not by the use of sentiments carefully prepared beforehand, but with the thoughts of which your heart is full. If you feel drawn to love Him, tell Him so. Also tell Him all the evil you know about yourself. God's mercies or your own miseries will always give you enough to talk to Him about.

François de la Mothe Fénelon (1651-1715)

The God of patience and comfort will support you, if you are diligent in seeking to maintain His presence within your heart in childlike love. He who has counted the hairs of your head, letting not one fall uselessly to the ground, counts your every trial-hour. He is faithful to His promises and His love. He will not suffer pain to try you beyond what you can bear, but will work your advancement out of temptation and trial. Give yourself up to Him; let Him do as He wills. Take up the dear Cross, which will be so precious to you if you carry it aright. One who has never been tempted knows neither the goodness of God nor one's own weakness.

François de la Mothe Fénelon (1651-1715)

How often we look upon God as our last and feeblest resource! We go to Him because we have nowhere else to go. And then we learn that the storms of life have driven us, not upon the rocks, but unto the desired haven.

George Macdonald (1824-1903)

In all things it behoved Him to be made like unto His brethren,
that He might be a merciful and faithful High Priest.

Hebrews 2:17

It is good to remember that He who is the bread hungered; He who gives the living water thirsted; He who invites to rest was weary; He who opens the pathway to glory was put to shame; He who calls us to *all spiritual blessings in heavenly* places suffered the curse; He who bestows life eternal went down into death. Be assured, then, that He will minister these divine benefits with a loving, understanding and sympathetic heart.

Anonymous

Christ gathered unto Himself every form of pain, of misery, of weariness, of burden, which can weigh upon and wear out a human spirit; and no single ingredient that ever made any person's cup distasteful was left out. We know not by what mysterious process the Son learned obedience by the things which He suffered; nor can we understand how it was that the High Priest, who would never have become the High Priest had He not been merciful, became yet more merciful by His own experience of human sorrow. Comfort drops but coldly from lips that have never uttered a sigh or a groan; and for our poor human hearts it is not enough to have a merciful God far off in the heavens. We need a Christ who can be touched with the feeling of our infirmities before we come boldly to the Throne of Grace, assured of there finding grace in time of need. He became like us in our sorrows that we might become like Him in His gladness.

Alexander Maclaren (1826-1910)

> This, this is the God we adore,
> our faithful, unchangeable Friend,
> Whose love is as great as His power,
> and neither knows measure nor end.

Joseph Hart (1712-1768)

Keep your heart with all diligence; for out of it are the issues of life.
Proverbs 4:23

The heart is a *lamp* which the High and Holy One has entrusted to our care: keep it well trimmed then, keep it with all diligence: let it not resemble those of the foolish virgins who took no oil with them: but rather look unto God for fresh supplies of His grace.

The heart is a *ship*; keep it with all diligence. Look to the hull and the rudder, the masts, the sails, and the rigging. Have an eye to the crew, and take especial care what merchandise you put aboard; mind that you have plenty of ballast, and that you carry not too much sail. Mind that you have a heavenly Pilot at the helm. Be prepared for storms.

The heart is a *temple*. Have care that you keep it with all diligence: keep it pure and undefiled. Let the Ark of the Covenant be found within it. Let your prayers be set forth as incense, and the lifting up of your hands as the evening sacrifice. Dedicate the temple of your heart to the Lord of lords and King of kings, and use all diligence in seeking that it may be filled with His glory.

The heart is a *besieged city*, and liable to attacks on all sides. While you defend one part, keep a good look-out on the other; while you build up the bastion here, let not the gateway be left defenseless there. Be alive! be diligent! post your sentinels! have a watchword! take care whom you let in, and whom you allow to go out.

Humphrey Sydenham (1637)

> Give Me thine heart as I
>   have given Mine to purchase thine.
> I halved it not when I did die,
>   but gave Myself wholly to set thee free.
>
> Francis Quarles (1592-1644)

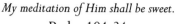

My meditation of Him shall be sweet.
Psalm 104:34

Picture the Lord close beside you. See how lovingly, how humbly He is teaching you. Practise it! I am not asking you to produce great thoughts nor to feel deep devotion. I only ask you to look at Him. Place yourself in the presence of Christ and converse with Him without wearying yourself in searching out reasons. We should ever reflect on the greatness and majesty of our God. We shall advance more by contemplating the Divinity than by keeping our eyes fixed on ourselves. I think we shall never learn to know ourselves except by endeavouring to know God, for beholding His greatness we are struck by our own baseness. His purity shows our foulness, and by meditating on His humility, we find how far we are from being humble. Always begin and finish your prayer with the thought of your own nothingness.

Teresa of Åvila (1515-1582)

The contemplation of Christ's glory is the universal remedy and cure, the only balsam, for all our distresses. Whatever presses, urges, perplexes, if we can but retreat in our minds to a view of this glory and a due consideration of our own interest therein, comfort and support will be administered to us.

John Owen (1616-1683)

When I feel I cannot make headway in devotion, I open my Bible at the Psalms and... let myself be carried along in the stream of devotion which flows through the whole book. The outreach always sets toward God and is deep and strong.

James Gilmour (1843-1891)

> Speak to Him, then, for He hears,
> and spirit with Spirit can meet—
> Closer is He than breathing,
> and nearer than hands and feet

Alfred Tennyson (1809-1892)

August 11th

I bow my knees unto the Father of our Lord Jesus Christ.
Ephesians 3:14

My God, how wonderful Thou art,
Thy majesty how bright!
How beautiful Thy mercy seat,
In depth of burning light!

How dread are Thine eternal years,
O everlasting Lord,
By prostrate spirits day and night
Incessantly adored!

How beautiful, how beautiful
The sight of Thee must be,
Thine endless wisdom, boundless power,
And awful purity!

O how I fear Thee, living God,
With deepest, tenderest fears
And worship Thee with trembling hope
And penitential tears!

Yet I may love Thee, too, O Lord,
Almighty as Thou art,
For Thou hast stooped to ask of me
The love of my poor heart.

No earthly father loves like Thee;
No mother, e'er so mild,
Bears and forbears as Thou hast done
With me, Thy sinful child.

Father of Jesus, love's reward,
What rapture will it be
Prostrate before Thy throne to lie,
And gaze and gaze on Thee! Amen.

Frederick W. Faber (1814-1863)

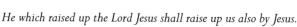

He which raised up the Lord Jesus shall raise up us also by Jesus.
2 Corinthians 4:14

Come fellow Christians, let us contentedly commit these bodies to the grave; that prison grave shall not long contain them. Lay down freely this natural body; you shall receive it again a celestial, spiritual body. Though you lay it down in dishonour, you shall receive it in glory. Though you are separated from it through weakness, it shall be raised again in mighty power. When the trumpet of God shall sound the call, *Arise you dead, and come away*, and when He shall call to the earth and the sea, *O earth, give up thy dead, O sea, give up thy dead*, who shall resist the powerful command? The first that shall be called are the saints that sleep; and then the saints that are alive shall be changed. Triumph now, O Christian, in these promises; you shall shortly triumph in their fulfillment. The grave that could not keep our Lord shall not keep us: He arose for us, and by the same power shall we arise. Let us never look at the grave, but let us see the resurrection beyond it. Faith is quick-sighted and can see as far as eternity. Therefore let our hearts rejoice; let our flesh also rest in hope; for He will not leave us in the grave. Christian, because Christ sanctified the grave by His burial and conquered death by His resurrection, the grave is not now a horrid spectacle to the believing eye. Death shall not dissolve the union between Him and us nor turn away His affections from us. But in the morning of eternity, He will send His angels, yes, come Himself, and roll away the stone, and unseal our grave, and reach forth His hand, and deliver us alive to our Father.

Richard Baxter (1615-1691)

One step more and the race is ended;
  One word more, and the lesson's done;
One toil more and a long rest follows
  At set of sun.

Christina Rossetti (1830-1894)

August 13th

He had in His right hand seven stars....
He laid His right hand upon me, saying unto me, Fear not.
Revelation 1:16, 17

Did you ever fear a little as you thought of the difficulties ahead? Did you ever think, He has so many to take care of, how will He have time to think of me? We have the answer to our thoughts here in this verse. It is the Hand that holds the seven stars (the seven churches, all the worlds and the Heaven of heavens); it is the Hand that is laid upon each one of us, and to each one the word is the same, *Fear not.*

Amy Carmichael (1867-1951)

John was here favoured with an unusual vision of his glorified Lord; his fear was far more in the ascendant than holy joy, for the Lord said to him *Fear not.* The knowledge of Jesus is the best remedy for fears: when we are better acquainted with our Lord we part company with half our doubts. Jesus in His person, work and offices, and relations, is a mine of consolation; every truth which is connected with Him is an argument against fear. Study then your Lord. Let your thoughts of Christ be high, and your delight in Him will be high too; your sense of security will be strong, and with that sense of security will come the sacred joy and peace which always keep the heart which confidently reposes in the Mediator's hands. If you would be raised, let your thoughts of Christ be raised. Earth sinks as Jesus rises.

C.H. Spurgeon (1834-1892)

> Is God for me? I fear not, though all against me rise;
> I call on Christ my Saviour, the host of evil flies.
> My friend the Lord Almighty, and He who loves me, God,
> What enemy shall harm me, though coming as a flood?
> At all times, in all places, He standeth at my side,
> He rules the battle fury, the tempest and the tide.
>
> Paul Gerhardt (1606-1676)

He is the exact likeness of the unseen God.
Colossians 1:15 (Williams)

Christ is the visible image of an invisible God. We cannot allow God to be out of mind because He is out of sight. We *walk by faith, not by sight*. How difficult an acquirement, for we are creatures of sense. Because we are chiefly affected by the visible, how soon we forget. And so it is in matters which affect our eternal well-being. We need to live by faith in the invisible. Things seen are paltry and passing; grandeur and endurance belong to the unseen. The soul is unseen; this precious jewel of immortality lies concealed within its fragile fleshly casket. Hell and heaven are unseen; the eternal world is unseen, death is unseen, the devil is unseen. Jehovah is an invisible God. *Lord, show us the Father, said Philip. Jesus said, He that has seen Me has seen the Father.* Seen Me weeping with the living and weeping for the dead, seen Me receiving little children into my arms to bless them, seen Me inviting the weary to rest, pitying all human suffering, patient under the greatest wrongs, encouraging the penitent, and ready to forgive the vilest sinners. In Me, my character and works, you have a living, visible, perfect *image of the invisible God.*

Thomas Guthrie (1803-1873)

Thou art the Everlasting Word, the Father's only Son;
God manifestly seen and heard, and Heaven's beloved One.

In Thee most perfectly expressed, the Father's glories shine;
Of the full Deity possessed, eternally Divine.

True image of the infinite, whose essence is concealed;
Brightness of uncreated light; the heart of God revealed.
Worthy, O Lamb of God, art Thou
That every Knee to Thee should bow

Josiah Conder (1789-1855)

August 15th

But the LORD was with Joseph, and showed him mercy,
and gave him favour in the sight of the keeper of the prison.
Genesis 39:21

That is one of the most eloquent 'buts' of Scripture. The prison is light when God is there, and chains do not chafe if He wraps His love round them. Many a prisoner for God since Joseph's time has had this experience repeated, and received tenderer tokens from Him in a dungeon than ever before. Paul the prisoner, John in Patmos, Bunyan in Bedford jail, George Fox in Lancaster Castle, Rutherford in Aberdeen, and many more, have found the Lord with them and showing them kindness. We may all be sure that, if ever faithfulness to conscience involves us in difficulties, the faithfulness and the difficulties will combine to bring us strong tokens of God's approval and presence, the winning of which will make a prison a palace and a gate of heaven. Joseph had come 'out of prison to reign,' and as we all find, if we are God's servants, to reign means to serve, and the higher the place the harder the task. The long years of waiting had nourished powers which the seven years of busy toil tested. We must make ourselves, by God's help, ready in obscurity, for whatever may be laid on us in after days.

Alexander Maclaren (1826-1910)

Our brightest visions often come in our hardest trials. The Valley of the Shadow of Death is often the way to the land of Beulah and Delectable Mountains. Often, from a pillow of stones, as to Jacob at Bethel, come the brightest visions of the soul. From weariness and pain and trouble arise the steps that lead to heaven. Life's Pisgahs and Mounts of Transfiguration are built of the hardest rocks of affliction and trial.

Francis Nathan Peloubet (1831-1920)

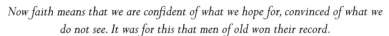

Now faith means that we are confident of what we hope for, convinced of what we do not see. It was for this that men of old won their record.
Hebrews 11:1, 2 (Moffatt)

When sentenced to exile for his faith, John Chrysostom (345 – 407) responded: "What can I fear? Will it be death? But you know that Christ is my life, and that I shall gain by death. Will it be exile? But the earth and all its fullness is the Lord's. Will it be loss of wealth? But we brought nothing into the world and carry nothing out. Thus all the terrors of the world are contemptible in my eyes, and I smile at all its good things. Poverty I do not fear. Riches I do not sigh for. Death I do not shrink from, and life I do not desire, save only for the progress of your souls.... And so, if they banish me, I shall be like Elias; if they throw me into the mire, like Jeremiah; if they stone me, it is Stephen that I shall resemble; John the forerunner, if they cut off my head; Paul, if they beat me with stripes; Isaiah, if they saw me asunder.".... In exile he wrote letters that reveal to us a picture of a good and great man confronting his destiny in the purest spirit, and cheered by the sense of God's presence.... He was driven from place to place, endured great trials and was finally dragged to his death. He died with these memorable words on his lips, Glory to God for all things. Amen.

F. W. Farrar (1831-1903)

True faith is not only a certain knowledge, whereby I hold for truth all that God has revealed to us in his word, but also an assured confidence, which the Holy Spirit works by the gospel in my heart; that not only to others, but to me also, remission of sin, everlasting righteousness and salvation, are freely given by God, merely of grace, only for the sake of Christ's merits.

Heidelberg Confession (1563)

The blood of Jesus Christ, His Son, cleanses us from all sin.
1 John 1: 7

Luther felt depressed. It seemed to him that he saw a hideous and malignant form inscribing the record of his own transgressions round the walls of his room. There was no end to the list. Luther bowed his head and prayed. When he looked again, the writer had paused and turned, facing him. "Thou hast forgotten one thing!" said Luther. "And what is that?" asked his tormentor. "Take thy pen once more and write across it all: *The blood of Jesus Christ, His Son, cleanses me from all sin.*

Gray & Adams Commentary (1951)

Great as He is, there are some things that even God cannot do. He cannot pass over sin as though it did not matter. He must deal with it in some way. But there are some things which God can do. He can forgive sin as soon as it is confessed. He can give peace to the troubled spirit. He can give the assurance of salvation. He can keep those who commit themselves to Him. He will forgive sin and utterly blot it out and forget it if we confess and forsake it. He will silence the guilty conscience and give rest to the soul. He will impart the joy of salvation. He will cleanse and sanctify the heart so that we are made fit to live in a better world when death takes us away from this.

General Booth (1829-1912)

Almighty and everlasting God, you hate nothing that you have made, and forgive the sins of all those who are penitent. Create and make in us new and contrite hearts, that, lamenting our sins and acknowledging our wretchedness, we may receive from you, the God of all mercy, perfect forgiveness and peace: through Jesus Christ our Lord. Amen.

Thomas Cranmer (1498-1556)

August 18ᵗʰ

Blessed be God, which has not turned away my prayer nor His mercy from me.
Psalm 66:20

Let prayer nourish your soul as your meals nourish your body. Let your times of prayer keep you in God's presence through the day, and as His presence is frequently remembered, it will be an ever fresh spring of prayer. Such loving recollections of God renew our whole being, quiet our passions, supply light and counsel in difficulty, gradually subdue the temper, and cause us to possess our souls in patience. Every morning get some quiet time for brief meditation–this will feed you through the day. Let this meditation be more a matter of the heart than intellect, less of argument than simple affection, less of methodical arrangement than of faith and love. How strong we are in God when we realize our own weakness! Why should we daily say *Our Father, Which art in Heaven*, if we do not want to be held in His arms as tender, simple, obedient children?

Grace is to the soul what food is to the body. And prayer is to the soul's life as the digestive organ is to the body. Love digests everything, absorbs everything, and assimilates all it receives; it nourishes and leads to good deeds. As the digestion forms blood, flesh, and power for arms and legs, so love in prayer renews the spirit of life for all its course. It forms patience, gentleness, humility, purity, temperance, sincerity, and all other virtues. If you strive to apply such virtues externally, you only produce a formal method, a superstitious exterior, a collection of works, a lifeless form. It will be a mere whitened sepulchre; the outside may be garnished with the marble of virtues, but within will only be dry bones. The interior will be lifeless, lacking the Holy Spirit's power.

François de la Mothe Fénelon (1651-1715)

Hear our prayer, O heav'nly Father, for the dear Redeemer's sake. Amen.

Traditional prayer

My tongue shall speak of Thy righteousness and of Thy praise all the day long.
Psalm 35:28

O for a thousand tongues to sing my dear Redeemer's praise,
The glories of my God and King, the triumphs of His grace!

My gracious Master and my God, assist me to proclaim,
To spread through all the earth abroad the honours of Thy Name.

Jesus! the Name that charms our fear, that bids our sorrows cease,
'Tis music in the sinner's ears, 'tis life and health and peace.

He breaks the power of cancelled sin, He sets the prisoner free;
His blood can make the foulest clean, His blood availed for me.

He speaks, and listening to His voice, new life the dead receive,
The mournful broken hearts rejoice, the humble poor believe.

Hear Him, ye deaf; His praise, ye dumb, your loosened tongues employ;
Ye blind, behold your Saviour come; and leap, ye lame, for joy.

See all your sins on Jesus laid: the Lamb of God was slain;
His soul was once an offering made for every soul of man.

Glory to God, and praise, and love be ever, ever given
By saints below and saints above, the Church in earth and heaven.
Charles Wesley (1707-1788)

No one can hinder our private addresses to God. Everyone can build a chapel in their breast; one's self, the priest; the heart, the sacrifice; the earth one treads, the altar.
Jeremy Taylor (1613-1667)

Take my voice and let me sing always only for my King. Take my lips and let them be filled with messages from Thee. Amen
Frances Havergal (1836-1879)

Let us not be weary in well doing: for in due season we shall reap, if we faint not.
Galatians 6:9

Every day that passes leaves life's margin a little less for each of us. Our allotment of time is ever shortening. We must work while the day lasts. We must do good while our hearts are warm. We must speak the words of life before our lips grow dumb. We must scatter kindnesses in the world before our hands grow feeble. We must pour out love to bless the lonely before our pulses are stilled. We must not crowd God's work out of our busy days, hoping to have time for it by-and-by, when leisure comes. Ah! by-and-by it will be too late. Those who need us now will not need us then. The deeds of love which we should do today we cannot do tomorrow. The neighbor who now longs for our warm sympathy and gentle ministry may not need us when our tasks have been banished and we have leisure.

J.R. Miller (1840-1912)

Living for others -- planning for them, serving them, doing your utmost for them -- you will find that your heart is so full of joy, that you are deeply and intensely happy.

Gray & Adams Commentary (1951)

Eternity is crying out to you louder and louder as you near its brink. Rise, be doing; count your resources; learn what you are not fit for, and give up wishing for it; learn what you can do, and do it.

F. W. Robertson (1816-1853)

Let me to Thy glory live; my every sacred moment spend in publishing the sinners' Friend. Enlarge, inflame and fill my heart with boundless charity divine: so shall I all my strength exert, and love them with a zeal like Thine; and lead them to Thy open side, the sheep for whom their Shepherd died. Amen.

Charles Wesley (1707-1788)

August 21st

By the law is the knowledge of sin. But now
the righteousness of God without the Law is manifested.
Romans 3:20, 21

God imparts righteousness to the believer by the Spirit of grace without the work of the Law, or without the help of the Law. Through the Law God opens our eyes so that we see our helplessness and by faith take refuge to His mercy and so are healed.

Augustine of Hippo (354-430)

The law does nothing more than remind us of our sin and slay us by it, and make us liable to eternal wrath; and, all this is taught and experienced by our conscience, when it is really smitten by the law. Therefore we must have something else than the law, and more than the law, to make us righteous and save us.

Martin Luther (1483-1546)

Justification is an act of God's free grace wherein He pardoneth all our sins, and accepteth us as righteous in His sight, only for the righteousness of Christ imputed to us and received by faith alone.

Westminster Shorter Catechism (1647)

Not the labours of my hands can fulfill Thy law's demands.
Could my zeal no respite know, could my tears for ever flow,
All for sin could not atone; Thou must save, and Thou alone.

Nothing in my hand I bring; simply to the Cross I cling;
Naked, come to Thee for dress; helpless, look to Thee for grace;
Foul, I to the fountain fly; wash me, Savior, or I die.

Rock of ages, cleft for me, let me hide myself in Thee;
Let the water and the blood, from Thy river side which flowed
Be of sin in the double cure, cleanse me from its guilt and power

Augustus Toplady (1740-1778)

August 22nd

For everybody has sinned and continues to come short of God's glory,
but anybody may have right standing with God as a free gift of
His undeserved favor, through the ransom provided in Christ Jesus.
Romans 3:23-25 (Williams)

God does not justify us freely by His grace in such a way that He did not demand any atonement to be made, for He gave Jesus Christ into death for us, in order that He might atone for our sins. So now He justifies freely by His grace those who have been redeemed by His Son.

Martin Luther (1483-1546)

By justification a believer is put in the place of a righteous person in the eye of the law, and is entitled on Christ's account to all the advantages of righteousness. As these advantages comprise peace with God, His favour, access to Him, His guardian care for this life, and for the life to come the unfading inheritance and Eternal Kingdom – it is evident how unspeakably rich is the grace given to us in justification. And just as certainly as justification rests on the work and sufferings of Christ as its righteous basis, so also is it certain that it is a free and pure act of Divine Grace. They who are justified are in no way of themselves entitled to the place of righteous ones. They are the "ungodly," the "condemned," sinners, those who are morally impotent.

David Gracey (1894)

Abraham was justified not by works but from faith. At the end of life, it will be of no profit to have performed good works, unless we have faith. The Apostle Paul says you have been justified in the name of the Lord: you have been made by Him to be as Himself; and you have been tempered according to His power by the Holy Spirit.

Clement of Alexandria (150-213)

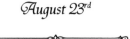

It is a good thing to give thanks unto the Lord.
Psalm 92:1

Almighty God, Father of all mercies, we Thine unworthy servants do give Thee most humble and hearty thanks for all Thy goodness and loving-kindness to us and all people. We bless Thee for our creation, preservation and all the blessings of this life; but above all, for Thine inestimable love in the redemption of the world by our Lord Jesus Christ; for the means of grace, and for the hope of glory. And, we beseech Thee, give us that due sense of all Thy mercies that our hearts may be unfeignedly thankful, and that we may show forth Thy praise, not only with our lips, but in our lives; by giving up ourselves to Thy service, and by walking before Thee in holiness and righteousness all our days. Amen.

Book of Common Prayer (1822)

When all Thy mercies, O my God, my rising soul surveys,
Transported with the view, I'm lost in wonder, love, and praise.

O how shall words, with equal warmth, the gratitude declare
That glows within my ravished heart? But Thou canst read it there.

Ten thousand thousand precious gifts my daily thanks employ;
Nor is the least a cheerful heart that tastes these gifts with joy.

When worn with sickness, oft has Thou with health renewed my face;
And, when in sins and sorrows sunk, revived my soul with grace.

Through every period of my life Thy goodness I'll pursue;
And after death, in distant worlds, the glorious theme renew.

When nature fails, and day and night divide Thy works no more,
My ever grateful heart, O Lord, Thy mercy shall adore.

Joseph Addison (1672-1719)

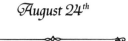

Though I am the foremost of sinners, I obtained mercy.
1 Timothy 1:15 (Moffatt)

The men and women who willingly and joyfully share the fellowship of Christ's sufferings are vividly conscious of the unspeakable reality of their own personal redemption. They never forget the pit out of which they have been digged, and they never lose the remembrance of the grace that saved them. *He loved me, and gave Himself for me; therefore, I glory in tribulation!* When Henry Martyn (1781-1812) reached the shores of India he made this entry in his journal, "I desire to burn out for my God," and at the end of the far-off years the secret of his grand enthusiasm stood openly revealed. "Look at me, the vilest of sinners, but saved by grace! Amazing that I can be saved!" It was that amazement wondering all through his years that made him such a fountain of sacrificial energy in the service of his Lord.

J.H. Jowett (1863-1923)

In proportion as the Holy Spirit imparts a sense of personal sinfulness, there will be the heart's appreciation of the value and sufficiency of the Lord Jesus As the conviction of our lost and undone condition deepens, as sin's exceeding sinfulness unveils, as the purity and extent of God's law opens, as the utter helplessness and impotence of self is forced upon the mind, the glory, the worth, the suitableness, and the preciousness of Jesus will, through the teaching of the Spirit, present itself vividly to the mind and heart, as constituting the one only foundation and hope of the soul!

Octavius Winslow (1808-1878)

A person who has learned their own sinfulness will find no occasions for complaint in God's dealings with them. Get near to God in heart-knowledge of Him, and that will teach our sinfulness.

Alexander Maclaren (1826-1910)

Great peace have they which love Thy law: and nothing shall offend them.
Psalm 119:165

To experience this great peace there must be a good conscience toward God. The pleasures of a good conscience are the paradise of souls, the joy of angels, a garden of delights, a field of blessing, the temple of Solomon, the court of God, the habitation of the Holy Spirit.

Bernard of Clairvaux (1090-1153)

Amidst the storms and tempests of the world, there is a perfect calm in the breasts of those who not only do the will of God, but who love to do it. They are at peace with God, by the blood of reconciliation; at peace with themselves, by the answer of a good conscience, and the subjection of those desires which war against the soul; at peace with all people, by the spirit of charity; and the whole creation is so at peace with them that all things work together for their good. No external troubles can rob them of this great peace -- no offences or stumbling blocks, which are thrown in their way by persecution or temptation, by the malice of enemies, by the apostasy of friends, or by anything which they see, hear or feel. Heavenly love surmounts every obstacle, and runs with delight the way of God's commandments.

James Martin (1878)

There is a connection between integrity of purpose and clearness of perception, insomuch that a conformity to what is right is generally followed up by a steady and luminous discernment of what is true. If we have but grace to *do* as we ought, we shall be made to *see* as we ought. It is a lesson repeatedly affirmed by Scripture: *The path of the just is as the shining light, that shines more and more unto the perfect day.*

Thomas Chalmers (1780-1847)

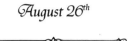

It is God which works in you both to will and to do of His good pleasure.
Philippians 2:13

The common thought is that the life *hid with Christ in God* is to be lived in the emotions, and consequently all the attention of the soul is directed toward them, and as the emotions are satisfactory, the soul rests or is troubled. The truth is that this life is not to be lived in the emotions at all, but in the will; if the will be kept steadfastly abiding in its centre -- God's will -- the varying states of emotion do not disturb or affect the reality of the life. Fenelon says, "Pure religion resides in the will." By this he means that, as the will is the governing power in our nature, if the will is set right, all the rest of our nature must come into harmony.... If God is to take possession of us, it must be into this central will or personality that He enters. If He is reigning there by the power of His Spirit, all the rest of our nature comes under His sway; and as the will is, so is the person. Cease to consider your emotions, for they are only servants; and regard your will which is the real king in your being.... Put your will over completely into the hands of your Lord, surrendering to Him the entire control of it. Say, "Yes, Lord, YES!" to everything, and trust Him to work in you to bring your whole wishes and affections into conformity with His own lovable and most lovely will. It is wonderful what miracles God works in wills that are utterly surrendered to Him. He turns hard things into easy and bitter things into sweet. It is not that He puts easy things in the place of the hard, but He actually changes the hard thing into an easy one.

Hannah Pearsall Smith (1832-1911)

Every instance of obedience, from right motives, strengthens us spiritually, whilst every act of disobedience weakens us spiritually.

George Müller (1805-1898)

Whether we live or die, we are the Lord's.
Romans 14:8

Should all the hosts of death and powers of hell unknown
Put their most dreadful forms of rage or malice on,
 I shall be safe;
For Christ displays superior power and guardian grace.
Isaac Watts (1674-1748)

I creep under my Lord's wings in the great shower, and the waters cannot reach me. We may sing, even in our winter's storm, in the expectation of a summer's sun at the turn of the year. No created powers in hell or out of hell, can mar our Lord's work, or spoil our song of joy.
Samuel Rutherford (1600-1661)

No angel and no heaven, no throne, nor power, nor might
No love, no tribulation, no danger, fear, nor fight,
No height, no depth, no creature that has been or can be,
Can drive me from Thy bosom, can sever me from Thee.
The source of all my singing is high in Heaven above;
The Sun that shines upon me is Jesus and His love.
Paul Gerhardt (1607-1676)

Father, I know that all my life is portioned out for me, and the changes that are sure to come I do not fear to see; but I ask Thee for a present mind, intent on pleasing Thee. Amen.
Anna Laetitia Waring (1820-1910)

'Tis Jesus, the first and the last,
 whose Spirit shall guide us safe home;
We'll praise Him for all that is past,
 and trust Him for all that's to come.
Joseph Hart (1712-1768)

Lord, if any have to die this day, let it be me, for I am ready.
Billy Bray (1794-1868)

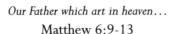

Our Father which art in heaven...
Matthew 6:9-13

The Lord's Prayer is beautiful. The form of petition breathes a filial spirit — *Our Father*; a reverential spirit — *Hallowed be Thy Name*; a missionary spirit — *Thy kingdom come*; an obedient spirit — *Thy will be done on earth*; a dependent spirit — *Give us this day our daily bread*; a forgiving spirit — *and forgive us our trespasses as we forgive them that trespass against us*; a cautious spirit — lead us not into temptation but deliver us from evil; a confidential and adoring spirit — *for Thine is the kingdom, and the power and the glory, for ever and ever. Amen.*

Henry Ward Beecher (1813-1887)

The name we use for God in prayer is very important. It is not the same whether we call Him King, Creator, Judge, or Father. If we think of Him as our King, royalty is suggested — majesty, splendour, and power; but not tenderness, not ease of access, not love. If we call Him Creator, the name carries us back to the beginning when all things came from the Divine hand, and we think of strength, wisdom, goodness, beauty; but He is not brought near to our heart.... When we speak to God, however, as our Father, the vision which arises assures us of welcome when we come to Him. In the midst of the splendors of royalty, when those of highest rank are admitted to the king's presence only at the king's pleasure, the children of the king's household always have free access. No court rules shut them away or prescribe any ceremonious manner in which they must approach the throne. The king is their father. To be a child of God is to have assurance of access to Him at all times. This golden gate of prayer, "Our Father," opens into the innermost sanctuary, into the very secret place of the Most High; and it is shut neither day nor night to any child of God.

J.R. Miller (1840-1912)

August 29th

*Blessed are those servants, whom the lord when He comes
shall find watching.... And if He shall come in the second watch...
and find them so, blessed are those servants.*

Luke 12:37, 38

The second watch was from 10:00 at night till 2:00 a.m. We live
life under the discipline of uncertainty, the indefinite and the
unexpected. The Master of the house may return at any time. That is
enough to keep the servants alert all the time. Vigilance cannot for
one single moment be relaxed. What if He shall come in the second
watch? There are periods in our life that correspond to the second
watch.... In the second watch we shall be tested along the line of
endurance. It is always simple to begin a thing. The difficulty is when
you are in between start and finish. It is then that your staying power
is put to the test. Most failures in life occur in the second watch....
It is the witness of a patience untiring, through the second watch,
that is going to impress the life of our country and the vaster world
beyond.

John Macbeath (n.d.)

> Go, labour on: spend and be spent,
> Thy joy to do the Father's will;
> It is the way the Master went;
> Should not the servant tread it still?
> > Toil on, faint not, keep watch, and pray;
> > Be wise the erring soul to win;
> > Go forth into the world's highway,
> > Compel the wanderer to come in.
> Toil on, and in thy toil rejoice;
> For toil comes rest, for exile home;
> Soon shalt thou hear the Bridegroom's voice,
> The midnight peal, "Behold, I come!"

Horatius Bonar (1808-1889)

August 30th

It is better to trust in the Lord than to put confidence in man.
Psalm 118:8

It is grand to trust in the promises, but it is grander still to trust in the Promiser. The promises may be misunderstood or misapplied, and at the moment when we are leaning all our weight upon them they may seem utterly to fail us. But no one ever trusted in the Promiser and was confounded. The little child does not always understand the mother's promises, but it knows its mother, and childlike trust is founded not on her word, but upon herself.

Hannah Pearsall Smith (1832-1911)

All make this acknowledgement, and yet there is scarcely one among a hundred who is fully persuaded that God alone can afford sufficient help. That person has attained a high rank among the faithful who, resting satisfied in God, never ceases to entertain a lively hope, even when one finds no help upon earth.

John Calvin (1509-1564)

Trust in yourself, and you are doomed to disappointment; trust in your friends, and they will die and leave you; trust in money, and you may have it taken from you; trust in reputation, and some slanderous tongue may blast it; but trust in God, and you are never to be confounded in time or eternity.

D.L. Moody (1837-1899)

> The heart that trusts, forever sings,
> And feels as light as it had wings;
> A well of peace within it springs
> Come good or ill,
> What'er today or morrow brings
> It is His will.

Isaac Williams (1802-1865)

It is better to trust in the Lord than to put confidence in princes.
Psalm 118:9

David knew this verse by experience, for he confided in Saul his king; at another time in Achish the Philistine; at another time in Ahithophel, his own most prudent minister; besides many others. They all failed him; but he never trusted in God without feeling the benefit of it.

Robert Bellarmine (1542-1621)

When John Huss (1372-1415) was summoned before the Council of Constance in 1414 to give account for his reformist views, he was provided guides by King Wenceslaus and promised safe conduct by Emperor Sigismund. Yet he said: "I confide altogether in my Saviour. I trust that He will accord me His Holy Spirit to fortify me in His truth, so that I may face with courage temptations, prison, and if necessary a cruel death." The emperor failed to keep his promise. Huss was condemned, imprisoned and burned at the stake.

"This is my psalm, my chosen psalm. I love them all; I love all Holy Scripture, which is my consolation and my life. But this psalm is nearest my heart, and I have a peculiar right to call it mine. It has saved me from many a pressing danger from which neither emperor, nor kings, nor sages, nor saints could have saved me. It is my friend, dearer to me than all the honors and power of the earth." Those were the words of Martin Luther on the 15th of April, 1521. This was the day on which, as a poor monk, son of a German miner, he was ushered before the potentates of Europe, bishops, knights, lords, dukes, ambassadors and princes. "I may not and will not recant, because to act against conscience is unholy and unsafe; here I stand, I can do no other; God help me!" At that moment the Reformation was secured. And he proved that *it is better to trust in the Lord than to put confidence in princes.*

F. W. Farrar (1831-1903)

September

September 1st

Every good gift is from above, and comes down from the Father, who is the source of all Light. In Him there is no variation nor the shadow of change.
James 1:17 (Weymouth)

In 1808 a grand performance of the "Creation" took place in Vienna. Haydn himself was there, but so old and feeble that he had to be wheeled into the theatre in a chair. His presence roused intense enthusiasm among the audience, which could no longer be suppressed as the chorus and orchestra burst in full power upon the passages, *And there was light.* Amid the tumult of the enraptured audience, the old composer was seen striving to raise himself. Once on his feet, he mustered up all his strength, and in reply to the applause of the audience, he cried out as loud as he was able, "No, no! not from me, but," pointing to heaven, "from thence – from heaven above – comes all!"

Biblical Illustrator (1887)

The sun does not shine for a few trees and flowers, but for the wide world's joy. The lonely pine on the mountain-top waves its sombre boughs and cries, "Thou art my sun;" and the little meadow violet lifts its cup of blue, and whispers with its perfumed breath, "Thou art my sun." So God sits in heaven, not for a favored few, but for the universe of life; and there is no creature so poor or so low that we may not look up with child-like confidence and say, "My Father, Thou art mine."

H.W. Beecher (1813-1887)

> But oh, Thou bounteous Giver of all good!
> Thou art of all Thy gifts Thyself the crown!
> Give what Thou canst, without Thee we are poor;
> And with Thee rich, take what Thou wilt away.
> William Cowper (1731-1800)

September 2nd

⸎ ———————◆——————— ⸎

He is before all things, and by Him all things consist.
Colossians 1:17

God's work of providence is "most holy, wise and powerful, preserving and governing, of all his creatures and all their actions." It has no Sabbath. No night suspends it, and from its labors God never rests.... How great that Being whose hand paints every flower, and shapes every leaf; who forms every bud on every tree, and every infant in the darkness of the womb; who throws open the golden gates of day, and draws around a sleeping world the dusky curtains of the night; who measures out the drops of every shower, the whirling snow-flakes, and the sands of our eventful life; who determines alike the fall of a sparrow and the fate of a kingdom; and so overrules the tide of human fortunes, that whatever befall us, come joy or sorrow, the believer says, *It is the Lord: let Him do what seems to Him good.*

By Him all things consist. In the hands that were once nailed to the cross, it places the sceptre of universal empire; and on those blessed arms that, once thrown around a mother's neck, now tenderly enfold every child of God, it hangs the weight of worlds. Great is the mystery of godliness! By Him the angels keep their holiness, and the stars their orbits; the tides roll along the deep, and the seasons through the year; kings reign, and princes decree justice; the church of God is held together, riding out at anchor the rudest storms; and by Him, until the last of His elect are plucked from the wreck, and His purposes of mercy are all accomplished, this guilty world is kept from sinking under a growing load of sins.

Thomas Guthrie (1803-1873)

But chance is not; or is not where Thou reignest:
Thy Providence forbids that fickle power.

William Cowper (1731-1800)

September 3rd

Thy word have I hid in mine heart, that I might not sin against Thee.
Psalm 119:11

In proportion as the word of the King is present in the heart, "there is power" against sin. Where the word of a king is, there is power (Eccles. 8:4). Let us use this means of absolute power more, and more life and holiness will be ours.

Frances Havergal (1836-1879)

The worldlings have their treasure in jewels without them; the Christian has them within. Neither is there any receptacle wherein to receive and keep the word of consolation but the heart only. If you have it in the mouth only, it shall be taken from you; if you have it in your book only, you shall miss it when you have most need of it; but if you lay it up in your heart, as Mary did the words of the angel, no enemy shall ever be able to take it from you.

William Cowper (1731-1800)

In my heart – bodily bread in the cupboard may be eaten of mice, or mould and waste; but when it is taken down into the body, it is free from danger. If God enables you to take your soul-food into your heart, it is free from all hazards.

Bernard of Clairvaux (1090-1153)

> Order my footsteps in Thy Word,
> And make my heart sincere;
> Let sin have no dominion, Lord,
> But keep my conscience clear.
>
> Isaac Watts (1674-1748)

Do not leave my cry unanswered. Whisper words of truth in my heart, for You alone speak truth. Amen.

Augustine of Hippo (354-430)

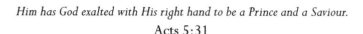

Him has God exalted with His right hand to be a Prince and a Saviour.
Acts 5:31

He left a grave to ascend the throne; He exchanged the side of a dying thief for the right hand of God; He dropped a reed to assume the sceptre of earth and heaven; He put off a wreath of thorns to put on a sovereign's crown. He who died to save the chief of sinners is made *Head over all things to the church.* On raising our eyes to Jesus, we see Him exalted, crowned, enthroned, with the government upon His shoulder. Our mind reverts by way of contrast to Calvary, to the day when He sank beneath the weight, and expired amid the agonies of the cross. If He, who now bears the weight of worlds, once staggered under the burden of our sins, oh! what an incalculable, mysterious load of guilt must there be in sin! It bent the back that bears with ease the burden of ten thousand worlds. Believer, what are you doing, going groaning through the world beneath a load of fears and cares? What should discourage or disturb your peace? What ruffles the calm spirit of a person who knows that the hands once nailed for us to the tree now hold the helm of our fortunes; and that the blessed Saviour, who by love's sceptre reigns within our heart, holds sovereign sway over earth and heaven; and by both bitter and sweet providences, by coffins and cradles, by disappointments and joys, by losses and gains, shall make all things work together for good to them that love God.

Thomas Guthrie (1803-1873)

Christ's exaltation consisteth in His rising again from the dead on the third day, in ascending up into heaven, in sitting at the right hand of God the Father, and in coming to judge the world at the last day.

Westminster Shorter Catechism (1647)

We glory in tribulations also: knowing that tribulation works patience; and patience, experience; and experience hope: and hope makes not ashamed.

Romans 5:3

Tribulation works patience. Naturally it works impatience, and impatience misses the fruit of experience, and sours into hopelessness. When the heart is renewed by the Holy Spirit, tribulation works patience. Patience is a pearl which is only found in the deep seas of affliction; and only grace can find it, bring it to the surface, and adorn the neck of faith therewith. This patience works in us experience: the more we endure, the more we test the faithfulness of God. The more we prove His love, the more we perceive His wisdom. Anyone who has never endured may believe in the sustaining power of grace, but has never had experience of it. You must put to sea to know the skill of the Divine Pilot, and be buffeted with tempest before you can know His power over winds and waves. What better wealth can a person have than to be rich in experience? And experience works hope. How wonderfully does Divine alchemy fetch fine gold out of baser metal! The Lord in His grace spreads a couch for His own on the threshing-floor of tribulation, and there we take our rest. Out of the foam of the sea of sorrow He causes to arise the bright spirit of *hope that makes not ashamed.*

C.H. Spurgeon (1834-1892)

My God, I have never thanked Thee for my thorn. I have thanked Thee a thousand times for my roses, but not once for my thorn. I have been looking forward to a world where I shall get compensated for my cross – but I have never thought of my cross as itself a present glory. Teach me the glory of my cross. Teach me the value of my thorn. Show me that my tears made my rainbow. Amen.

George Matheson (1842-1906)

Seek the Lord while He may be found, call upon Him while He is near.
Isaiah 55:6

O Lord, I am ashamed to seek Thy face
  As tho' I loved Thee as Thy saints love Thee;
    Yet turn from those Thy lovers, look on me.
Disgrace me not with uttermost disgrace;
But pour on me ungracious, pour Thy grace
    To purge my heart and bid my will go free,
    Till I too taste Thy hidden Sweetness, see
Thy hidden Beauty in the holy place.
O Thou Who callest sinners to repent,
    Call me Thy sinner unto penitence,
    For many sins grant me the greater love;
    Set me above the waterfloods, above
Devil and shifting world and fleshly sense,
Thy Mercy's all-amazing monument.

Christina Rossetti (1830-1894)

Almighty God, Father of our Lord Jesus Christ, Maker of all things, Judge of all people, I acknowledge and bewail my manifold sins and wickedness, which I from time to time most grievously have committed by thought, word and deed against thy divine Majesty: provoking most justly thy wrath and indignation against me. I do earnestly repent, and am heartily sorry for these my misdoings, the remembrance of them is grievous unto me, the burden of them is intolerable. Have mercy upon me, have mercy upon me most merciful Father; for thy Son our Lord Jesus Christ's sake, forgive me all that is past, and grant that I may ever hereafter serve and please Thee in newness of life, to the honour and glory of thy Name, through Jesus Christ our Lord. Amen.

John Cosin (1595-1672)

September 7th

Pride goeth before destruction, and a haughty spirit before a fall.
Better it is to be of a humble spirit.
Proverbs 16:18, 19

Pride is based on falsity; it is irreverent and ungrateful; it is ugly and offensive in the sight of people; it is repeatedly and severely condemned by God as a serious sin. Humility, on the other hand, is founded on a true view of our own hearts; it is admirable in itself; it is the very gateway into the kingdom of God; it is an attribute of Christian character which commends us to the love and to the favor of our Lord; it is the only ground on which we are safe. Pride is a slippery place, where we are sure to slip and fall; humility is the ground where devotion finds its home, where God is ready with the shield of his guardianship, where human souls attain to their maturity in Jesus Christ their Lord.

David Clarkson (1621-1686)

It is a strange truth that God should dwell in a human heart at all, but it is almost self-evident that if He is to dwell in any human heart it must be in one which has been emptied of all pride, one which has thrown down all the barriers of self-importance, and laid itself open to the incoming Spirit. If we cling to ever so little of our natural egotism; if we dwell on any imagined excellence, purity, or power of our own; if we are conscious of any elation, any springing sense of merit... how could the High and Lofty One that inhabits Eternity enter in? That thought of vanity would seek to divide our nature with Him, would enter into negotiations for a joint occupation, and the insulted Spirit of God would depart.

J. Whitecross (1858)

John Bunyan's (1628-1688) Pilgrim sang: "The person that is down need fear no fall, the one that is low no pride."

September 8th

*Who shall change our vile body, that it may be fashioned
like unto His glorious body, according to the working
whereby He is able to subdue all things unto Himself.*

Philippians 3:21

Paul is telling us of a change yet to pass over us, over these bodies, altogether inconceivable in kind and degree. They are to be transformed into conformity to the body of our Saviour's glory. It is unthinkable. How can these things be? Scripture does not invite us to "conceive" it, in the sense of thinking it out. What it does is something better; it invites us to trust a personal Agent who understands all that He has undertaken, and who *is able to subdue all things unto Himself*. The method of the Bible is to give us ample views of what Jesus Christ is, and then to ask us to trust Him to do what he says He can. We do not know how. But we know Him. Shall we not rest here? It is good ground.

And what is true of His power and promise in this great matter of our resurrection and our glory, is true all round the circle of His undertakings. *He can subdue all things*. Not only death, the grave, the mysteries of matter, but our hearts, our affections, our wills. He can *bring every thought into captivity* to the holy rule of His thought. He can subdue our iniquities. And He can subdue all that we know as circumstance and condition, making the crooked straight, and the rough places plain.

This is *unto Himself*. What a word of rest and power! Our expectation of His victories in us and for us does not terminate upon ourselves. It rises and rests in Himself. Our glorification, body and soul, is, ultimately, unto Him. Our being will be fully liberated that it may fully serve day and night in His temple.

H.C.G. Moule (1841-1920)

September 9th

The gospel... is the power of God unto salvation.
Romans 1:16

In Pilgrim's Progress, John Bunyan (1628-1688) sees Christian running with a great load on his back: "He ran thus till he came to a place somewhat ascending; and upon that place stood a cross, and a little below, in the bottom, a sepulchre. So I saw in my dream, that just as Christian came up with the cross, his burden loosed from off his shoulders, and fell from off his back, and began to tumble, and so continued to do till it came to the mouth of the sepulchre, where it fell in, and I saw it no more. Then was Christian glad and lightsome, and said with a merry heart, 'He hath given me rest by His sorrow, and life by His death.' Then he stood still awhile to look and wonder; for it was very surprising to him that the sight of the cross should ease him of his burden. He looked therefore, and looked again, even till the springs in his head sent the water down his cheeks."

We were so proud that no one could humble us; we were so hard that no earthly power could have melted us. But one day a power seized us which we tried to wrench ourselves from, but could not. It flung us to our knees, and when we arose we were changed. We glory in the cross, because there was no other way of making an end of sin and making reconciliation for iniquity. It has put away our sins, blessed be God, so that this load no more weighs us down.

Biblical Illustrator (1887)

Let us run after God, for we may be sure He will not fly from us. He is nailed upon the cross, and infallibly we shall find Him there. Let us convey Him into our hearts, and then shut the door that He retire not thence.

St. John of the Cross (1542-1591)

Give thanks to the Lord for… His wonderful deeds.
Psalm 107:8

For the beauty of the earth, for the glory of the skies,
For the love which from our birth over and around us lies:
Lord of all, to Thee we raise this our hymn of grateful praise.

For the beauty of each hour of the day and of the night,
Hill and vale, and tree and flower, sun and moon, and stars of light;
Lord of all, to Thee we raise this our hymn of grateful praise.

For the joy of human love, brother, sister, parent, child,
Friends on earth, and friends above; for all gentle thoughts and mild:
Lord of all, to Thee we raise this our hymn of grateful praise.

For Thy church, that evermore lifteth holy hands above,
Offering up on every shore her pure sacrifice of love:
Lord of all, to Thee we raise this our hymn of grateful praise.

For Thyself, best Gift Divine! To our race so freely given;
For that great, great love of Thine, peace on earth and joy in heav'n:
Lord of all, to Thee we raise this our hymn of grateful praise.

Folliott S. Pierpoint (1835-1917)

Grant most merciful Father that in your presence my spirit may receive wisdom, and my powers of action the glory of triumph; in your presence, where there is no danger, but many mansions and the perfect concord of wills; where there is the charm of Springtime, the light of Summer, the fruitfulness of Autumn, and the repose of Winter. Amen.

Thomas Aquinas (1225-1274)

Great is the comfort that comes by singing with grace in our hearts.
John Trapp (1601-1669)

Consider Him... so that you will not grow weary and lose heart.
Hebrews 12:3

All heaven considers or looks at Christ. The angels look at Him with reverence and adoring wonder as their Lord and King. The devils look at Him with terror and alarm, as the Judge and Author of their punishment. But neither heaven nor hell can get such precious views of Christ as can those whom Christ came to redeem. They consider Him as the Lawgiver who shows the path of duty, as the Redeemer who shows the way of life; as the Physician who heals their spiritual diseases, as the Pattern after which they are themselves to copy. They consider Him who endured the contradiction of sinners, in order that they may not be wearied nor faint in their minds. Christ is rich and precious, but only to those who know Him. They are made better, wiser, holier, happier, by it. Looking unto Jesus is the attitude of spiritual health, the posture of spiritual activity, the habit of spiritual enjoyment. It is a blessed exercise – it strengthens the soul, it animates the heart, it enlivens the whole frame of the inner person. And it is peculiarly beneficial to all those who are in distress or perplexity. The contemplation of Him, who suffered the contradiction of sinners hinders the mind from becoming weary and faint....

By looking at the afflictions of Christ we derive encouragement because we could not of ourselves do what Christ has done for us; and we derive encouragement because we should not expect to be treated better than He Himself was. By considering Him, we are further encouraged because as He triumphed over all His enemies, so shall we if we be partakers of His salvation. Christians are one with their Redeemer.

Biblical Illustrator (1887)

❧───────◆───────☙

Here is the patience and the faith of the saints.
Revelation 13:10

Patience is the guardian of faith, the preserver of peace, the cherisher of love, the teacher of humility. Patience governs the flesh, strengthens the spirit, sweetens the temper, stifles anger, extinguishes envy, and subdues pride; she bridles the tongue, restrains the hand, tramples upon temptations, and endures persecutions. She teaches us to forgive those who have injured us, and to be the first in asking forgiveness of those whom we have injured; she delights the faithful, and invites the unbelieving.... Behold her appearance and her attire. Her countenance is calm and serene as the face of heaven unspotted by the shadow of a cloud, and no wrinkle of grief or anger is seen on her forehead. Her eyes are as the eyes of doves for meekness, and on her eyebrows sit cheerfulness and joy. Her mouth is lovely in silence; her complexion and color that of innocence and security. She is clothed in the robes of martyrs, and in her hand she holds a sceptre in the form of a cross. She rides not in the whirlwind and stormy tempest of passion, but her throne is the humble and contrite heart, and her kingdom is the kingdom of peace.

George Horne (1730-1792)

It is in the course of our feeble and very imperfect waiting that God Himself, by His hidden power, strengthens us and works out in us the patience of the saints, the patience of Christ Himself.

Andrew Murray (1828-1917)

But think not thou, by one wild bound, to clear
the numberless ascensions, more and more,
of starry stairs that must be climbed, before
thou comest to the Father's likeness near.

George Macdonald (1824-1903)

While I was musing the fire burned.
Psalm 39:3

My soul, is there no secret pavilion into which thou canst go and warm thyself? Is there no holy of holies where thou canst catch a glow of impulse that will make thee strong? Is it not written of the Son of Man that as He prayed the fashion of His countenance was altered? Yes; it was from His prayer that His transfigured glory came. It was from the glow of His heart that there issued the glow of His countenance. O my soul, wouldst thou have thy life glorified, beautified, transfigured to the eyes of people? Get thee up into the secret place of God's pavilion, where the fires of love are burning. Thy life shall shine gloriously to the dwellers on the plain. Thy prayers shall be luminous; they shall light thy face like the face of Moses when he wist not that it shone. Thy words shall be burning; they will kindle many a heart journeying on the road to Emmaus. Thy path shall be lambent; when thou hast prayed in Elijah's solitude thou shalt have Elijah's chariot of fire.

George Matheson (1842-1906)

The end of all prayer and meditation is to see Jesus, to be united with Jesus, to work in Him. The final object of our musing is to adhere to Jesus, to put on Christ, to abide in Christ, to live with Christ, to live the life of Christ risen from the dead, to go by the Spirit of Christ and to do all things in His Name, to put on the character and virtues of Christ living in Heaven.

Secret of the Saints (1933)

Those who set out on prayer should labour to have the deepest apprehension of the presence of God and of the incomparable greatness of the majesty which they approach.

Teresa of Avila (1515-1582)

September 14th

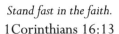

Stand fast in the faith.
1 Corinthians 16:13

In 257 A.D. an edict was published that bishops were to be banished and Christian assemblies forbidden. Cyprian (200-258) was summoned and asked what he had to say. "I am a Christian, and I recognize the one true God," was his answer. He was banished. In 258 he was again ordered to appear. He felt he could render no grander service than by dying for his faith. He wished all his flock should see how deep had been his sincerity when he had repeatedly counseled them to stand fast in the Lord even unto death. He was marched to the place of execution in the midst of a great multitude. There was no cry of exultation, no demonstration of hostility among the pagans. Wherever his eye fell it was met with looks of sympathy and respect.... At the place of execution, he knelt in prayer. Rising, he gave a sign of forgiveness to the executioner and asked his friends to give the executioner twenty-five pieces of gold. It was September 14, 258. So perished the first martyr bishop of Northern Africa. His words *stand fast in the faith...* forever ring in the ears of his followers.

F.W. Farrar (1831-1903)

Paul had greatly set his heart on being suddenly caught up to be forever with the Lord. It was not to be by the triumphant path of the air, but by the darksome path of death and the grave. It was a matter of small importance what the method of his home-going would be, he was only too thankful to be able to say *I have finished my course, I have kept the faith.*

F.B. Meyer (1847-1929)

When imprisoned, Madame Guyon (1648-1717) said: I feel no anxiety in view of what my enemies will do to me. I have no fear of anything but of being left to myself. So long as God is with me, neither imprisonment nor death will have any terrors.

275

Thou will keep him in perfect peace, whose mind is stayed on Thee.
Isaiah 26:3.

The author of this peace is none other than God Himself. Earthly honors, riches and friendships leave the heart devoid of enduring peace because they can do nothing to dispel the sense of guilt and the consequent apprehensions of the future. We cannot have peace unless we have God for our portion. The peace which God imparts to His people is "perfect" – in its source, in its measure, in its adaptation to our needs. It erects its brightest monuments on the ruins of earthly hopes. If this perfect peace is to be ours we must link ourselves to God by a simple, earnest, childlike faith. This is essential; this is sufficient.

Gray & Adams Commentary (1951)

Do not look forward to the changes and chances of this life in fear; rather look to them with full hope that, as they arise, God, whose you are, will deliver you out of them. He has kept you hitherto. Do hold fast to His dear hand, and He will lead you safely through all things; and when you cannot stand, He will bear you in His arms. Do not look forward to what may happen tomorrow. Our God will give you strength to bear it.

Francis de Sales (1567-1622)

Happy the one who sees a God employed
        In all the good and ill that chequer life.
William Cowper (1731-1800)

The end of discipline is not to make us critical, facetious, pedantic, pharisaic, self-sufficient; the end of all life-discipline is to make us complete, and completeness is peace. Where there is want of peace there is want of completeness.

Joseph Parker (1830-1902)

September 16th

He has put a new song in my mouth.
Psalm 40:3

Praise to the Lord, the Almighty, the King of creation;
O my soul, praise Him, for He is thy health and salvation:
All ye who hear, brothers and sisters draw near,
Praise Him in glad adoration.

Praise to the Lord, who o'er all things so wondrously reigneth,
Shelters thee under His wings, yea, so gently sustaineth:
Hast thou not seen how thy entreaties have been
Granted in what He ordaineth?

Praise to the Lord, who doth prosper thy work, and defend thee;
Surely His goodness and mercy here daily attend thee:
Ponder anew what the Almighty can do,
If with His love He befriend thee.

Praise to the Lord, who, when tempests their warfare are waging,
Who, when the elements madly around thee are raging,
Biddeth them cease, turneth their fury to peace,
Whirlwinds and waters assuaging.

Praise to the Lord, who, when darkness of sin is abounding,
Who, when the godless do triumph, all virtue confounding,
Sheddeth His light, chaseth the horrors of night,
Saints with His mercy surrounding.

Praise to the Lord! O let all that is in me adore Him!
All that hath life and breath come now with praises before Him!
Let the Amen sound from His people again:
Gladly for aye we adore Him.

Joachim Neander (1640-1680)

The angels never sing our song – theirs is jubilant, but ours is triumphant; their theme is creation, ours is grace; they praise God in his works, we adore and love Him in His Son.

J. Vaughan (1878)

God forbid that I should glory, save in the cross of our Lord Jesus Christ.
Galatians 6:14

Oh, do not study God in the jeweled heavens, in the sublimity of the mountain, in the beauty of the valley, in the grandeur of the ocean, in the murmurs of the stream, or in the music of the winds. God made all this, but all this is not God. Study Him in the cross of Jesus! Look at Him through this wondrous telescope, and although through a glass darkly, you will behold His glory; you will see the Godhead in awful eclipse, the Sun of His Deity setting in blood. Yet that rude and crimsoned cross more fully reveals the mind of God, more harmoniously discloses the perfections of God, more perfectly unveils the heart of God, and more fully exhibits the glory of God -- than the combined power of ten thousand worlds. Study God in Christ, and Christ on the cross! Oh the marvels that meet in it! The glory that gathers round it! The streams of blessing that flow from it! The deep refreshing shadow it casts in the happy experience of all who look to Jesus and embrace that blessed hope of eternal life which God promised before the world began.

Octavius Winslow (1808-1878)

The Cross!
There, and there only, is the power to save,
There no delusive hope invites despair,
No mockery meets you, no deception there,
All vanish there, and fascinate no more.

The Cross once seen is death to every vice:
Else He that hung there suffered all His pain,
Bled, groaned and agonized, and died, in vain.

William Cowper (1731-1800)

*For Thou, Lord, art good, and ready to forgive; and plenteous in mercy
unto all them that call upon Thee.*

Psalm 86:5

*As high as the heavens are above the earth, so high are His thoughts above
your thoughts, and His ways above your ways.* Your sin is of great
measure, but there is no measure to His grace. His mercy is so great
that it forgives great sins to great sinners, after great lengths of time,
and then gives great favors and great privileges, and raises them up
to great enjoyments in the great heaven of the great God. As John
Bunyan (1628-1688) well says, "It must be great mercy or no mercy, for
little mercy will never serve my turn."

When David spoke of his enemies, he said they were more in
number than the hairs of his head; he had, therefore, some idea of
their number, and found a figure suitable to set it out; but in the case
of the Lord's covenant mercies, he declares, I know not the number,
and does not venture upon any sort of comparison. To creatures belong number and limit, to God and His grace there is neither.

C.H. Spurgeon (1834-1892)

All other mercies are as nothing in comparison to the love of God
in giving His Son to be our Saviour; they are all swallowed up in this
love, as the light of candles when brought into the sunshine.

J. Flavel (1627-1691)

Well may we wonder that the great God should stoop so low, to
enter into such a covenant of grace and peace, founded upon such
a Mediator as Christ, with such utter enemies. This mercy is the
wonder of angels, and will be the topic of our admiration and of our
praising God for all eternity.

R. Sibbes (1577-1635)

September 19th

You have died, and your life is hidden with Christ in God.
Colossians 3:3 (Weymouth)

This truth is for Christians to use amidst the formidable facts of the devil, the world and the flesh. We are to remember that because Christ died, we died, and are in that sense dead to sin's doom and dominion through our crucified Lord. We died with Him and have our new life in Christ.... This is Paul's prescription for the blessed life, the transfigured life. Live in heaven, not in the sense of the poet, but in recollecting our union with Him, who is in heaven and at the same time in you, your Life. Continually tell your soul that you died in His death and live in His life, and are with Him – by the law of union – on His throne. Take these things as facts into your life. You will find that in Him you can be holy, and you can walk at liberty and in perpetual and delightful service.

H.C.G. Moule (1841-1920)

Rejoice, believer, in the Lord,
Who makes your cause His own;
The hope that's built upon His Word
Can ne'er be overthrown.
>   Though many foes beset your road,
>   And feeble is your arm:
>   Your life is hid with Christ in God,
>   Beyond the reach of harm.

Weak as you are, you shall not faint,
Or, fainting, shall not die;
Jesus, the strength of every saint,
Will aid you from on high.
>   As surely as He overcame,
>   And triumphed once for you;
>   So surely you, that love His name,
>   Shall triumph in Him too.

John Newton (1725-1807)

September 20th

Christ Jesus... is made unto us wisdom, and righteousness,
and sanctification, and redemption.
I Corinthians 1:30

Let us steadfastly look unto the blood of Christ; and let us see how precious unto God is His blood which, being shed on account of our salvation, has offered to the whole world the grace of repentance.... We, called through God's will in Christ Jesus, are not justified through our own wisdom, understanding, piety, or works which we have done in holiness of heart, but through faith. Through faith the Almighty God justifies all that ever lived; to Whom be glory for ever. Amen.

Clement of Rome (30-100)

Christ is the person who, by God the Father, was made unto us righteousness. Happy are they who even now exalt in this righteousness, and are thus exhilarated in their consciences! When righteousness is brought in, He is brought in, who of God was *made unto us righteousness*. Shall I plead my own righteousness? Lord, I will make mention of Thy righteousness alone. Thy righteousness is my righteousness.

Bernard of Clairvaux (1090-1153)

And can it be that I should gain
An int'rest in the Savior's blood?...
No condemnation now I dread,
Jesus, and all in Him, is mine;
Alive in Him, my living Head,
And clothed in righteousness divine,
Bold I approach the eternal throne,
And claim the crown, through Christ my own.
Charles Wesley (1707-1788)

Oh! I am my Beloved's and my Beloved is mine! He brings a poor vile sinner into His house of wine. I stand upon His merit, I know no other stand.

Samuel Rutherford (1600-1661)

Though I spake with the tongues of men and angels, and yet had no love, I were even as sounding brass: or as a tinkling cymbal. And though I could prophesy, and understood all secrets, and all knowledge: yea, if I had all faith, so that I could move mountains out of their places, and yet had no love, I were nothing. And though I bestowed all my goods to feed the poor, and though I gave my body even that I burned, and yet had no love, it profiteth me nothing. Love suffereth long, and is courteous. Love envieth not. Love doth not frowardly, swelleth not, dealeth not dishonestly, seeketh not her own, is not provoked to anger, thinketh not evil, rejoiceth not in iniquity: but rejoiceth in the truth, suffereth all things, believeth all things, hopeth all things, endureth in all things. Though that prophesying fail, other tongues shall cease, or knowledge vanish away, yet love falleth never away. For our knowledge is unperfect and our prophesying is unperfect. But when that which is perfect is come, then that which is unperfect shall be done away. When I was a child, I spake as a child, I understood as a child, I imagined as a child. But as soon as I was a man, I put away childishness. Now we see in a glass, even in a dark speaking: but then shall we see face to face. Now I know unperfectly: but then shall I know even as I am known. Now abideth faith, hope, and love, even these three: but the chief of these is love.

1 Corinthians 13
William Tyndale's translation (1525).

The greatest thing a person can do for their Heavenly Father is to be kind to His other children. How much the world needs it. How easily it is done. How instantaneously it acts. How infallibly it is remembered. How superabundantly it pays itself back – for there is no debtor in the world so superbly honourable as love.

Henry Drummond (1851-1897)

Help me to spread Your fragrance everywhere I go. Let me preach You without preaching, by my example, by the sympathetic influence of what I do, and by the evident fullness of the love my heart bears for You. Amen

John Newman (1801-1890)

September 22nd

The Lord Jesus shall be revealed from heaven with His mighty angels.
2 Thessalonians 1:7

We preach not only one advent of Christ, but also a second, far more glorious than the former. For the former gave a view of His patience; but the latter brings with it the crown of a divine kingdom.... In His former advent, He was wrapped in swaddling clothes in the manger; in His second, He covereth Himself with light as with a garment. In His first coming, He endured the Cross, despising shame; in His second, He comes attended by a host of Angels, receiving glory. In the first He came teaching with persuasion; but this time all people will of necessity have Him for their King, even though they wish it not....

The things then which are seen shall pass away, and there shall come the things which are looked for, things fairer than the present. But as to the time let no one be curious. *It is not for you*, He says, *to know times or seasons, which the Father hath put in His own power.* Venture not to declare when these things shall be, nor on the other hand supinely slumber. For He saith, *Watch, for in such an hour as you expect not the Son of Man cometh....* Let us then wait and look for the Lord's coming upon the clouds from heaven. Angelic trumpets shall sound; the dead in Christ shall rise first, the godly persons who are alive shall be caught up in the clouds, receiving as the reward of their labors more than human honour; according as the Apostle Paul writes, *For the Lord Himself shall descend from heaven with a shout, with the voice of the Archangel, and with the trump of God: and the dead in Christ shall rise first. Then we which are alive and remain shall be caught up together with them in the clouds, to meet the Lord in the air; and so shall we ever be with the Lord.*

Cyril of Jerusalem (315-389)

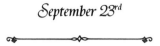

Behold the Lamb of God which takes away the sin of the world.
John 1:29

The two Galilean youths who heard these words from John the Baptist, followed the retreating footsteps of Jesus. He gently asked, *What seek you?* It was the beginning of His ministry: as yet they could not know Him for all that He was; as yet they had not heard the gracious words that proceeded out of His lips. It was more than the two young Galileans could answer, more than they knew or understood. But their answer showed they were in earnest, *Rabbi, where are you staying?* Again His words were so simple, *Come and see.* They came and saw where Jesus dwelt. And before they lay down to sleep that night they knew in their hearts that the kingdom of heaven had come; that the hopes of long centuries were now fulfilled; that they had been in the presence of Him who was the desire of all nations, the Priest greater than Aaron, the Prophet greater than Moses, the King greater than David, the true Star of Jacob, and the Sceptre of Israel.

It was the first care of Andrew to find his brother Simon, and tell him of their great find. How was it that these youths of Galilee were brought at once – brought, as it were, by a single look, by a single word – to the Saviour's feet? How came they to recognise in the carpenter of Nazareth, the Messiah of prophecy, the Son of God, the Saviour of the world? "Certainly, a flame of fire and starry brightness flashed from His eye, and the majesty of the Godhead shone in His face," said St Jerome (340-420). This view may be regarded as certain; for amazement is the expression most used by the Evangelists to express the effect produced by His presence upon His enemies and friends alike.

F.W. Farrar (1831-1903)

You call me Master and Lord: and you say well; for so I am.
John 13:13

Make me a captive, Lord, and then I shall be free;
Force me to render up my sword, and I shall conqueror be.
I sink in life's alarms when by myself I stand;
Imprison me within Thine arms, and strong shall be my hand.

My heart is weak and poor until its master find
It has no spring of action sure-- it varies with the wind.
It cannot freely move, till Thou has wrought its chain;
Enslave it with Thy matchless love, and deathless it shall reign.

My power is faint and low till I have learned to serve;
It wants the needed fire to glow, it wants the breeze to nerve;
It cannot drive the world, until itself be driven;
Its flag can only be unfurled when Thou shalt breathe from heaven.

My will is not my own till Thou hast made it Thine;
If it would reach a monarch's throne it must its crown resign;
It only stands unbent, amid the clashing strife,
When on Thy bosom it has leant and found in Thee its life.

George Matheson (1842-1906)

Lord, when Thou wilt, where Thou wilt, as Thou wilt.

Richard Baxter (1615-1691)

You must do as well as you can whatever God gives you to do; that is the best possible preparation for what He may want you to do next.

Thomas Chalmers (1780-1847)

Let us choose life that we and our seed may live, by obeying His voice and cleaving to him, for he is our life and prosperity.

John Withrop (1588-1649)

*Consider the work of God: for who can make straight that
which He has made crooked?*
Ecclesiastes 7:13

A just view of afflicting incidents is altogether necessary to a Christian deportment under them; and that view is to be obtained only by faith. It is the light of the word alone that represents them justly, discovering in them the work of God. *Consider the work* (or, see the doing) of God in the crooked, rough, and disagreeable parts of thy lot, the crosses thou findest in it. Thou seest very well the cross itself; yea, thou turnest it over and over in thy mind, and leisurely viewest it on all sides; thou lookest to this and the other cause of it, and so thou art in a foam and fret. But if thou wouldst be quieted and satisfied in the matter, lift up thine eyes towards heaven, see the doing of God in it, the operation of His hand. Eye the first cause of the crook in thy lot; behold how it is the work of God, His doing. Only He who made it can mend it or make it straight. While we are here, there will be cross events as well as agreeable ones. Sometimes things are softly and agreeably gliding on; but, by-and-by there is some incident which alters that course, grates us, and pains us. There is no perfection here, no lot out of heaven without a crook. Sin so bowed our hearts and minds, that they became crooked in respect of the holy laws; and God justly so bowed our lot, that it became crooked too. This crook inseparably follows our sinful condition, till, dropping this body of sin and death, we get within heaven's gates.

Thomas Boston (1676-1732)

Every joy or trial falleth from above,
Traced upon our dial by the Sun of Love;
We may trust him fully, all for us to do—
They who trust Him wholly find Him wholly true.

Frances Havergal (1836-1879)

September 26ᵗʰ

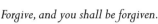

Forgive, and you shall be forgiven.
Luke 6:37

If you are coming to the altar – that is, approaching God – *and remember that your brother has aught against you, leave there your gift and first be reconciled.* Here comes a man with a lamb to offer. He approaches solemnly, reverently, towards the altar of God. But as he comes there flashes across his mind the face of that man. The shortest way to God for the man is not the way to the altar, but around by *that* man's house. In Matthew 6 our Lord gives us what we call the Lord's prayer. At the close He stops to emphasize just one of the seven petitions; the one about forgiveness. Peter later asks a question. *Master, how many times must I forgive? Seven times?* Apparently Peter thinks he is growing in grace. But the Master says, "Peter, you haven't caught the idea. Forgiveness is not a question of mathematics; not a matter of keeping tab on somebody; *not seven times but seventy times seven.*"… Some persons and some things you cannot forgive of yourself, but if one allows the Spirit of Jesus to sway the heart He will make you love persons you cannot like.

S.D. Gordon (1859-1936)

See if you are in charity with all people. It is no use trying to explain away your daily words, *Forgive us our trespasses, as we forgive them that trespass against us,* for Christ Himself has explained and emphasized them. He said, *But if you forgive not their trespasses, neither will your Father forgive your trespasses.* There is no evading this. There is no forgiveness for you, if you do not forgive…. Look at the example of perfect forgiveness – hear the smitten King in His lonely death-agony saying, *Father, forgive them!* Oh, it is not hard to forgive anything when one looks away to the forgiveness of Jesus. *Then* come and offer thy gift.

Frances Havergal (1836-1879)

Godliness with contentment is great gain.
1 Timothy 6:6

Peace in this life springs from acquiescence even in disagreeable things, not in the exemption from bearing them.

François de la Mothe Fénelon (1651-1715)

I entreat your lordship, and that by the Lord Jesus, that if I am to remain here in prison for the winter, you would beg the Commissary to be so kind as to send me, from the things of mine which he has, a warmer cap; I feel the cold painfully in my head; also a warmer cloak, for the one I have is very thin; also some cloth to patch my leggings. My overcoat is worn out, my shirts are threadbare. The Commissary has a woolen shirt of mine if he will be so kind as to send it. But most of all I entreat your kindness to be so good as to send me my Hebrew Bible, grammar and vocabulary, that I may spend my time in that pursuit.

William Tyndale (1490-1536)

My prison [Aberdeen] is my palace, my sorrow is with child of joy, my losses are rich losses, my pain easy pain, my heavy days are holy and happy days. Oh, if I could set all tongues to work, to help me to sing a new song of my Well-Beloved! A cross for Christ should have another name; yea, a cross, especially when He cometh with His arms full of joys, is the happiest hard tree that ever was laid upon my weak shoulder.

Samuel Rutherford (1600-1661)

All the way may Savior leads me, What have I to ask beside?
Can I doubt His tender mercy who through life has been my Guide?
Heavenly peace, divinest comfort, here by faith in Him to dwell,
For I know whate'er befall me, Jesus doeth all things well.

Fanny Crosby (1820-1915)

This is life eternal, that they might know Thee the only true God,
and Jesus Christ, whom Thou hast sent.

John 17:3

Study God in Jesus Christ. This is the most glorious subject of contemplation; there we find God infinitely just and yet merciful, pardoning sinners and yet salving the authority of the law; there we see God and humanity in one person, and the beams of divine majesty allayed by the veil of human nature. In the godhead of Christ we see His power, in His human nature His love and condescension. He is our Lord, and yet our brother; a man, and yet God's fellow and equal.... He would have a mother on earth, that we might have a Father in heaven; our relation and alliance to heaven groweth by Him. In Christ only can we look upon God as a father, otherwise we should be overwhelmed with despair and perish .... Oh! how should we, by the deliberate gaze of faith, reflect upon this glorious mystery, fit for angels to look into! When we know God in Christ, and Christ in us, this is to know Him indeed; not only by hearsay but acquaintance, to know Him so as to love Him and enjoy Him.

Thomas Manton (1620-1677)

Let us become like Christ, since Christ became like us. Let us become God's for His sake, since He for our sake became Man. He assumed the worse that He might give us the better; He became poor that we through His poverty might be rich; He took upon Him the form of a servant that we might receive back our liberty; He came down that we might be exalted; He was tempted that we might conquer; He was dishonoured that He might glorify us; He died that He might save us; He ascended that He might draw to Himself us, who were lying low in the Fall of sin. Let us give all, offer all, to Him Who gave Himself a Ransom and a Reconciliation for us.

Gregory Nazianzen (329-390)

Lift up your eyes and look on the fields; for they are white already to harvest.
John 4:35

It was noon, and weary as He was with the long journey, possibly also with the extreme heat, our Lord sat on the well. This implies that the Wayfarer was quite tired out, and in His exhaustion flung His limbs wearily on the seat, anxious, if possible, for complete repose. His disciples had gone to the neighboring city to buy what was necessary for their wants; and, hungry and thirsty, He who bore all our infirmities, sat wearily awaiting them, when His solitude was broken by the approach of a woman coming to draw water. The Lord was thirsty and fatigued, and having no means of reaching the cool water deep below the well's mouth, He said to the woman, *Give Me to drink*. The request only elicited from the woman of Samaria an expression of surprise that it should have been made, for the Jews have no dealings with the Samaritans. Gently, and without a word of rebuke, our Lord tells her that had she known the gift of God, and who it was who said unto her *Give Me to drink*, she would have asked Him, and He would have given her living water. She becomes the suppliant now. He had asked her a little favour, which she had delayed or half declined; He now offers her an eternal gift. The disciples returned and begged Him to eat. *I have food to eat which you know not* was His response. And then pointing to the inhabitants of Sickem, as they streamed to Him over the plain, He continued, *You talk of there being yet four months to harvest. Look at these fields, white already to harvest.*

F. W. Farrar (1831-1903)

God loved the world of sinners lost and ruined by the fall;
Salvation full, at highest cost, He offers free to all.

Martha Stockton (1821-1885)

September 30th

Bless the LORD, O my soul: and all that is within me, bless His holy name.
Bless the LORD, O my soul, and forget not all His benefits.
Psalm 103:1, 2

All prayer does not consist of petitions arising from the sense of need. Prayer is often spoken of as if it consisted of nothing but a series of demands addressed to God -- to give fine weather, or to take away disease, or in some other way to alter our circumstances in accordance with our wishes. But it is not by those who pray that prayer is thus spoken of. In the prayers of those who pray most and best, petitions proper occupy only an inconsiderable place. Much of prayer expresses the fullness of the soul rather than its emptiness. It is the overflow of the cup. Prayer at its best is, if one may be allowed the expression, conversation with God, the confidential talk of a child who tells everything to its father.

James Stalker (1848-1927)

O my God, what shall I say unto Thee! I love Thee above all the powers of language to express! I love Thee for what Thou art to thy creatures. But oh I adore Thee yet far more for what Thou art in Thyself, for those stores of infinite perfection which can never be exhausted, that makes Thee thine own happiness.... I rejoice in beholding thy face, O Lord, and in calling Thee my Father in Christ. Such Thou art, and such Thou wilt be, for time and for eternity. What have I more to do, but to commit myself to Thee for both? Leaving it to Thee to choose my inheritance and to order my affairs, while all my business is to serve Thee and all my delight to praise Thee. I shall press on towards Thee till all my desires be accomplished in the eternal enjoyment of Thee. Amen.

Philip Doddridge (1702-1751)

It is true prayer to seek the Giver more than the gift.

J.R. Miller (1840-1912)

October

October 1st

⟡————————◇————————⟡

Thy statutes have been my songs in the house of my pilgrimage.
Psalm 119:54

Warmth is expected in the poet, in the musician, in the scholar, in the lover... but warmth in religion is sometimes branded as enthusiasm. Why is it condemned in the concerns of the soul – a subject which, infinitely above all others, demands and deserves all the energy of the mind? Is the redeemed sinner to walk forth from bondage, unmoved, unaffected, without gratitude or joy? No, *You shall go out with joy... and all the trees of the field shall clap their hands* (Isaiah 55:12). Travelers were accustomed to relieve the tediousness of their journey with a song. And of the righteous it is said, *The redeemed of the Lord shall come to Zion with songs; and everlasting joy shall be upon their heads* (Isaiah 51:11).

William Jay (1769-1853)

The one who sings prays twice. Let your life be an Alleluia from head to toe.

Augustine of Hippo (354-430)

Every thing is beautiful in its season; we must not be merry when God calls to mourning, so we must not frighten and afflict ourselves when God gives us occasion to rejoice. Even sorrow for sin must not grow so excessive as to hinder our joy in God and our cheerfulness in service. The joy of the Lord was to be the strength for service. Holy joy is like oil in the wheels of our obedience.

Matthew Henry (1662-1714)

Such songs have power to quiet the restless pulse of care,
And come like the benediction that follows after prayer.

Henry Wadsworth Longfellow (1807-1882)

October 2ⁿᵈ

But godliness with contentment is great gain.
1 Timothy 6:6

Seek the blessedness of godly contentment. No doubt contentment apart from godliness is a good thing; it is not contentment, however, which is inculcated here so much as *godliness with contentment.* Many a person has been content without being godly, who might have been saved had their contentment been disturbed and destroyed. To be content we must entertain a lowly estimate of things. *We brought nothing into this world.* However precious worldly things may seem, it is certain we can carry nothing out of the world. It is a narrow bed which will form the last resting-place even for the owner of a province or the ruler of a nation.

Biblical Illustrator (1887)

The road to contentment lies not in despising what we have not got. Let us acknowledge all good, all delight that the world holds, and be content without it. But this we can never do but by possessing the one thing – without which no one can be content – the Spirit of the Father.

George Macdonald (1824-1903)

Lord, it belongs not to my care whether I die or live; to love and serve Thee is my share, and that Thy grace must give.

Richard Baxter (1615-1691)

> I think we are too ready with complaint
> in this fair world of God's. Had we no hope
> indeed beyond the zenith and the slope
> of yon gray blank of sky, we might be faint
> to muse upon Eternity's constraint
> round our aspirant souls. But since the scope
> must widen early, is it well to droop,
> for a few days consumed in loss and taint?

Elizabeth Browning (1806-1861)

October 3rd

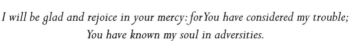

I will be glad and rejoice in your mercy: for You have considered my trouble;
You have known my soul in adversities.

Psalm 31:7

Yes, though we have lost our rich attire, and come to Him in rags; though our forms be wasted because of grief, and waxed old; though sickness and sorrow have consumed our beauty like a moth; though blushes, and tears, and dust overspread our face, He still recognizes and is not ashamed to own us. Comfort yourself with this, for what harm will it do you at last, though people disown, if God the Lord has not forgotten you.

Christian Scriver (1629-1693)

God owns His saints when others are ashamed to acknowledge them; He never refuses to know His friends. He thinks not the worse of them for their rags and tatters. He does not misjudge them and cast them off when their faces are lean with sickness, or their hearts heavy with despondency. Moreover, the Lord Jesus knows us in our pangs in a peculiar sense, by having a deep sympathy towards us in them all, when no others can enter into our griefs, from want of understanding them experimentally. Jesus dives into the lowest depths with us, comprehending the direst of our woes, because He has felt the same.... Many saints have had their greatest enlargement of soul when their affairs have been in the greatest straits. Their souls have been in a large room when their bodies have been lying in some narrow dungeon. Grace has been equal in every emergency. There is a large place for the children of God. In their natural state they are confined. Hedged in by doubt, fear, habit, etc., their deliverance can only come from one quarter -- God. When He delivers He brings into a wide place of liberty, grace, safety, joy, and hope.

C.H. Spurgeon (1834-1892)

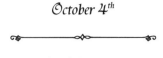

Into your hands I commit my spirit.
Psalm 31:5

Into Thy hands, my Father and my God, I commend my spirit, soul, body, powers, and desires. I offer all that I have hitherto been, that Thou mayest forgive and restore my wounds; my blindness, that Thou mayest enlighten it; my coldness, that Thou mayest inflame it; my erring ways, that Thou mayest set me forth in the right path; and all my evils, that Thou mayest uproot them from my soul.... I offer into Thy sacred Hands what I am, which Thou knowest far better than I can know.... Receive me and make me to become what He, the divine Lamb, would have me to be. In your loving Hands, I shall sleep and rest in peace because the Lamb, in dying for me, placed me within your Hands and left me hope in them as my only refuge. ....
Make me continually to live through your Hands, and from them at last to receive the crown. Amen.

Fra Thomé de Jesu (1582)

> My name from the palms of His hands
>   eternity will not erase;
> Impressed on His heart it remains,
>   in marks of indelible grace.
> Yes, I to the end shall endure,
>   as sure as the earnest is given;
> More happy, but not more secure,
>   the glorified spirits in heaven.

Augustus Montague Toplady (1740-1778)

Blessed are they who die not only for the Lord as martyrs, not only in the Lord as all believers, but likewise with the Lord, as breathing forth their lives in these words, *Into Thy hands I commit my spirit.*

Martin Luther (1483-1546)

October 5th

Stand still, and consider the wondrous works of God.
Job 37:14

Job tells us that it was the Holy Spirit who beautified the heavens, *By His Spirit he hath garnished the heavens* (26:13).... He bespangled them with stars by night, and painted them with the light of the sun by day.... If the pavement be so richly inlaid, what must the palace be! If the visible heavens be so glorious, what are those that are out of sight! From the beauteous garniture of the antechambers, we may infer the precious furniture of the presence-chamber. If stars be so bright, what are angels!

Matthew Henry (1662-1714)

> These are Thy glorious works, thou Source of good,
> How dimly seen, how faintly understood!
>> Thine, and upheld by Thy paternal care,
>> This universal frame, thus wondrous fair;
>> Thy power divine, and bounty beyond thought,
>> Adored and praised in all that Thou hast wrought,
>> Absorbed in that immensity I see,
>> I shrink abased, and yet aspire to Thee;
> Instruct me, guide me to that heavenly day
> Thy words, more clearly than Thy works, display.
>> That, while Thy truths my grosser thoughts refine,
>> I may resemble Thee, and call Thee mine.

William Cowper (1731-1800)

There are so many things I see and understand about the grandeurs of God and of His providence, that almost any time I begin to think about it my intellect fails me, as when one sees things that are far beyond one's ability to understand; and I remain in recollection.

Teresa of Avila (1515-1582)

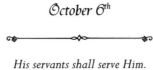

October 6ᵗʰ

His servants shall serve Him.
Revelation 22:3

Service is not confined and limited to this earthly existence. Death does not put a period to our energies and activities. Heaven is not a dreamland of repose, an everlasting sleep. The life on the other side will be a normal, healthy, active existence. In the parables of our Lord which deal with service, the description of the rewards for faithfulness are noteworthy... *Well done, good and faithful servant; I will make you ruler over many things. Enter into the joy of your Lord.* Entrance into the joy of the Lord did not mean discharge from duty but more responsibility and service of greater magnitude....

A company of monks had been reading the book of Revelation together. At the end they discussed the relative attractiveness of the promises therein. One chose, *God shall wipe away all tears.* Another, *To him that overcomes will I grant to sit with Me on My throne.* A third claimed, *His servants shall serve Him.* The third was Thomas à Kempis (1380-1471). How near his choice came to the centre of things.

John Macbeath (1933)

His servants -- such is the title of the glorified. In heaven there is no emancipation from the bonds of God. The holy nations are eternally bound to the will of God and of the Lamb.... The scriptures are full of the idea of the service of God; a service not the less real as service because it can also be viewed as 'perfect freedom' in the light of knowledge and love.

Handley G. Moule (1841-1920)

That we shall serve forever Thyself, Thyself alone;
Shall serve Thee, and forever, oh hope most sure, most fair;
The perfect love outpouring in perfect service there.

Frances Havergal (1836-1879)

October 7th

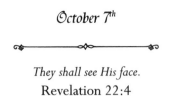

They shall see His face.
Revelation 22:4

Here on earth we see by faith, but yonder there will be a vision.... of the revealed Godhead manifest in Jesus Christ. There we shall see His face. *They shall serve Him* – that is work. *They shall see His face* – that is contemplation. These two, the life of work and the life of devout communion – the Martha and Mary of the Christian experience shall be blended together. In all our activity we shall not lose the vision of His face, nor in all the blessedness of our gaze upon Him shall we slack the diligence of the unwearied hands, or the speed of willing feet.

Alexander Maclaren (1826-1910)

Our thoughts of Him, even at the best, are most imperfect: we see through a glass darkly – catching here and there a feature of His character, a glimpse of His beauty – all through the dim and distorting medium of earthly conceptions. But it is the glory of that land that we will behold Him as He is, and the sight will make us like Him. *We shall be like Him; for we shall see Him as He is.* Our minds, familiar with earthly objects, tremble at the thought.... *God manifest in the flesh* is the sight most coveted by those who know and love Him as their own Saviour. It is a solemn thing to look forward to leaving this world, and launching forth into the unknown scenes of a great eternity; but Jesus will meet His own people there, and He who was their God and their Guide in life will be with them in death also, not as a stranger, but as their trusted Friend – the Man Christ Jesus. A dying woman, rich in faith, expressed it in a way to which other Christian hearts will respond: "I know I am soon going; but what a comfort it is to think that when I enter the other world I shall see a Human Face!"

Sunday at Home Magazine (1870)

October 8th

I will confess my transgressions unto the LORD.
Psalm 32:5

God, unto Whom all hearts are open, unto Whom all wills do speak, from Whom no secret thing is hidden, I beseech Thee so to cleanse the purpose of my heart with the unutterable gift of Thy grace that I may perfectly love Thee, and worthily praise Thee. Amen.

Cloud of Unknowing (14th century)

The confession of evil works is the first beginning of good works.

Augustine of Hippo (354-430)

It is not the sin that I have done, it is the sin that I am. No one was ever yet condemned for the sins that they have done, they are condemned because they will not leave them. *This is the condemnation, that light is come into the world, and men love darkness rather than light because their deeds are evil.*

George MacDonald (1824-1903)

Above all, let us keep up the constant habit of at once detaching ourselves by confession, from every seed of sin as soon as ever we perceive anything contrary to God's Will.

Anonymous

Lord Jesus, our Saviour, let us now come to you:
Our hearts are cold; Lord, warm them with your selfless love.
Our hearts are sinful; cleanse them with your precious blood.
Our hearts are weak; strengthen them with your joyous Spirit.
Our hearts are empty; fill them with your divine presence.
Lord Jesus, our hearts are yours; possess them always and only for yourself. Amen.

Augustine of Hippo (354-430)

October 9th

⟨ornamental divider⟩

Cast your burden upon the Lord, and He shall sustain you;
He will never suffer the righteous to be moved.
Psalm 55:22

There is a myth about the birds, that when they were first created they had no wings; and the story is that God made the wings, put them down before the birds, and said, "Now, come and take the burdens up and bear them." The birds had beautiful plumage and voices; they could sing and shine, but they could not soar; but they took up their wings with their beaks and laid them upon their shoulders, and at first they seemed to be a heavy load, and rather difficult to bear. But as they cheerfully and patiently bore them, and folded them over their hearts, lo! the wings grew fast, and that which they once bore, now bore them. The burdens became pinions, and the weights became wings. We are the wingless birds, and our duties are the pinions; and when at first we assume them, they seem loads; but if we cheerfully bear them, going after Jesus, the burdens change to pinions, and we, who once thought we were nothing but servants bearing loads, find that we are children and heirs of God, free to mount up with wings as eagles, running without being weary, walking without being faint.

A.T. Pierson (1837-1911)

Oh, wonderful story of deathless love!
Each child is dear to that heart above.
　　He fights for me when I cannot fight,
　　He comforts me in the gloom of night;
　　He lifts the burden, for He is strong,
　　He stills the sigh and awakens the song;
The sorrows that bowed me down He bears,
And love and pardons because He cares.

Marianne Farningham (1834-1909)

October 10ᵗʰ

Grace be with all them that love our Lord Jesus Christ in sincerity.
Ephesians 6:24

We can exaggerate about many things; but we can never exaggerate our obligation to Jesus or the compassionate abundance of the love of Jesus to us. All our lives long we might talk of Jesus, and yet we should never come to an end of the sweet things that might be said of Him. Eternity will not be long enough to learn all He is, or to praise Him for all He has done, but then, that matters not; for we shall be always with Him, and we desire nothing more.

Frederick Faber (1814-1863)

Jesus, the very thought of Thee with sweetness fills my breast;
But sweeter far Thy face to see, and in Thy presence rest.

Nor voice can sing, nor heart can frame, nor can the memory find
A sweeter sound than Thy blest Name, O Saviour of mankind.

O Hope of every contrite heart, O Joy of all the meek,
To those who fall how kind Thou art, how good to those who seek!

But what to those who find? ah, this no tongue nor pen can show;
The love of Jesus, what it is none but His loved ones know.

Jesus, our only joy be Thou, as Thou our prize wilt be;
Jesus, be Thou our glory now and through eternity.

Let Jesus be ever born not upon your shoulders as a burden, but before your eyes; so shall you easily and readily bear your burdens through His help, Who is the Bridegroom of the Church, above all, God blessed for ever.

Bernard of Clairvaux (1091-1153)

October 11th

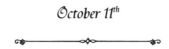

Hear me, O Lord, hear me, that this people may know that Thou art the Lord God.
1 Kings 18:37

There is a greatness of prayer that rises to be intercession. Our power of prayer is a faculty full of high possibilities. It may rise even to this – to go beyond all self-spheres and become intercessory. When prayer keeps in the self-sphere there is a certain narrowness and even meanness about it. It is concerned with what we want and what we feel, and we are greatly comforted if we have any fervor or emotion in such prayer. But daily prayer from which the interceding element is removed would be most injurious to the spiritual life. It lacks the generous, sympathetic, unselfish element, and it will very soon lack fervor and faith. No one can long keep up a prayerful life, and persist in praying altogether about one's self. Power comes, love grows, when prayer includes intercession. The prayers of Scripture are, for the most part, intercessory – Abraham's for Sodom; Moses', Joshua's and Samuel's for the people of Israel. Daniel prays with the window open towards desolate Jerusalem, that he may be reminded of the captive people. Our last sight of Job finds him in the attitude of the mediator, praying for God's mercy on his mistaken friends.

Gray & Adams Commentary (1951)

Perhaps we do not think enough what an effective service intercessory prayer is. It can help those we would serve, penetrating the hearts we cannot open, shielding where we cannot guard, teaching where we cannot speak, comforting where our words have no power to soothe; following the steps of our beloved through the toils and perplexities of the day, lifting their burdens with an unseen hand at night. No ministry is so like that of an angel as this -- silent, invisible, known but to God.

Elizabeth Rundle Charles (1827-1896)

You shall love the LORD *your God with all your heart, and with all your soul,*
and with all your strength, and with all your mind.

Luke 10:27

God deserves to be loved very much, yea, boundlessly, because
He loved us first; He infinite and we nothing, loved us miserable
sinners, with a love so great and so free. This is why... the measure
of our love to God is to love immeasurably. For since our love is
toward God, who is infinite and immeasurable, how can we bound
or limit the love we owe Him? Besides, our love is not a gift but
a debt. And since it is the Godhead who loves us, Himself boundless,
eternal, supreme love, of whose greatness there is no end, yea, and
His wisdom is infinite, whose peace passeth all understanding; since
it is He who loves us, I say, can we think of repaying Him grudgingly?
I will love Thee, O Lord, my strength. He is all that I need, all that I long for.

My God and my help, I will love Thee for Thy great goodness; not
so much as I might, surely, but as much as I can. I cannot love Thee as
Thou deservest to be loved, for I cannot love Thee more than my own
feebleness permits. I will love Thee more when Thou deemest me
worthy to receive greater capacity for loving; yet never so perfectly
as Thou hast deserved of me. *Thine eyes did see my substance, yet being
unperfect; and in Thy book all my members were written.* Yet Thou recordest
in that book all who do what they can, even though they cannot do
all what they ought.

Bernard of Clairvaux (1091-1157)

Now to Him who loved us, gave us every pledge that love could give,
freely shed His blood to save us, gave His life that we might live, be
the kingdom and dominion, and the glory evermore. Amen.

Samuel Waring (1792-1827)

You crown the year with your goodness: and your paths drop fatness.
Psalm 65:11

God has surrounded this year with His goodness, "compassed and enclosed it" on every side. He has given us instances of His goodness in every thing that concerns us; so that, turn which way we will, we meet with the tokens of His favour; every part of the year has been enriched with the blessings of heaven, and no gap has been left open for any desolating judgment to enter by.

Matthew Henry (1662-1714)

God's works of providence are most holy, wise and powerful, preserving and governing all His creatures and all their actions.

Westminster Shorter Catechism (1647)

> How good is the God we adore,
> our faithful, unchangeable Friend!
> His love is as great as His power,
> and knows neither measure nor end!
> 'Tis Jesus the First and the Last,
> whose Spirit shall guide us safe home;
> We'll praise Him for all that is past,
> we'll trust Him for all that's to come.

Joseph Hart (1712-1768)

Lord, send rain out of Thy treasures upon those places which stand in need of it. Renew and make glad the face of the earth that it may bring forth and rejoice in the rain-drops. Raise the waters of the river to their just height; renew and make glad the face of the earth by its ascent; water the furrows and increase their produce. Bless, O Lord, and crown the year with the riches of thy goodness, for the sake of the poor, the widow, the fatherless, and the stranger. Amen.

Church of Alexandria (3rd century)

October 14th

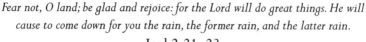

Fear not, O land; be glad and rejoice: for the Lord will do great things. He will
cause to come down for you the rain, the former rain, and the latter rain.

Joel 2:21, 23

The former and the latter rain marked respectively the beginning and the close of the wet season, October to November, and then March and April. The 'former' rain moistens the earth and fits it to receive the seeds which are sown shortly afterwards: the 'latter' rain is important for giving fullness and strength to the ripening crops. *He shall come down like rain upon the mown grass.* This is spoken and promised of Christ. He is the former and the latter rain. He comes by the gracious influences of His Holy Spirit, refreshing our souls. Christless souls are like the dry ground; without the moisture of saving grace their hearts are hard. They are without the fountain of grace and spiritual influences. Before the fall, our soul was like a well-watered garden, beautiful, green, and fragrant. But, in Adam our first head, the springs of grace and holiness are quite dried up in the soul, and there is no curing of this drought but by the soul's union with a new head, Christ, our second Adam. Christ comes down as the rain, by His Spirit of regeneration and brings the springs of grace into the soul. He is the first and immediate receptacle of the Holy Spirit and all regenerating and sanctifying influences, and out of His fullness we must by faith receive them. O how pleasant are the effects of rain to languishing plants, to make them green and beautiful, lively and strong and fragrant. So the effects of Christ's influences are most desirable to drooping souls, for enlightening and enlivening them, for confirming and strengthening them, for comforting and enlarging them, for appetizing and satisfying them, transforming and beautifying them.

John Willison (1680-1750)

October 15th

To obey is better than sacrifice, and to hearken than the fat of rams.
1 Samuel 15:22

It is not our actions considered in themselves which please Him, but the spirit in which they are done, more especially the constant ready obedience to every discovery of His will even in the minutest things, and with such a suppleness and flexibility of mind as to turn and move in any direction where He shall call.

Jeanne Marie de la Mothe Guyon (1648-1717)

Conformity to what is right is generally followed up by a steady and luminous discernment of what is true. If we have but grace to do as we ought, we shall be made to see as we ought.

Thomas Chalmers (1780-1847)

Sincerity drives but one design, and that is to please and enjoy God; and what can more establish and fix the soul in the hour of temptation than this?... Persons of only one design put out all strength to carry it; nothing can stand before them. Sincerity brings one's will into subjection to the will of God; and this being done, the greatest danger and difficulty is over. This is that holy oil which makes the wheels of the soul run nimbly, even in the difficult paths of obedience.

John Flavel (1627-1691)

Lord, you are Truth, and you are everywhere present where all seek counsel of you.... The answer you give is clear, but not all hear it clearly. All ask you whatever they wish to ask, but the answer they receive is not always what they want to hear. Those who serve you best are the ones who are less intent on hearing from you what they will to hear than on shaping their wills according to what they hear from you. Amen.

Augustine of Hippo (354-430)

October 16th

My grace is sufficient for you, for my strength is made perfect in weakness.
2 Corinthians 12:9

In infinite wisdom God permitted the messenger of Satan to buffet His servant all through that first missionary journey. There were perils of robbers, waters, mountain-passes, and violent crowds; but in addition to all these, there was the lacerating thorn. Was it during this journey that he besought the Lord on three occasions for deliverance, and received the assurance that though the thorn was left, more than sufficient grace would be given? If so, like a peal of bells he must have heard the music of those tender words: *My grace is sufficient*, Sufficient, SUFFICIENT for you! Sufficient when friends forsake and foes pursue; sufficient to make you strong against a shower of stones; sufficient for excessive labours of body, and conflicts of the soul; sufficient to enable you to do as much work, and even more, than if the body were perfectly whole – *for my strength is made perfect* only amid the conditions of mortal weakness. Ah, afflicted ones, your disabilities were meant to unite with God's enablings.... Do not sit down before that mistaken marriage, that uncongenial business, that unfortunate partnership, that physical weakness, that hesitancy of speech, that disfigurement of face, as though they must necessarily maim and conquer you. God's grace is at hand – sufficient – and at its best when human weakness is most profound. Appropriate it and learn that those that wait on God are stronger in their weakness than those in their stoutest health and vigour.

F.B. Meyer (1847-1929)

His grace is sufficient for sickness, sustaining and making me whole;
His grace is sufficient when sorrows like billows roll over the soul.
His grace is sufficient for service, it sets us from selfishness free,
And sends us to tell to the tried ones, His grace is sufficient for thee.

A.B. Simpson (1843-1919)

I determined not to know any thing among you, save Jesus Christ and Him crucified.
1 Corinthians 2:2

What we think about the Cross of Christ is of the utmost importance. Heaven or hell, happiness or misery, life or death, blessing or cursing in the last day – all hinges on what we think about the Cross of Christ. And Paul gloried only in the Cross. He could have gloried in his national privileges, his own works, his knowledge, his graces and his churchmanship. Paul was a man who went to and fro on the earth, proclaiming to sinners that the Son of God had shed His own heart's blood to save their souls. *I delivered unto you first of all that which I also received, how that Christ died for our sins*, was his message. Furthermore, this is what he lived upon all his life, *for the life that I now live in the flesh I live by the faith of the Son of God, who loved me and gave Himself for me.* This is what made him so strong to labor, willing to work, unwearied in endeavoring to save some, persevering and patient. The secret of it all was that he was always feeding by faith on Christ's body and blood. Jesus crucified was the meat and drink of his soul. For all our life and service, we need the cross.

J.C. Ryle (1816-1900)

> In the cross of Christ I glory,
> towering o'er the wrecks of time;
> All the light of sacred story
> gathers round its head sublime.
>
> Bane and blessing, pain and pleasure,
> by the cross are sanctified;
> Peace is there that knows no measure,
> joys that through all time abide.
>
> John Bowring (1792-1872)

October 18ᵗʰ

I will never leave you, nor forsake you.
Hebrews 13:5

These words have been a staff in the hand of believers throughout all ages; and they will continue to be so, if we lean on them. This is a borrowed promise. It is borrowed from what God said to Jacob, *Behold, I am with you, and will keep you in all places whither you go... I will not leave you until I have done that which I have spoken to you of.* David said to Solomon his son, *Be strong and of a good courage... for the Lord God, even my God, will be with you. He will not fail you nor forsake you.* The same staff is put into Joshua's hand, *As I was with Moses, so will I be with you, I will not fail you nor forsake you. Therefore be strong and of good courage... for the Lord God, even my God, will be with you: He will not fail you nor forsake you.* When God speaks to one believer, He speaks to all. In the Old Testament it is addressed to individuals, but here it is addressed to all believing Joshuas, to the end of time. This is true because God is the same yesterday, today and forever... *I am the Lord, I change not.* All believers are one body, and therefore what belongs to one, belongs to all. We are all branches on one vine.

Robert Murray M'Cheyne (1813-1843)

> The soul that on Jesus hath leaned for repose,
> I will not, I will not desert to the foes;
> That soul, though all hell should endeavour to shake,
> I'll never, no never, no never forsake.
>
> 'Fear not, I am with thee; O be not dismayed!
> I, I am thy God, and will still give thee aid;
> I'll strengthen thee, help thee, and cause thee to stand,
> Upheld by My righteous omnipotent hand.
>
> John Rippon (1751-1816)

With my whole heart have I sought You.
Psalm 119:10

It is a wondrous and a lofty road wherein the faithful soul must tread; on that high path the soul is free, she knows no care nor ill, for all God's will desireth she, and blessed is His will.

Mechthild of Helfide (?-1277)

Thou Breath from still eternity
Breathe o'er my spirit's barren land--
The pine-tree and the myrtle-tree
Shall blossom amidst the desert sand;
And where Thy living water flows
The waste shall blossom as the rose.

O Spirit, Stream that by the Son
Is opened to us crystal pure,
Forth flowing from the heavenly Throne
To waiting hearts and spirits poor,
Athirst and weary do I sink
Beside Thy waters, there to drink.

My spirit turns to Thee and clings,
All else forsaking, unto Thee;
Forgetting all created things,
Remembering only "God in me."
O living Stream; O gracious Rain,
None wait for Thee, and wait in vain.

Gerhard Tersteegen (1697-1769)

To worship is to quicken the conscience by the holiness of God, to feed the mind with the truth of God, to purge the imagination by the beauty of God, to open the heart to the love of God, to devote the will to the purpose of God.

William Temple (1881-1944)

October 20th

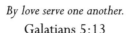

By love serve one another.
Galatians 5:13

Condescend to all the weaknesses and infirmities of your fellow creatures, cover their frailties, love their excellencies, encourage their virtues, relieve their wants, rejoice in their prosperities, be compassionate in their distress, receive their friendship, overlook their unkindness, forgive their malice; be a servant of servants, and condescend to do the lowest offices to the lowest of humanity.

William Law (1686-1761)

'Tis but as we draw nigh to Thee, my Lord, we can draw nigh to each other and not hurt.

George Macdonald (1824-1903)

Lord, make me an instrument of your peace. Where there is hatred, let me sow love; where injury, pardon; where there is doubt, let me sow faith; where despair, hope; where there is darkness, let me sow light; where sadness, joy. O Master, grant that I may not seek to be consoled as to console, not to be understood, as to understand; not to be loved, as to love. For it is in giving that we receive, it is in pardoning that we are pardoned, it is in dying that we are born to eternal life.

Francis of Assisi (1181-1226)

Forgive us if this day we have done or said anything to increase the pain of the world. Pardon the unkind word, the impatient gesture, the hard and selfish deed, the failure to show sympathy and kindly help where we had the opportunity, but missed it; and enable us so to live that we may daily do something to lessen the tide of human sorrow, and add to the sum of human happiness.

F. B. Meyer (1847-1929)

October 21st

Mercy shall be built up forever:
Psalm 89:2

This glorious and gracious scheme... is our salvation, founded in the eternal purpose of God – carried into execution by the labours and death of Jesus Christ, and then applied and brought home to the heart by the illuminating and converting power of the Holy Spirit. This is that "mercy" which is "built up forever." It was planned from everlasting, and will know no ruin or decay through the illimitable line of eternity itself. And God alone is the builder of it. This house will never fall, nor ever be taken down. Fire cannot injure it; storms cannot overthrow it; age cannot impair it. It stands on a rock, and is immoveable as the rock on which it stands – the three-fold rock of God's inviolable decree, of Christ's finished redemption, and the Spirit's never-failing faithfulness.

Augustus Montague Toplady (1740-1778)

Say not that any crime was e'er too great to be forgiven. Can we within our little span, grasp the viewless mind of Heav'n? Shall we attempt with puny force to lash back ocean with a rod? Arrest the planets in their course, or weigh the mercies of a God?

Gray & Adams Commentary (1951)

> Faithful, O Lord, Thy mercies are, a rock that cannot move!
> A thousand promises declare thy constancy and love.
> Throughout the universe it reigns, unalterably sure;
> And while the truth of God remains, the goodness must endure.
>
> Charles Wesley (1707-1788)

Our prayer and God's mercy are like two buckets in a well; while the one ascends, the other descends.

Ezekiel Hopkins (1633-1690)

October 22nd

In my distress I called upon the Lord, and cried unto my God:
He heard my voice out of His temple, and my cry
came before Him, even into His ears.

Psalm 18:6

Prayer is not eloquence, but earnestness; not the definition of helplessness, but the feeling of it; it is the cry of faith to the ear of mercy.

Hannah Moore (1745-1833)

Prayer is that way upward from the pit of despair to which the spiritual miner flies at once when the floods from beneath break forth upon him. He calls and then cries; prayer grows in vehemence as it proceeds. He first invokes God under the name of Jehovah, and then advances to a more familiar name, my God. Thus faith increases by exercise. Far up within the bejewelled walls, and through the gates of pearl, the cry of the suffering suppliant was heard. Music of angels and harmony of seraphs availed not to drown or even impair the voice of that humble call. The King heard it... and lent a willing ear to the cry of His own beloved child. The operation of prayer with God is immediate and personal. We may cry with confident and familiar importunity, while our Father Himself listens.

C.H. Spurgeon (1834-1892)

The unconscious needs of the world are all appeals and cries to Him.... He does not wait to hear the voice of conscious want. The mere vacancy is a begging after fullness; the mere poverty is a supplication for wealth; the mere darkness cries for light.... Alas for us if God helped us only when we knew we needed Him and went to Him with full self-conscious wants! Alas for us if every need which we knew not, had not a voice for Him, and did not call Him to us! Our hope is in the ear which God has for simple need; so that mere emptiness cries out to Him for filling; mere poverty for wealth.

Phillips Brooks (1835-1893)

October 23rd

The Lord of hosts is with us; the God of Jacob is our refuge.
Psalm 46:7

A mighty fortress is our God, a bulwark never failing;
Our helper He amid the flood of mortal ills prevailing.
For still our ancient foe doth seek to work us woe—
His craft and pow'r are great, and, armed with cruel hate,
On earth is not his equal.

Did we in our own strength confide, our striving would be losing,
Were not the right man on our side, the man of God's own choosing.
Doest ask who that may be? Christ Jesus, it is He—
Lord Sabaoth His name, from age to age the same,
And He must win the battle.

And tho this world, with devils filled, should threaten to undo us,
We will not fear, for God hath willed His truth to triumph thru us.
The prince of darkness grim, we tremble not for him—
His range we can endure, for lo, his doom is sure:
One little word shall fell him.

That word above all earthly pow'rs, no thanks to them, abideth;
The Spirit and the gifts are ours thru Him who with us sideth.
Let goods and kindred go, this mortal life also—
The body they may kill; God's truth abideth still:
His kingdom is forever. Amen.

Martin Luther (1483-1546)

We cannot be tested without the knowledge and watchfulness of God.
God is always mightier than the circumstances; and all the world forces
which pull us downward are also under His control, if we live in right
relationship to Him.

G. Campbell Morgan (1863-1945)

October 24th

She has done what she could.

Mark 14:8

The great Head of the church likes "doing" Christians. Satan will tell some that they are too young to do anything; you are too old, it is too late, you have no gifts, no talents, no influence, no opportunities, no open door on any side. But have you not the power of doing good by your life? You may work wonders by steady consistency and patient continuance in well-doing. I have but to give a cup of cold water to one of Christ's little ones. Paths of service are sure to open before willing feet. When the Spirit of God puts a benevolent impulse in the soul, the providence of God will open a channel for its overflowing. The works which Christ accounts to be "good" spring from faith in and love to Him.

J.C. Ryle (1816-1900)

> Master, to do great work for Thee, my hand
> Is far too weak! Thou givest what may suit,
> Some little chips to cut with care minute,
> Or tint, or grave, or polish. Others stand
> Before their quarried marble, fair and grand,
> And make a life work of the great design
> Which Thou hast traced; or many skilled combine
> To build vast temples, gloriously planned.
> Yet take the tiny stones which I have wrought
> Just one by one, as they were given by Thee,
> Not knowing what came next in Thy wise thought:
> Set each stone by Thy master-hand of grace;
> Form the mosaic as Thou wilt for me,
> And in Thy temple-pavement give it place.

Frances Havergal (1836-1879)

We ought not to be weary of doing little things for the love of God, who regards not the greatness of the work, but the love with which it is performed.

Brother Lawrence (1605-1691)

October 25th

We give thanks to God always for you all... remembering without ceasing your work
of faith, and labour of love, and patience of hope in our Lord Jesus Christ.
1 Thessalonians 1:2, 3

Faith is the hand that grasps. It is the means of communication; it is the channel through which the life, which is grace, comes to us. It is the open door by which the angel of God comes in with gifts. It is like the petals of the flowers, opening when the sunshine kisses them, and by opening, laying bare the depths of their calyxes to be illuminated and coloured, and made to grow by the sunshine which itself has opened them. So faith is the basis of everything.

Then again, out of faith rises love. No person can love God unless they believe that God loves them.... My love is the reverberation of the primeval voice, the echo of God's.... If you wish to love, do not try to work yourself into an hysteria of affection, but take into your hearts and minds the Christian facts, mainly the fact of the Cross, which will set free the frozen and imprisoned fountains of your affections, and cause them to flow out abundantly in sweet water. First faith, then love; and get at love through faith.

The topmost shoot in this plant is hope. Hope is faith directed to the future. Hope helps us both to bear and to do. The hope of the Christian is but the inference from one's present faith or trust, and the joy and sweetness of one's present love.

Alexander Maclaren (1826-1910)

Give me the love that leads the way, the faith that nothing can dismay, the hope no disappointments tire, the passion that will burn like fire. Let me not sink to be a clod: make me Thy fuel, Flame of God.

Amy Carmichael (1867-1951)

October 26th

Repent... and be converted, that your sins may be blotted out.
Acts 3:19

Conversion is not changing from one set of principles to another.... Others think that they are converted because they have reformed their lifestyle. However, reformation is not renovation. The outside of the platter may be washed while the inside remains filthy. A person may turn from profaneness to morality and therefore believe that he is converted, yet his heart is still unrenewed.... What is conversion then? In order to be truly converted, a person must become a new creature and be converted from his own righteousness to the righteousness of the Lord Jesus Christ. Conviction will always precede spiritual conversion. You may be convicted without being converted, but you cannot be converted without being convicted.... True conversion means turning not only from sin but also from depending on self-made righteousness. Those who trust in their own righteousness for conversion hide behind their own good works.... We talk in vain about being converted until we see ourselves as lost sinners and come to the Lord Jesus Christ to be washed in His blood and to be clothed in His imputed righteousness. The consequence of this application of Christ's righteousness to the soul will be a conversion from sin to holiness. The Bible says, "If any man be in Christ, he is a new creature: old things are passed away; behold, all things are become new" ....

The author of conversion is the Holy Spirit. It is not based on free will or moral persuasion. Nothing short of the influence of the Spirit of the living God can effect this change in a person's heart. Therefore, we are said to be "born again" and "born of the Spirit".... Have you experienced it? If you are not yet converted, upon what other grounds do you hope for conversion? You ought to repent and be converted, for until you do, you can never find true rest for your soul.

George Whitefield (1714-1770)

October 27th

For He is our God; and we are the people of His pasture, and the sheep of His hand.
Psalm 95:7

See how elegantly the psalmist hath transposed the order of the words. He said not "the sheep of His pasture" and "the people of His hand," which might be thought more congruous, since the sheep belong to the pasture; but he said, "the people of His pasture." The people themselves are sheep.... Our Lord made us; the people of His pasture, and the sheep of His hand, are the sheep which He hath deigned by His grace to create unto Himself.

Augustine of Hippo (354-430)

We are His people whom He feeds in His pastures, and His sheep whom He leads as by His hand. Here is a reason to constrain us to praise God; it is this, that not only has He created us, but that He also directs us by special providence, as a shepherd governs His flock. Jesus Christ, Divine Shepherd of our souls, who not only feeds us in His pastures, but Himself leads us with His hand. Loving Shepherd, who feeds us not only from the pastures of Holy Writ, but even with His own flesh. What subjects of ceaseless adoration for a soul penetrated by these great verities! What a fountain of tears of joy at the sight of such prodigious mercy!

P. Quesnel (1634-1719)

In the fields of heaven He is still the Shepherd, leading His flock to the living fountains of waters. And surely in the upper sky He will be forever the Star of the Morning, so far as He will be the eternal pledge and joy -- of a life that will be forever young; of energies that will accumulate without end; of service before the throne that will always deepen in its ardour and its triumph; of discoveries in the knowledge of the Eternal which will carry the experience of the blessed from glory to glory in a succession that cannot close. All is fleeting, Christ is the same.

H.C.G. Moule (1841-1920)

October 28ᵗʰ

Confess your faults one to another, and pray one for another,
that you may be healed.

James 5:16

It is not just *confess your faults one to another*, but also *pray one for another*. If we prayed more we should blame less; we should be far more tolerant; we should not suspect so much; we should not carry stories so much; we should not do wrong so much. By confessing our faults one to another and praying one for another, we learn humility on the one side, and on the other side that large charity which covers transgression and hides a multitude of sins. While we are striving to bear our own burdens and to sustain the faults and shortcomings of our fellows, let us remember every day what Christ is obliged to bear in and for us.

Henry Ward Beecher (1813-1887)

He prayeth best who leaves unguessed
The mystery of another's breast.
>Why cheeks grow pale, why eyes o'erflow,
>Or heads are white, thou need'st not know.
Enough to note by many a sign
That every heart hath needs like thine.
>>Pray for us!

John G. Whittier (1807-1892)

Though you continually pardon your neighbors for all their sins, as a drop of water to an endless sea, so much, or rather so much more, does your love to others come short in comparison with the boundless goodness of God.

John Chrysostom (347-407)

The decisive preparation for prayer lies not in the prayer itself, but in the life prior to the prayer.

H.C.G. Moule (1841-1920)

When you stand praying, forgive, if you have ought against any: that your Father
also which is in heaven may forgive you your trespasses.
Mark 11:25, 26

God's way of forgiving is thorough and hearty. And if thine be not so, thou hast no portion of His.

Archbishop Leighton (1611-1684)

The memory of God's precepts paves for our prayers a way unto heaven; of which precepts the chief is, that we go not up unto God's altar before we compose whatever of discord or offence we have contracted with our brethren. For how can you approach the peace of God without peace? the remission of debts while you retain them? How will you appease the Father when you are angry with a brother, when from the beginning "all anger" is forbidden us?... Ever if we must be angry, our anger must not be maintained beyond sunset, as the apostle admonishes. But how rash is it either to pass a day without prayer, while you refuse to make satisfaction to your brother; or else, by perseverance in anger, to lose your prayer?

Tertullian of Carthage (150-212)

They who cannot forgive others break the bridge over which they must pass themselves.

George Herbert (1593-1632)

For still in mutual sufferance lies
The secret of true living,
Love scarce is love that never knows
The sweetness of forgiving.

John G. Whittier (1807-1892)

Forgive us our sins; for we also forgive everyone that is indebted to us
Luke 11:14

And when they had sung an hymn, they went out into the mount of Olives.
Mark 14:26

The Lord Jesus has just instituted the sacred ordinance of His love – the Lord's Supper – and according to custom at the Feast of the Passover, He commences with His disciples the "Hallel" or great song of praise, which consisted of Psalms 115-118. The Lord thereby forever consecrates vocal music in His Church. Singing –this language of the feelings, this exhalation of an exalted state of mind, this pinion of an enraptured soul – is heaven's valuable gift to earth. It has the power to raise us high above the foggy atmosphere of daily life; to transport us so wondrously, even into the precincts of heaven; to expand the heart; to banish sorrow and burst the bonds of care. A thousand times has it restored peace in the midst of strife, banished Satan, and annihilated his projects. Like a genial breeze of spring, it has blown across the stiff and frozen plain, and has caused stony hearts to melt and rendered them capable of receiving the seed of eternity.

F. W. Krummacher (1796-1868)

Praise is the believer's help in trials and companion after trial. Jehoshaphat's army sang praises before the battle. David sang praises in the cave. Daniel, when the trap was set for his life, prayed and gave thanks three times a day. Jesus, before He went to the garden, sang a hymn with His disciples.

Thomas Fuller (1608-1661)

Only Begotten, Word of God eternal, Lord of creation, merciful and mighty, List to thy servants when their tuneful voices rise to thy presence. God in three persons, Father everlasting, Son co-eternal, ever-blessed Spirit, Thine be the glory, praise and adoration, now and for ever.

Latin hymn (9th century)

October 31st

The harvest is the end of the world; and the reapers are the angels.

Matthew 13:39

Come, ye thankful people, come,
Raise the song of harvest-home:
All is safely gathered in,
Ere the winter storms begin;
God, our Maker, doth provide
For our wants to be supplied:
Come to God's own temple, come,
Raise the song of harvest-home.

> All this world is God's own field,
> Fruit unto His praise to yield;
> Wheat and tares together sown,
> Unto joy or sorrow grown;
> First the blade, and then the ear,
> Then the full corn shall appear:
> Lord of harvest, grant that we
> Wholesome grain and pure may be.

For the Lord our God shall come;
And shall take His harvest home;
From His field shall in that day
All offences purge away;
Give His angels charge at last
In the fire the tares to cast;
But the fruitful ears to store
In His garner evermore.

> Even so, Lord, quickly come
> To Thy final harvest home:
> Gather Thou Thy people in,
> Free from sorrow, free from sin;
> There, for ever purified,
> In Thy presence to abide:
> Come, with all Thine angels, come,
> Raise the glorious harvest-home. Amen.

Henry Alford (1810-1871)

November

November 1st

May they all be one!... that the world may believe Thou hast sent Me.
John 17:21 (Moffatt)

The unity of believers results from their inclusion in the ineffable union of the Father and the Son. Jesus prays that they may be one, and that they also may be one in Us. Their unity is no mere matter of formal external organization nor of unanimity of creed, but it is a deep, vital unity.

Alexander Maclaren (1826-1910)

By this shall all know that you are My disciples. Not by the creed you recite. Not by the livery you wear. Not by the hymns you sing. Not by the ritual you observe. But by the fact that you love one another. It was Seneca who declared in the early days of the church, "See how these Christians love one another."

G. Campbell Morgan (1863-1945)

I wish all names among the saints of God were swallowed up in that one name of Christian. Are you Christ's? If so, I love you with all my heart.

John Wesley (1703-1791)

I think if I had a drop of sectarian blood in my veins, I would open a vein and let that drop out.

D.L. Moody (1837-1899)

> May the grace of Christ our Saviour,
> and the Father's boundless love,
> With the Holy Spirit's favor,
> rest upon us from above.
> Thus may we abide in union,
> with each other and the Lord,
> And possess, in sweet communion,
> joys which each cannot afford.

John Newton (1725-1807)

November 2nd

Thy throne, O God, is for ever and ever.
Hebrews 1:8

The God of Abraham praise, Who reigns enthroned above,
Ancient of everlasting days, and God of love.
Jehovah, great I Am! By earth and heaven confessed,
I bow, and bless the sacred Name for ever blest.

The God of Abraham praise, at whose supreme command
From earth I rise, and seek the joys at His right hand.
I all on earth forsake—its wisdom, fame, and power—
And Him my only portion make, my shield and tower.

He by Himself hath sworn, I on His oath depend:
I shall, on eagle's wings upborne, to heaven ascend;
I shall behold His face, I shall His power adore,
And sing the wonders of His grace for evermore.

There dwells the Lord our King, the Lord our Righteousness,
Triumphant o'er the world and sin, the Prince of Peace;
On Zion's sacred height His Kingdom He maintains,
And glorious with His saints in light for ever reigns.

The whole triumphant host give thanks to God on high;
'Hail, Father, Son, and Holy Ghost!' they ever cry.
Hail, Abraham's God, and mine!—I join the heavenly lays—
All might and majesty are Thine, and endless praise. Amen.
Thomas Olivers (1725-1799)

When thou shalt have put off the mortal and put on the incorruption,
then shall thou see God worthily. For God will raise thy flesh immortal
with thy soul; and then, having become immortal, thou shalt see the
Immortal, if now you believe on Him.
Mathetes (130)

And we know that all things work together for good to them that love God,
to them who are the called according to His purpose.

Romans 8:28

The privilege of the saints is that all things work together for good, that is, all the providences of God that concern us.... Either directly or indirectly, every providence has a tendency to spiritual good, breaking us off from sin, bringing us nearer to God, weaning us from the world, fitting us for heaven. There is a harmony of Providence in its uniform designs. It is not from any specific quality in the providences themselves, but from the power and grace of God working in, with, and by these providences.

Matthew Henry (1662-1714)

Remember nothing can touch you but God's will for you. Rest in it. I'm lying down in the centre of the will of God.

Jeanne Marie de la Mothe Guyon (1648-1717)

Affliction may refine, but cannot waste that heart wherein His love is fixed fast.

Francis Quarles (1592-1644)

Thou alone knowest what is expedient for me; Thou art my Sovereign Master and Lord; guide and govern me at Thy pleasure. Give me or take from me as shall seem best to Thy providence; but in all things conform my will to Thine, and grant that with a humble and perfect submission and a holy confidence, I may dispose myself to receive the orders of Thy eternal wisdom, and may equally reverence and adore the most different events which Thou shalt please to accomplish in me. Amen.

Blaise Pascal (1623-1662)

Thee will I love, beneath thy frown or smile, thy sceptre or thy rod. What though my flesh and heart decay? Thee shall I love in endless day.

Johann Scheffler (1624-1677)

I am the way and the truth and the life.
No one can come to the Father except through Me.
John 14:6 (Williams)

Christ is the way through whom the soul has admittance to God, and without Him it is impossible that so much as one desire should come into the ears of the Lord.... And to come through Christ is for the sinner to be enabled of God to hide under the shadow of the Lord Jesus, as a person hides under a thing for safeguard.... Those then that come to God through Christ must have faith, by which they put on Christ, and appear before God in Christ's merits, in His blood, righteousness, victory, intercession, and so stand before Him being *accepted in the Beloved.*

John Bunyan (1628-1688)

It was a wonderful word about prayer that Jesus spoke to His disciples on the night before His crucifixion, (Whatsoever you shall ask in My name, that will I do, that the Father may be glorified in the Son. If you ask anything in My name, I will do it.) Prayer in the name of Christ has power with God. God is well pleased with His Son Jesus Christ. He hears Him always, and He also hears always the prayer that is really in His name. There is a fragrance in the name of Christ that makes acceptable to God every prayer that bears it.... To pray in the name of Christ is to pray on the ground, not of my credit, but His; to renounce that thought that I have any claims on God whatsoever, and approach Him on the ground of Christ's claims. Praying in the name of Christ is not merely adding the phrase "I ask these things in Jesus' name" to my prayer. I may put that phrase in my prayer and really be resting in my own merit.... But when I really do approach God, not on the ground of my merit, but on the ground of Christ's merit, not on the ground of my goodness, but on the ground of the atoning blood, God will hear me.

R.A.Torrey (1856-1928)

He entered heaven itself, now to appear in the presence of God on our behalf.
Hebrews 9:24 (Weymouth)

Before the throne of God above
I have a strong, a perfect plea;
A great high priest, whose name is Love,
who ever lives and pleads for me.
My name is written on His hands,
my name is hidden in His heart:
I know that while in heaven He stands
no power can force me to depart.

When Satan tempts me to despair
and tells me of the guilt within,
Upward I look, and see Him there
who made an end of all my sin.
Because the sinless Saviour died,
my sinful soul is counted free:
For God, the just, is satisfied to look
on Him and pardon me.

Behold Him there! The risen Lamb,
my perfect, sinless Righteousness,
The great unchangeable I AM,
the King of glory and of grace!
One with my Lord I cannot die:
my soul is purchased by His blood,
My life is safe with Christ on High,
with Christ, my Saviour and my God.

Charitie L. de Chenez (1841-1892)

Luther saw ground enough for what he said, when he cried out, "I will have nothing to do with an absolute God, a God without Christ." Woe, and alas! forevermore, to that person that meets a just and righteous God without a Mediator.

John Flavel (1627-1691)

cNovember 6th

Weeping may endure for a night, but joy comes in the morning.
Psalm 30:5

Our mourning shall last but till morning. God will turn the winter's night into a summer's day, our sighing into singing, our grief into gladness, our mourning into music, our bitter into sweet, our wilderness into a paradise. The life of the Christian is filled up with interchanges of sickness and health, weakness and strength, want and wealth, disgrace and honour, crosses and comforts, miseries and mercies, joys and sorrows, mirth and mourning; all honey would harm us, all wormwood would undo us; a composition of both is the best way in the world to keep our souls in a healthy constitution. It is best for the health of the soul that the south wind of mercy, and the north wind of adversity, do both blow upon it.

Thomas Brooks (1608-1680)

Christ will have joy and sorrow sharing in the life of the saints, as the night and the day are kindly partners of time.... But if sorrow be the greedier half of our days here, I know that joy's day shall dawn.... We fools would have a cross of our own choosing, and would have our gall and wormwood sugared, our fire cold, and our death and grave warmed with heat of life; but He who has brought many children to glory, and lost none, is our best Tutor. I take His cross in my arms with joy; I bless it, I rejoice in it.

Samuel Rutherford (1600-1661)

Brief life here our portion, brief sorrow, short-lived care;
The life that knows no ending, the tearless life is there.
There God, our King and Portion, in fullness of His grace,
We then shall see forever, and worship face to face.

Bernard of Cluny (1091-1153)

November 7th

When the Spirit of truth is come, He will guide you into all truth.
John 16:13

There is an impressiveness of character present in those who walk in the fellowship of the Holy Spirit. It is a certain convincing aroma, self-witnessing, like the perfume of a flower. It is independent of mental equipment, and it makes no preference between a plenteous and a penurious estate. It works without the aid of speech. It sways the lives of others when mere words would miserably fail. A miner said of his vicar, "You have only to shake that man's hand to feel that he is full of the Holy Spirit." Ours is the Pentecostal inheritance. Let us assume the Pentecostal attitude of zealous and hungry reception. Above all, let us cultivate a sensitive intimacy with the Holy Spirit.

J.H. Jowett (1864-1923)

The Spirit moves us when we do not perceive it. There is none in heaven or earth nearer to us than the Holy Spirit; yet there is none whose presence is more deeply hidden. Unseen because He is so near, unrecognized for very intimacy, there is no depth of personality whither He will not come; and even the soul which He purifies and strengthens may only discern Him in its own new purity and strength. But though He is hidden, though we cannot tell whence He cometh or whither He goeth, we may watch and forward and pray for His work, in others and in ourselves.

Dean Paget (1851-?)

> Holy Spirit, truth Divine, dawn upon this soul of mine;
> Word of God, and inward light, wake my spirit, clear my sight.
> Holy Spirit, love Divine; glow within this heart of mine;
> Kindle every high desire; perish self in Thy pure fire.
> Holy Spirit, joy Divine, gladden Thou this heart of mine;
> In the desert ways I'll sing; spring, O Well, for ever spring!
>
> Samuel Longfellow (1819-1892)

November 8th

Why standeth Thou afar off, O LORD? Why hidest Thou thyself in times of trouble?
Psalm 10:1

Have thy prayers been followed by a calm stillness? That is God's voice -- a voice that will suffice thee in the meantime till the full disclosure comes. Has He moved not from His place to help thee? Yet, His stillness makes thee still, and He has something better than help to give thee.

George Matheson (1842-1906)

It may be you will be kept in darkness, but darkness is not always the frown of God; it is only Himself – *His shade on thy right hand.*

Henry Martyn (1781-1812)

God has wisely kept us in the dark concerning future events and reserved for Himself the knowledge of them, that He may train us up in a dependence upon Himself and a continued readiness for every event.

Matthew Henry (1662-1714)

He will do marvels if you will learn the mystery of His silence, and praise Him, for every time He withdraws His gifts it is that you may better know and love the Giver.

Anonymous

Although God has no other desire than to impart Himself to you, He frequently conceals Himself for a purpose. It may be to arouse you from laziness, or perhaps you have not been seeking Him in faith and love. But for whatever reason, He does so out of His abundant goodness and faithfulness to you. Often these apparent withdrawings of Himself are succeeded by the caresses of His love.

Jeanne Marie de la Mothe Guyon (1648-1717)

November 9ᵗʰ

Watch and pray that you enter not into temptation.
Matthew 26:41

Nothing will so tend to loosen you from the world as His Presence. It is when beholding God that we realize the emptiness of the world, which will ere long pass away like a cloud; all grandeur and pomp will vanish as a dream, the proud will be brought low, the powerful laid helpless, the mighty bowed beneath the Eternal Majesty of God. In His judgment-day He will extinguish all that glitters now, as the rising sun puts out the starlight. Then we shall see nought save God; seek as we may, we shall find nought save Him. Where, we shall ask in that day, are the pleasant things which lured us? What were they? What remains of them? Not even a token by which to trace them! They have melted away like the mist before the sun; we can scarce say that they ever were, they did but appear for an instant, and are gone!

François de la Mothe Fénelon (1651-1715)

O let me feel Thee near me; the world is ever near;
I see the sights that dazzle, the tempting sounds I hear;
My foes are ever near me, around me and within;
But, Jesus, draw Thou nearer, and shield my soul from sin.
John B. Bode (1816-1874)

The devil may place the soul in peril and temptation, but can never make it sin. It is the devil's part to suggest, it is ours not to consent.

Augustine of Hippo (354-430)

God alone can give spiritual life at the first, and keep it up in the soul afterwards.

George Müller (1805-1898)

November 10th

I am... the bright and morning star.
Revelation 22:16

The imagery here is lifted to the scenery of the firmament; He who is the Vine and the Shepherd, now also reveals Himself as the Star of Stars in a spiritual sky. We may be sure that the word, with all its radiant beauty, is no mere flight of fancy. Prophecy, not poetry, underlies these last oracles of the Bible.... He qualifies the word by this one bright epithet as to show Himself as not the King merely, but the King of the morning.... He is not Hesperus that sets, but Phosphorus that rises, springing into the sky through the earliest dawn; the pledge of reviving life and growing light, and all the energies and all the pleasures of a happy day. It indicates the delights of hope along with those of fruition; a happiness in which one of the deep elements is always the thought of something yet to be revealed; light with more light to follow, joy to develop into further joy, as the dawn passes into the morning and then into the day.

H.C.G. Moule (1841-1920)

The Morning Star upon us gleams,
How full of grace and truth His beams,
How passing fair His splendor!
Good Shepherd, David's proper heir,
My King in heaven, Thou does me bear
Upon Thy bosom tender. Nearest, Dearest,
Highest, Brightest, Thou delightest still to love me,
Thou so high enthroned above me.
Strike deep into this heart of mine
Thy rays of love, Thou Star divine,
And fire its dying embers:
And grant that naught have power to part
Me from Thy body, Lord, who art
The life of all Thy members.

Philipp Nicolai (1556-1608)

Give Me your heart.

Proverbs 23:26

Thou callest for my heart, oh that it were any way fit for Thine acceptance! I am unworthy, O Lord, everlastingly unworthy to be Thine. But since Thou wilt have it so, I freely give my heart to Thee. Take it, it is Thine, oh that it were better! But Lord, I put it into thy hands, who alone canst mend it. Mould it after Thine own heart; make it as Thou wouldst have it, holy, humble, heavenly, soft, flexible, and write thy law upon it. I deliver myself up to Thee. Receive me; write thy name, O Lord, upon me and upon all that I have. Set thy mark upon me and upon every member of my body and every faculty of my soul. Amen.

Joseph Alleine (1634-1668)

When Walter Raleigh (1552-1618) had laid his head upon the block, he was asked by the executioner whether it lay right. With the faith of a Christian, he returned an answer, the power of which we shall all feel when our own head is tossing and turning on death's uneasy pillow: "It matters little, my friend, how the head lies, provided the heart is right."

Thomas Guthrie (1803-1873)

"Give Me thy heart," says the Father above,
No gift so precious to Him as our love;
"Give Me thy heart," says the Saviour of all,
Calling in mercy again and again;
"Give Me thy heart," says the Spirit divine,
"All that thou hast to my keeping resign."

Eliza E. Hewitt (1851-1920)

Only in beholding and loving God can we learn forgetfulness of self.... Love God, and you will be humble; love God, and you will throw off the love of self; love God, and you will love all that He gives you to love for love of Him.

François de la Mothe Fénelon (1651-1715)

November 12th

The cloak that I left at Troas with Carpus, when you come,
bring with you, and the books, but especially the parchments.

2 Timothy 4:13

This verse has been criticised as trivial, as unworthy the dignity of inspiration.... How little could we spare this verse! What a light it throws on the last sad days of the persecuted Apostle! The fact that these necessary possessions, perhaps the whole that the Apostle could call his own in this world, had been left at the house of Carpus, may indicate his sudden arrest. Now he is settled again, though his home is but a prison, winter is coming on, and winter in a Roman prison, as he knows from experience, may be very cold.

A simple message, about an old cloak and some books, but very touching. They may add a little comfort, a little relief, to the long-drawn tedium of those last dreary days. Perhaps St. Paul had woven the cloak himself of the black goat's hair of his native province. Doubtless it was an old companion – wetted many a time in the water-torrents of Asia, whitened with the dust of Roman roads, stained with the brine of shipwreck. He may have slept in its warm shelter on the chill Phrygian uplands, under the canopy of stars, or it may have covered his bruised and trembling limbs in the dungeon at Philippi. Poor inventory of a saint's possessions! But he is much more than content. His soul is joyful in God. If he has the cloak to keep him warm, and the books and parchments to teach and encourage him, and Mark to help him in various ways, and if, above all, Timothy will come himself, then life will have shed on him its last rays of sunshine. Did Paul ever get that cloak, and the papyri and the vellum rolls? Did Timothy ever reach him? None can tell us. With the last verse of the Second Epistle to Timothy we have heard Paul's last word.

F. W. Farrar (1831-1903)

cNovember 13th

The Lord Jesus Christ be with your spirit. Grace be with you. Amen.
2 Timothy 4:22

It was a mellowed and softened old age. Lonely so far as dear companions were concerned; full of privations, without cloak or books or tendance, shivering in the prison, waiting to be offered.... He wanted once more to see his beloved son in the faith, and wrote to speed his steps. It was very pathetic, very beautiful, very human. But the ray of an indomitable courage and faith is flung across the heaving waters, and he has kept his Lord's deposit, and knows that the deposit which he had made years before had been no less safely kept.

F.B. Meyer (1847-1929)

"God buries His workmen, but carries on their work." Paul's faith had never wavered amid life's severest trials, nor his hope grown dim amid its most bitter disappointments; and when he passed from the dungeon and martyrdom to his crown of righteousness, he left the life which he had sown to be quickened by the power of God in the soil of the world's history, where it shall continue to bear fruit until the end of time, amid the ever-deepening gratitude of generations yet unborn.

F.W. Farrar (1831-1903)

To Him be glory for ever and ever. Amen (2 Timothy 4:18). Here is a doxology to the Son that the Apostle used to sustain himself, not merely Divine truth wherewith to enlighten his soul; he also had a Divine Person wherewith to share his life. And therefore, with a heart full of thankfulness to the Master who has shared his sufferings and will share his bliss, he leaves us this doxology, and then his last words, The Lord Jesus Christ be with your spirit, Grace be with you. Amen.

John Chrysostom (345-407)

November 14th

The preaching of the cross... is the power of God.
1 Corinthians 1:18

O ur method of proclaiming salvation is this: to point out to every heart the loving Lamb who died for us, and although He was the Son of God, offered Himself for our sins.... When preaching of His blood, and of His love unto death, even the death of the cross, we ought never, either in discourse or in argument, to digress even for a quarter of an hour from the loving Lamb: to name no virtue except in Him, and from Him and on His account; to preach no commandment except faith in Him; no other justification but that He atoned for us; no other sanctification but the privilege to sin no more; no other happiness but to be near Him, to think of Him and do His pleasure; no other self denial but to be deprived of Him and His blessings; no other calamity but to displease Him; no other life but in Him.

Nicolaus von Zinzendorf (1700-1760)

Stop your ears when any one speaks to you at variance with Jesus Christ, who was descended from David and was also of Mary; who was truly born, and did eat and drink. He was truly persecuted under Pontius Pilate; He was truly crucified and truly died in the sight of beings in heaven, and on earth, and under the earth. He was also truly raised from the dead, His Father quickening Him, even as after the same manner His Father will so raise us who believe in Christ Jesus, apart from whom we do not possess the true life.

Ignatius of Antioch (50-107)

Whoever has the Lord Jesus has both the motive and the message. When you get Him, you get your message and the message gets you, and you must give it out.... It is a message of a Christ who died.

S.D. Gordon (1859-1936)

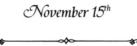

I will restore to you the years that the locust has eaten.
Joel 2:25

L ost years can never be restored literally. Time once past is gone for ever.... We cannot have back our time; but there is a strange and wonderful way in which God can give back to us the wasted blessings, the unripened fruit of years over which we mourned. The fruit of wasted years may yet be ours. God can give His repentant people larger grace in the present and in the future, can make the life which has hitherto been blighted and eaten up with the locust, and the caterpillar, and the palmer-worm of sin, and self, and Satan, yet to be complete, and blessed and useful. It is a great wonder; but Jehovah is a God of wonders, and in the kingdom of His grace miracles are common things. It is a divine work. Those dead years, those doleful years, those desponding years – all the harvest of them, God can give back to us. The Lord can bring so much good out of evil, so much light out of the darkness, so much joy out of sorrow, that we will say, "I thank God that I was shut up in Doubting Castle, I thank God I did sink in the deep mire where there was no standing, for He has restored to me the years that the locust has eaten." We do not want the locusts at all: we cannot endure sin, or doubt or trifling. We want every year to be fruitful. But if the evils have come, let us turn to God with penitence and faith, and He can yet restore to us the losses they have caused.

C.H. Spurgeon (1834-1892)

Not what I am, O Lord, but what Thou art!
That, that alone, can be my soul's true rest;
Thy love, not mine, bids fear and doubt depart,
And stills the tempest of my tossing heart
Horatius Bonar (1808-1889)

November 16ᵗʰ

The Lord's hand is not shortened that it cannot save.
Isaiah 59:1

H is is infinite power that can do all things. No circumstances are so low, but that He can raise them; so entangling and perplexing, but He can unravel them; so hopeless, but He can remedy them. Be our case what it will, it is never past reach with Him to help; it is the most proper season for Him to take it in hand, when all others have given it over.... His is infinite goodness inclining to help. He is good and gracious in His nature and therefore His power is a spring of comfort.... In His wisdom He may see it necessary to put His own in humbling circumstances, and keep them there for a time, but it is not possible He can leave them therein altogether. His is infinite wisdom that does nothing in vain, and therefore will not needlessly keep one in humbling circumstances.

Thomas Boston (1676-1732)

Believe under a cloud, and wait for Him when there is neither moonlight nor starlight. Let faith live and breathe, and lay hold of the sure salvation of God, when clouds and darkness are about you.... Take heed of unbelieving hearts, which can father lies upon Christ. Beware of the question: *does His promise fail for evermore?* Who dreameth that a promise of God can fail, fall aswoon or die? Who can make God sick or His promises weak? When we are pleased to seek a plea with Christ, let us plead that we hope in Him. Job's stout word of faith was, *Though He slay me, yet will I trust in Him.* An epitaph, written upon the grave-stone of a departed believer, said, "I died hoping, and my dust and ashes believe in life!" Faith's eye can see through a frown of God, and under it read God's thoughts of love and peace. Hold fast to Christ in the dark; surely you will see the salvation of God.

Samuel Rutherford (1600-1661)

———◦◇◦———

Other sheep I have, which are not of this fold: them also I must bring,
and they shall hear My voice; and there shall be one fold, and one shepherd.

John 10:16

God who sees beneath the surface and beyond the present, beholds His sheep where we only see wolves. He sees an Apostle in the blaspheming Saul, a teacher for all generations in the sensual Augustine, a reformer in the eager monk Luther, a poet-evangelist in the tinker Bunyan. He sees the future saint in the present sinner.... A mighty Voice ought ever to be sounding in our ears, *Other sheep I have*; and the answer of our hearts and lives should be, "Them also, O Lord, will I try to bring." Not until the goal is accomplished shall we have a right to rest, and then we, with all those He has helped us gather to His side, shall be among that flock, whom He who is at once the Lamb and Shepherd, our Brother and our Lord, our Sacrifice and King, shall feed and lead by living fountains of waters, in the pastures of the upper world, where there are no ravening wolves nor false guides to terrify and bewilder His flock any more.

Alexander Maclaren (1826-1910)

We are not sent to proclaim the results of our own investigation, but the glorious provision of God. Not the subtleties of abstruse metaphysical reasoning, nor the teachings of learned scientists, but pardon for the guilty, a Saviour for the lost; we are to whisper into every ear, that the dying may hear it and never die, that the living may catch its message and live for ever.... The sacred privilege is to proclaim the mercy and grace of God, to give hope to the hopeless, courage to the faint, a Saviour to all. Every time a needy soul is met the word may be spoken, *Come to the fountain! Come to the bread of life!*

Biblical Illustrator (1887)

Christ in you, the hope of glory.
Colossians 1:27

Not only is our hope in Him, but He himself is our hope…. Christ Himself is our hope, as only Author of it; Christ is our hope, as the End of it; and Christ who is the Beginning and the End, is our hope also by the way. Each yearning of our hearts, each ray of hope which gleams upon us, each touch which thrills through us, each voice which whispers in our inmost hearts of the good things laid up in store for us, if we will love God, are the light of Christ enlightening us, the touch of Christ raising us to new life, the voice of Christ, *Whoso comes to me, I will in no wise cast out.* It is *Christ in us, the hope of glory,* drawing us by His Spirit who dwells in us, unto Himself our hope. For our hope is not the glory of heaven, not joy, not peace, not rest from labour, not fullness of our wishes, nor sweet contentment of the whole soul, not understanding of all mysteries and all knowledge, not only a torrent of delight; it is Christ our God, *the hope of glory*. Nothing which God could create is what we hope for; nothing which God could give us out of Himself, no created glory, bliss, beauty, majesty, or riches. What we hope for is our Redeeming God Himself, who hath loved us, to be our joy and our portion for ever.

Edward B. Pusey (1800-1882)

All for Jesus! All for Jesus!
All my being's ransomed powers;
All my thoughts and words and doings,
All my days and all my hours.

> Let my hands perform His bidding;
> Let my feet run in His ways;
> Let mine eyes see Jesus only;
> Let my lips speak forth His praise.

Since my eyes were fixed on Jesus,
I've lost sight of all beside;
So enchained my spirit's vision,
Looking at the Crucified.

Mary D. James (1810-1883)

See what wonderful love the Father has bestowed on us
in letting us be called God's children, and that is what we are!
1 John 3:1 (Williams)

Here is love vast as the ocean,
loving kindness as the flood,
When the Prince of life, our Ransom,
shed for us His precious blood.

Who his love will not remember?
Who can cease to sing His praise?
He can never be forgotten
throughout heav'n's eternal days.

On the mount of crucifixion,
fountains opened deep and wide;
Through the flood gates of God's mercy
flowed a vast and gracious tide.

Grace and love, like mighty rivers,
poured incessant from above,
And heav'n's peace and perfect justice
kissed a guilty world in love.

Robert Lowry (1826-1899)

All blessings are given to us through Christ.... By Him we look up to the heights of heaven. By Him we behold, as in a glass, His immaculate and most excellent visage. By Him are the eyes of our hearts opened. By Him our foolish and darkened understanding blossoms up anew towards His marvelous light. By Him the Lord has willed that we should taste of immortal knowledge, who, *being the brightness of His majesty, is by so much greater than the angels, as He hath by inheritance obtained a more excellent name than they.*

Clement of Rome (30-100)

You shall worship the Lord your God, and Him only shall you serve.
Matthew 4:10

There is no truth the Scriptures teach more frequently than that God is the only object of worship. To no mere creature on earth or in heaven may we bend the knee in prayer. *You shall have no other gods before Me....* It is a most wonderful fact that abject humanity that is fallen in iniquity, should have communion with the high and holy One. On the lips of a sinning creature, that fearful name, the LORD THY GOD, is a name of solemn import. O weigh the vast meaning of these words! Well may a holy fear take possession of the heart, and awe it into reverence as it approaches the King Eternal, Immortal, and Invisible. His greatness knows no bounds; His perfections are infinite; His spirituality is unmingled and pure; His existence has no beginning and will have no end. He is all-seeing, yet unseen; the most distant, yet the most near; comprehending all, and comprehended by none; containing all, while nothing contains Him. There is nothing but He controls by His power; nothing but what lives and moves within the compass of His immensity. Spotless cherubim, when they worship Him, cover their faces with their wings, and say one to another, *Holy, holy, holy is the Lord God of hosts*, the whole earth is full of His glory! The nearer the sinful come to Him, the nearer do they come to a consuming fire. To the guilty children of an apostate race, His throne might well be overshadowed with clouds and darkness, and made inaccessible.... Access to God as the Hearer of prayer is the effect only of that great work of redeeming mercy in which the second person of the ever-blessed Trinity came to seek and save those which were lost, and advance them to the privileges of children. We have nothing of our own to plead; yet in His name may our prayer go up as incense, and the lifting up of our hands as an acceptable sacrifice.

Gardiner Spring (1785-1873)

November 21st

He calls His own sheep by name, and leads them out.

John 10:3

A property of a good shepherd is skill to know and judge aright one's own sheep, and hence it is a usual thing to set a mark upon sheep, to the end that if they go astray, the shepherd may seek them and bring them home again. Christ affirms the same thing of Himself, *I know them and they follow Me.* Yea, doubtless, He that hath numbered the stars and calleth them all by their names, yes, the very hairs of our head, taketh special notice of His own children, the sheep of His pasture.

Samuel Smith (1588-?)

> Wheresoever I roam through valleys dreary
> Over mountains, or in pathless wood,
> Ever with me is a Friend to cheer me,
> Warning, comforting as none else could.
>> 'Tis the Shepherd, who once dying, bleeding,
>> Still through all eternity shall live;
>> Following His flock, protecting, feeding,
>> He the tend'rest care doth give.
>> C.O. Rosenius (1816-1868)

One of the great uses of the Incarnation was to humanize God that we might believe in His personal love. When a lone woman came up in a crowd to steal as it were some healing power He would not let her off in that impersonal, unrecognizing way. He even hunts up the youth He had healed of blindness and opens to him the secrets of His Messiahship; He calls us friends because He is on the private footing of personal confidence, and promises a friendship so personal that it shall be a cipher of mutual understanding, giving us a white stone and in the stone a new name which no person knoweth saving the one who receiveth it.

Horace Bushnell (1802-1876)

* * *

*I plead with you, by the compassion of God, to present all your faculties to Him as a
living and holy sacrifice acceptable to Him—a spiritual mode of worship.*
Romans 12:1 (Weymouth)

Eternal and ever-blessed God! I desire to present myself before
Thee, with the deepest humiliation of soul; sensible how
unworthy such a sinful one is to appear before the holy Majesty
of heaven.... I come acknowledging myself to have been a great
offender. I come, invited by the name of Thy Son, and wholly trusting
in His perfect righteousness; entreating that for His sake Thou wilt
be merciful to my unrighteousness, and wilt no more remember my
sins.... This day do I, with the utmost solemnity, surrender myself to
Thee. I renounce all former lords that have had dominion over me;
and I consecrate to Thee all that I am and all that I have; the faculties
of my mind, the members of my body, my possessions, my time, and
my influence over others; to be all used entirely for Thy glory, and
employed in obedience to Thy commands as long as Thou continuest
me in life....

To Thy direction also I resign myself, and all I am and have, to be
disposed of by Thee in such a manner as Thou shalt in Thine infinite
wisdom judge most subservient to the purposes of Thy glory. To Thee
I leave the management of all events and say without reserve, *Not
my will but Thine be done....* Use me, O Lord, I beseech Thee, as an
instrument for Thy service. Number me among Thy peculiar people.
Let me be washed in the blood of Thy dear Son. Let me be clothed
with His righteousness. Let me be sanctified by His Spirit. Transform
me more and more into His image. Impart to me, through Him, all
needful influences of Thy purifying, cheering and comforting Spirit.
And let my life be spent under those influences, and in the light of
Thy gracious countenance, as my Father and my God. Amen.

Phillip Doddridge (1702-51)

November 23ʳᵈ

He is altogether lovely. This is my beloved, and this is my friend.
Song of Solomon 5:16

I know not a thing worth the buying but heaven; and my own mind is, if comparison were made betwixt Christ and heaven, I would sell heaven with my blessing and buy Christ....

I am in sweet communion with Christ as a poor sinner can be; and I am only pained that He hath much beauty and fairness, and I little love; He has great power and mercy, and I little faith; He much light, and I bleared eyes. Alas, my riven dish, and running-out vessel can hold little of Jesus Christ....

Oh, if the heaven, and the heaven of heavens were paper, and the sea ink, and the multitude of mountains pens and brass, and I able to write that paper, within and without, full of the praises of my fairest, my dearest, my loveliest, my sweetest, my matchless and most peerless, and Well-beloved!...

If ten thousand thousand worlds of angels were created, they might all tire themselves in wondering at His beauty, and begin again to wonder anew. Oh that I could win nigh Him, to kiss His feet, to hear His voice, to feel the smell of His ointments! But oh, alas! I have little, little of Him. I long for more.

Samuel Rutherford (1600-1661)

Oh, what wonder! how amazing! Jesus, glorious King of kings,
Deigns to call me His beloved, lets me rest beneath His wings.

Mary D. James (1810-1883)

Dear Name! The Rock on which I build, my Shield and Hiding-Place, my never-failing Treasury filled with boundless stores of grace. Jesus! My Shepherd, Husband, Friend, Prophet, Priest, and King; my Lord, my Life, my Way, my End -- accept the praise I bring.

Bernard of Clairvaux (1091-1157)

November 24th

—◦—◦—◦—

I and my Father are one.
John 10:30

Jesus was the supreme mystic. The Unseen was the real to Him. He lived in God and God lived in Him…. But Jesus the mystic was amazingly concrete and practical…. He did not speculate on why temptation should be in the world – He met it, and after forty days' struggle with it in the wilderness He conquered and *returned in the power of the Spirit to Galilee.* He did not discourse on the dignity of labor – He worked at a carpenter's bench and His hands were hard with the toil of making yokes and ploughs…. As He came among people He did not try to prove the existence of God – He brought Him…. He did not argue the immortality of the soul – He raised the dead. He did not argue that God answers prayer – He prayed, sometimes all night, and in the morning the power of the Lord was present to heal. He did not paint in glowing colors the beauties of friendship and the need for human sympathy – He wept at the grave of His friend…. He did not teach in a didactic way about the worth of children – He put His hands upon them and blessed them, and setting one in their midst tersely said, *Of such is the kingdom of God.* He did not teach in the schoolroom manner the necessity of humility *– He girded Himself with a towel and kneeled down and washed His disciples' feet….* He did not prove how pain and sorrow in the universe could be compatible with the love of God – He took on Himself at the cross everything that spoke against the love of God…. He did not paint a Utopia, far off and unrealizable – He announced that the Kingdom of heaven is within us, and is at hand and can be realized here and now… He did not merely tell us that death need have no terror for us – He rose from the dead, and lo, now the tomb glows with light.

E. Stanley Jones (1884-1973)

November 25th

─────◦◦─────

To the saints and faithful brethren in Christ which are at Colossé....
Colossians 1:2

This familiar greeting puts before us the persons greeted from two very different points of sight. They were in Colossé. They were in Christ. From the one side they were the denizens of that small Asiatic-Greek town, probably its natives; habituated to the scenery of its streets, fields, rushing river, limestone chasms, and overlooking hills, and to the scenes of its daily life in home, shop and market. They were in it, hour by hour, as to all its unfavourable spiritual circumstances; its idolatry, pagan vice, provincialism, narrowness, decay.... But then on the other side, they were, while in Colossé, also in Christ. Here was their supernatural secret for life, power, purity, love, cheerfulness, and good hope. Their spiritual locality was the Lord. To Him they had come, and to Him by the Spirit, they were joined. And now, with Him, in God, their life... was hid. They moved about Colossé in Christ. They worked, served, kept the house, followed the business, met the neighbors, entered into their sorrows and joys, walked in wisdom towards them, suffered their abuse and insults – all in Christ. They carried about with them a "private atmosphere" which was not of Asia but of heaven. As then, so now for us who *have believed to the saving of the soul*; we are in some locality of earth's surface, where the will of God has set us. Perhaps in a spot familiar to us from the dawn of memory, made to be to us what it is by a thousand associations of love, loss, joy, grief.... Perhaps in some strange and alien place, remote in miles from the home of old, or remoter still in character and circumstances. We are not meant to ignore this locality, but to accept it. In order to do this aright we are called to remember our other and transcendent locality: we are in Christ.

H.C.G. Moule (1841-1920)

350

November 26th

Were there not ten cleansed? but where are the nine?
Luke 17:17

The nine lepers were more probably like children with a new toy, too delighted with their restored health and honour to think of the gracious friend to whom they owed it. In the case of some temporal blessings it is thus sometimes with us; the gift obscures the giver by its very wealth and profusion. So in spiritual things we are more likely to think of the gift. At bottom of our want of thankfulness there lies a radically imperfect estimate of the blessings of redemption, and until this is reversed we cannot seriously look in the face of Christ and thank Him for His inestimable love. Thanklessness is due to losing sight of our Benefactor, and of this the nine lepers were guilty. The nine men were not the men they would have been if they had accompanied the one who, when he saw that he was healed, turned back and with a loud voice glorified God, giving Him thanks.

Canon Lidden (1829-1890)

Now thank we all our God, with heart, and hands, and voices,
Who wondrous things hath done, in whom His world rejoices;
Who from our mother's arms hath blessed us on our way
With countless gifts of love, and still is ours today.

O may this bounteous God through all our life be near us,
With ever joyful hearts and blessed peace to cheer us;
And keep us in His grace, and guide us when perplexed,
And free us from all ills in this world and the next.

All praise and thanks to God the Father now be given,
The Son, and Him who reigns with them in highest heaven,
The one eternal God, whom earth and heaven adore;
For thus it was, is now, and shall be evermore. Amen.

Martin Rinckart (1586-1649)

November 27ᵗʰ

The hope of the righteous shall be gladness.

Proverbs 10:28

The righteous shall have what they hope for, to their unspeakable satisfaction. It is something future and unseen that they place their hope in, not what they have in hand, for we are saved by hope: but hope that is seen is not hope.... But if we hope for that we see not, then we do with patience wait for it. This hope will shortly be swallowed up in fruition, and it will be our everlasting gladness.

Matthew Henry (1662-1714)

> With a scrip on my back and a staff in my hand.
> I march on in haste through an enemy's land,
> The way may be rough, but it cannot be long,
> So I'll smooth it with hope, and I'll cheer it with song.
> Anonymous

He gives gladness. Some think of this gladness as a thing which God permits rather than gives; and some are driven from religion by a fancy that it is all gloomy and austere. This is not so. Thank God for what you have never associated with His gifts – your joys; passing gladness as well as spiritual ecstasy; for the sense of sight, hearing, taste and touch. Learn to feel God as near you when the sun shines as when the cloud depresses or the knell tolls. But remember that lasting gladness is dependent on union with Christ.

Biblical Illustrator (1887)

> My God, the spring of all my joys, the life of my delights,
> The glory of my brightest days, and comfort of my nights!
> The opening heavens around me shine, with beams of sacred bliss,
> If Jesus shows His mercy mine, and whispers I am His.
> In darkest shades, if Thou appear, my dawning is begun;
> Thou art my soul's bright morning star, and Thou my rising sun.
> Isaac Watts (1674-1748)

*Then shall we know, if we follow on to know the L*ORD*:*
His going forth is prepared as the morning;
and He shall come unto us as the rain....

Hosea 6:3

The Lord has brought us into the pathway of the knowledge of Him, and bids us pursue that path through all its strange meanderings until it opens out upon the plain where God's throne is. Our life is a following on to know the Lord. We marvel at some of the experiences through which we are called to pass, but afterwards we see that they afforded us some new knowledge of our Lord.

G. Bowen (1900)

His outgoings are prepared and secured to us as firmly as the return of the morning after a dark night, and we expect it as those who wait for the morning. It will come at the time appointed and will not fail; and the light of His countenance will be both welcome to us and growing upon us, unto the perfect day -- as the light of the morning is.

Matthew Henry (1662-1714)

Who is this who comes to meet me
On the desert way,
As the Morning Star foretelling
God's unclouded day?
He it is who came to win me
On the Cross of shame;
In His glory well I know Him
Evermore the same.
Oh the blessed joy of meeting,
All the desert past!

Gerhard Tersteegen (1697-1769)

Sun of my soul, Thou Saviour dear, it is not night if Thou be near. O may no earthborn cloud arise to hide Thee from Thy servant's eye. Amen.

John Keble (1792-1866)

November 29th

The soul of the wounded calls for help, and God does not regard it as foolish.
Job 24:12 (Rotherham)

Whatever the wounding be, however trivial it may appear so that the soul is ashamed to tell its inward distress, from whatever side the wind of unstablenesss blows, the soul of the wounded may call for help, and God will not regard it as foolish. Quick upon the call will come deliverance – if nothing outward, then something inward. Some little candle will be lit; the dull fog will lift.

Amy Carmichael (1867-1951)

I have had my trials, but I have laid hold on God, and so it has come that I have been sustained. It is not only permission, but positive command that He gives us to cast the burden upon Him. Cast your burden upon the Lord and He shall sustain you. Day by day I do it…. Come with your burdens, the burdens of your business, your profession, your trials and difficulties, and you will find help.

George Müller (1805-1898)

When this world's account is summed up, we shall find that we owe more to grief than we do to joy, and that sorrow has been the veiled angel of God come to teach us some of the deepest lessons which can ever be learned by human students.

Joseph Parker (1830-1902)

> The sweet times of refreshing come at last,
> My God shall fill my longing to the brim;
> Therefore I wait and look and long for Him;
> Not wearied though the work is wearisome,
> No fainting though the time be almost past.

Christina Rossetti (1830-1894)

November 30th

He is able to help those who are tempted and tried.
Hebrews 2:18 (Weymouth)

After the vision and glory of His baptism, *Jesus was led into the wilderness.* His human spirit filled with overpowering emotions, He sought for retirement to be alone with God, and once more to think over His mighty work. He was led – *driven* – by the Spirit into the wilderness. "He was led," says Jeremy Taylor, "by the Good Spirit to be tempted of the Evil Spirit." He was in the wilderness forty days and was with the wild beasts and He did eat nothing. It was then that Satan came to tempt Him. The struggle was powerful, personal, intensely real. Christ, for our sakes, met and conquered the tempter's utmost strength. The Captain of our salvation was *made perfect through sufferings,* in that He Himself has *suffered being tempted; He is able to help those who are being tempted.* The wilderness of Jericho and the Garden of Gethsemane – these witnessed His two most grievous struggles, and in these He triumphed wholly over the worst and most awful assaults of the enemy of souls, but during no part of the days of His flesh was He free from temptation, since otherwise His life had been no true human life at all. When the temptation in the wilderness was over, the foiled tempter left Him indeed, but left Him only for a season.

F. W. Farrar (1831-1903)

After being delivered from a period of hard temptation during his journey to the Celestial City, John Bunyan's Christian joyfully sang:

> O world of wonders! (I can say no less)
> That I should be preserved in this distress
> That I have met with here! O blessed be
> That hand that from it hath delivered me!

December

I will praise Thy name for ever and ever.
Psalms 145:2

Through all eternity to Thee, a joyful song I'll raise;
But, oh, eternity's too short, to utter all Thy praise!
Joseph Addison (1672-1719)

Praise is the only part of duty in which we at present engage, which is lasting. We pray, but there shall be a time when prayer shall offer its last litany; we believe, but there shall be a time when faith shall be lost in sight; we hope, and hope maketh not ashamed, but there shall be a time when hope lies down and dies, lost in the splendour of the fruition that God shall reveal. But praise goes singing into heaven, and is ready without a teacher to strike the harp that is waiting for it, to transmit along the echoes of eternity the song of the Lamb.
William Pushon (1824-1881)

Blessing and honour, thanksgiving and praise
more than we can utter be unto Thee,
O most adorable Trinity, Father, Son and Holy Ghost,
by all angels, all men, all creatures
for ever and ever, Amen and Amen.
To God the Father, who first loved us,
and made us accepted in the Beloved;
To God the Son who loved us,
and washed us from our sins in His own blood;
To God the Holy Ghost,
Who sheds the love of God abroad in our hearts,
be all love and all glory for time and for eternity. Amen
Thomas Ken (1637-1711)

I praise Thee for all things, I bless Thee, I glorify Thee, along with the everlasting and heavenly Jesus Christ, Thy beloved Son, with whom to Thee and the Holy Spirit, be glory both now and to all coming ages. Amen.
Polycarp of Smyrna (69-155)

December 2ⁿᵈ

There is no other name under heaven... whereby we must be saved.
Acts 4:12

Lean your whole weight day and night upon this saving name.
Make it your prayer and praise without ceasing.

Alexander Whyte (1836-1921)

> How sweet the Name of Jesus sounds in a believer's ear!
> It soothes his sorrows, heals his wounds, and drives away our fear.
>
> It makes the wounded spirit whole, and calms the troubled breast;
> 'Tis manna to the hungry soul, and to the weary rest.
>
> Dear Name! the rock on which I build, my shield and hiding place,
> My never-failing treasury, filled with boundless stores of grace.
>
> Jesus, my Shepherd, Brother, Friend, my Prophet, Priest, and King,
> My Lord, my Life, my Way, my End, accept the praise I bring.
>
> Weak is the effort of my heart, and cold my warmest thought;
> But, when I see Thee as Thou art, I'll praise Thee as I ought.
>
> Till then I would Thy love proclaim with every fleeting breath;
> And may the music of Thy Name refresh my soul in death. Amen.

John Newton (1725-1807)

The name of Jesus is a name of comfort to sinners when they call upon Him – it is honey in the mouth, harmony in the ear, melody in the heart.

Bernard of Clairvaux (1091-1157)

Faith in Jesus Christ is a saving grace, whereby we receive and rest upon Him alone for salvation, as He is offered to us in the gospel.

Westminster Shorter Catechism (1647)

December 3rd

Blessed are the pure in heart: for they shall see God.
Matthew 5:8

In the spiritual life, there is a law of action and reaction constantly at work. Those who are pure in heart see God; the vision of the Eternal intensifies the purity of their hearts; and this again increases their desire and capacity for fresh revelations. The pure in heart become purer and purer as the revelations of the divine become clearer and yet clearer, till at last they stand in His insufferable presence and behold with seraphic rapture the beauty of His face.

F. W. Boreham (1871-1959)

O Jesus Christ, grow Thou in me, and all things else recede; my heart be daily nearer Thee, from sin be daily freed. Make this poor self grow less and less, be Thou my life and aim. Oh, make me daily through Thy grace more worthy of Thy name.

Johann Casper Lavater (1741-1801)

The truth is that God wants nothing other than that we be made holy, for He loves us indescribably much. If He had not loved us so much, He would not have paid such a price for us. Be content then -- always, everywhere, and in all circumstances – because everything is a gift of love for you from the eternal Father. Rejoice in your troubles. Consider yourself unworthy to be sent by God along His Son's way. In everything give praise and glory to His name.

Catherine of Siena (1347-1380)

We taste Thee, O Thou Living Bread,
and long to feast upon Thee still:
We drink of Thee, the Fountainhead,
and thirst our souls from Thee to fill.

Bernard of Clairvaux (1090-1153)

Bringing into captivity every thought to the obedience of Christ.
2 Corinthians 10:5

Christ is the Word of God, the divine Reason in expression. All manifestation of the Godhead is the work of Christ.... It is Christ who conducts the march of human history.... He is the author, the subject, the end of the Old Testament revelation, and the New Testament is simply His emerging from behind the scenes where He has been invisibly managing the drama of history, to take visible part in the play, to become the leading actor in it, and to bring it to its fulfillment. The curtain has not fallen, and it will not fall until the end of the world. But that appearance of the incarnate, crucified, risen, ascending God has given us the key to human history.... God's holiness and love are focused in the cross, so that it reveals to us the heart of the Eternal, and teaches us more of Him than we can learn from all space and time besides.

A.H. Strong (1836-1925)

I believe in one Lord Jesus Christ, the only begotten Son of God, begotten of his Father before all worlds; God of God, Light of Light, very God of very God, begotten not made, being of one substance with the Father; by whom all things were made; who for us and for our salvation came down from heaven, and was incarnate by the Holy Spirit of the Virgin Mary, and was made man; and was crucified also for us under Pontius Pilate; He suffered and was buried; and the third day He rose again according to the Scriptures, and ascended into heaven, and sitteth on the right hand of the Father; and He shall come again with glory to judge both the quick and the dead; whose kingdom shall have no end.

Nicene Creed (325)

May the mind of Christ my Savior live in me from day to day,
By His love and pow'r controlling all I do and say.
Kate Wilkinson (1859-1928)

God has not appointed us to wrath, but to obtain salvation by our Lord Jesus Christ.
1 Thessalonians 5:9

If I should compare the natural state of humanity, I should conceive of an immense graveyard filled with yawning sepulchres and dying people. All round are lofty walls and massive iron gates. At the gate stands Mercy, sad spectatress of the melancholy scene. An angel flying through the midst of heaven, attracted by the awful sight, exclaims, "Mercy, why do you not enter?" Mercy replies, "Alas! I dare not enter; Justice bars the way." By her side a form appears like unto the Son of Man. "Justice," He cries, "what are your demands, that Mercy may enter and stay the carnival of death?" "I demand," says Justice, "pain for their ease, degradation for their dignity, shame for their honor, death for their life." "I accept the terms," says the Son of Man, "Now, Mercy, enter." Justice asks, "What pledge do you give for the performance of these conditions?" "My word, my oath," the Son replies. "When will you fulfill them?" And He responds, "... on the hill of Calvary."

At the foot of Calvary, behold the Incarnate Son of God! Justice, too, was there, presenting the dreadful bond and demanding its fulfillment. And Mercy was there and the weeping Church followed in His train. When He reached the summit, He did not tear the bond to pieces but nailed it to His cross. Justice sternly cried for the fire to come and consume the sacrifice.... The fire descended, consumed His humanity, but when it touched His deity, expired!

Christmas Evans (1766-1838)

> Had not the milder hand of mercy broke
> The furious violence of that fatal stroke
> Offended justice struck, we had been quite lost
> In the shadows of eternal night.
>
> Francis Quarles (1592-1644)

I am Alpha and Omega, the beginning and the end, the first and the last.
Revelation 22:13

We have here the names from the Greek alphabet, Alpha and Omega.... Long, long ago a startled shepherd was ordered to visit the court of the mightiest earthly potentate and to address him on matters of state in the name of the Most High. He was told to say, *I AM has sent me unto you.* "I AM-------!" "I AM ----- What?" For centuries and centuries that question stood unanswered; that sentence remained incomplete. It was a magnificent fragment. It stood like a monument that the sculptor had never lived to finish; like a poem that the poet had left with its closing stanzas unsung. But the sculptor was not dead; the singer had not perished. For, behold, He lives evermore! And in the fullness of time He reappeared and filled in the gap... *I am -- the Bread of Life, the Light of the world, the Door, the True Vine, the Good Shepherd, the Way, the Truth and the Life, the Resurrection and the Life -- the Alpha and Omega!* I am A to Z – the Alphabet. The whole of our literature consists of twenty-six letters arranged and rearranged. The alphabet is so inexhaustible. So, He cannot be exhausted.

For the love of God is broader than the measure of our mind;
And the heart of the Eternal is most wonderfully kind.

The alphabet is the most fluid, the most accommodating, the most plastic, the most adaptable contrivance on the planet. And the beauty of the alphabet is that it adapts itself to my individual need. And that is precisely the beauty of Jesus. He is the very Saviour I need.

F.W. Boreham (1871-1959)

O love of God, our shield and stay, through all the perils of our way;
Eternal love, in Thee we rest, forever safe, forever blest!

Horatius Bonar (1808-1889)

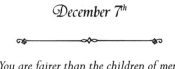

You are fairer than the children of men.

Psalm 45:2

He was fair in His conception, and a fair angel brought the news. He was fair in His nativity, born in the fullness of time and a fair star pointed to Him. He was fair in His childhood for He grew in grace and favour, and the doctors were much taken with Him. He was fair in His manhood; had there not been something admirable in His countenance and presence, some heavenly beauty, says St Jerome, the apostles and the whole world (as the Pharisees confessed) would not so suddenly have gone after Him. He was fair in His transfiguration, white as the light or as the snow, His face glittering as the sun, even to ravishing the very soul of Peter so that he knew not what he said.... He was fair in His passion; His very wounds, and the bloody prints of the whips and scourges drew from the mouth of Pilate: *Behold the man!* The sweetness of His countenance and carriage was in the midst of filth and spittle, whips and buffets. His very comeliness upon the cross and His giving up the ghost, made the centurion cry out, *He was the Son of God.* There appeared so sweet a majesty, so heavenly a lustre in Him through that very darkness that encompassed Him. And He was fair in His resurrection; with so subtle a beauty that mortal eyes, even the eyes of His own disciples, were not able to see or apprehend it. He was fair in His ascension; it made His disciples stand gazing after Him so long (as if they never could look long enough upon Him), till an angel was sent from heaven to rebuke them.

Mark Frank (1613-1664)

Beautiful Savior! King of creation!
Son of God and Son of Man!
Truly I'd love Thee, Truly I'd serve Thee,
Light of my soul, my joy, my crown.

German Hymn (1677)

"Blessed is the mother who bore you and nursed you!" But He said, "Yes, but better
still, blessed are those who listen to God's message and practice it!"
Luke 11:27, 28 (Williams)

Christ Himself when He was on earth declared the truth that there was no blessedness equal to that of obedience. More blessed even than to have been the earthly mother of our Lord, or to have carried Him in our arms and nourished Him in our bosoms, is to hear and do His will! Let your heart and your hand be as free to serve Him, as His heart and hand were to serve you. Say to Him each day, "Lord, enable me to regulate this day so as to please You! Give me spiritual insight to discover what is Your will in all the relations of my life. Guide me as to my pursuits, my friendships, my reading, my dress, my Christian work." Do not let there be a day nor an hour in which you are not consciously doing His will and following Him wholly.

Hannah Pearsall Smith (1832-1911)

> Master, speak, Thy servant heareth, waiting for Thy gracious word,
> longing for Thy voice that cheereth; Master, let it now be heard.
> I am listening, Lord, for Thee: what hast Thou to say to me?
> Speak to me by name, O Master, let me know it is to me;
> speak, that I may follow faster, with a step more firm and free,
> where the shepherd leads the flock in the shadow of the rock.
> Master, speak: and make me ready, when Thy voice is truly heard,
> with obedience glad and steady still to follow every word.
> I am listening, Lord, for Thee: Master, speak, O speak to me!
> Frances Havergal (1836-1879)

If we would please God we must watch every stroke and canvas of our lives.... We ought to live as miniature painters work, for they watch every line and tint.

C.H. Spurgeon (1834-1892)

December 9th

---◆---

To give unto them beauty for ashes, the oil of joy for mourning,
the garment of praise for the spirit of heaviness.

Isaiah 61:3

Two contrasted pictures are suggested: one of mourners with grey ashes strewed upon their disheveled locks, and their spirits clothed in gloom like a black robe; and to these there comes One who, with gentle hand smoothes the ashes out of their hair, trains a garland round their brows, anoints their heads with oil, and stripping off the trappings of woe, casts about them a bright robe fit for a guest at a festival.... He transforms sorrow because He transforms the mourner. Jesus does bring the 'joy of salvation' by a great change in a person's relations; yet in regard to the ordinary sorrows of life, He affects these not so much by an operation upon our circumstances as by an operation upon ourselves. He transforms the person who endures it. The landscape remains the same, the difference is in the colour of the glass through which we look at it. He can give the person with ashes on their head and gloom wrapped about their spirit, sources of joy altogether independent of external circumstances. We can have a patient acquiescence when we learn that the same Hand is working in all for the same end, and that all that contributes to that end is good.

Alexander Maclaren (1826-1910)

We bring the sin, He brings the salvation.
We bring the poverty, and He brings the riches.
We bring the broken heart, and He brings the healing.
We bring the captivity, and He brings the deliverance.
We bring the prison, and He brings the opening of the prison.
We bring the mourning, and He brings the joy.
We bring the ashes, and He brings the beauty.
We bring the spirit of heaviness, and He brings the garment of praise.

Alexander Whyte (1836-1921)

He heals the broken in heart and binds up their wounds.
He tells the number of the stars; He calls them all by their names.
Psalm 147:3, 4

The kings of the earth think to be great through their loftiness; but Jehovah becomes great by His condescension. Behold, the most High comes to the sick and the sorry, the wretched and the wounded! He walks in the hospitals as the good Physician! His deep sympathy with mourners is a special mark of His goodness. Few will associate with the despondent, but Jehovah chooses their company, and abides with them till He has healed them by His comforts. He deigns to handle and heal broken hearts; He himself lays on the ointment of grace and the soft bandages of love. Not only is Jehovah well acquainted with us but He tells the number of the stars and calls them all by their names. From stars to sighs is a deep descent! From worlds to wounds is a distance which only infinite compassion can bridge. Yet He who acts a surgeon's part with wounded hearts, marshals the heavenly host, and reads the muster-roll of suns and their majestic systems.

O Lord, it is good to praise Thee as ruling the stars, but it is pleasant to adore Thee as healing the broken heart!

C.H. Spurgeon (1834-1892)

O Thou who dry'st the mourner's tear,
How dark this world would be,
If, when deceived and wounded here,
We could not fly to Thee!
Oh! who could bear life's stormy doom,
Did not Thy wing of love
Come, brightly wafting through the gloom
Our peace-branch from above?
Thomas Moore (1779-1852)

Is not this the carpenter's son? is not his mother called Mary?
and his brethren, James, and Joses, and Simon, and Judas?
And his sisters, are they not all with us?
Whence then has this man all these things?
Matthew 13:55, 56

Extending from His early youth into the years of manhood, there is a great blank in our Lord's history. So far as this world and its inhabitants were concerned, Jesus passed His days in contented obscurity, unnoticed and unknown, save to the neighbors, whose esteem He could not fail to win by His pure life, gentle temper, and holy manners. *He grew in favour with God and man.* But their question remained, *Is not this the carpenter?*

Time was when He set His compass on the deep; time was when He stood and measured the earth; and now, with line, and compass, and plane, and hatchet, the sweat dropping from His lofty brow, He who made heaven and earth, and the sea, and all that in them is, in the guise of a common tradesman, bends at a carpenter's bench. How He stooped to save us! The Son of God stoops to toil. Here there is much for both people and angels to wonder at, and praise through all eternity.

Thomas Guthrie (1803-1873)

All praise to Thee, Eternal Lord,
Clothed in a garb of flesh and blood;
Choosing a manger for a throne,
While worlds on worlds are Thine alone!
All this for us Thy love has done;
By this to Thee our love is won;
For this we tune our cheerful lays,
And shout out thanks in ceaseless praise.

Martin Luther (1483-1546)

Lo, I come (in the volume of the book it is written of me), to do Thy will, O God,
Hebrews 10:7

The eternal Word became a human soul and emptied Himself of His world-embracing power as Ruler. He, the primary fount of love, did not regard even His own original and legitimate possession, the Divine form and Divine position, as something to be maintained at all costs, but surrendered it in order to save us. God became human that we might become godly.

The history of human salvation concentrates on the appearing of Christ as its central point. What took place before Him came to pass wholly in anticipation of Him; what took place after Him was accomplished in His name. His work on earth is the turning point of all development, and the history of His person is the essential content of all history. Therefore the incarnation of Christ is the coming out into view of the Divine basis of all that exists, the entrance of the Lord of history into the history itself; and the manger of Bethlehem, in conjunction with Golgotha, will forever be of all times – the turning point; of all love – the highest point; of all salvation – the starting point; of all worship – the central point.

But how in Christ these two, His deity and His humanity, unite in one, no one is able to explain. The secret of His self-humbling is forever unfathomable. Christ not only did wonders but was Himself a wonder, indeed, the wonder of all wonders, the original Wonder in person.... How then could we comprehend the... union of the infinite and the finite. No, there remains for us here only the one confession, in the words of Christian Gellert (1715-1769).

> When I this wonder contemplate
> My spirit doth in reverence wait;
> It worships, as it views this height—
> The love of God is infinite.

Erich Sauer (1899-1959)

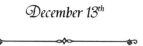

God sent His only begotten Son into the world, that we might live through Him.
1 John 4:9

God Himself, who is almighty, has sent from heaven and placed among us, Him who is the truth and the holy Word, and has firmly established Him in our hearts. He did not, as one might have imagined, send a servant, or angel, or ruler, or any one of those who bear sway over earthly things, or one of those to whom the government of things in the heavens has been entrusted. He sent the very Creator and Fashioner of all things -- by whom He made the heavens, by whom He enclosed the sea within its proper bounds; whose ordinances all the stars faithfully observe; from whom the sun has received the measure of its daily course; whom the moon obeys, being commanded to shine in the night, and whom the stars also obey, following the moon in her course; by whom all things have been arranged and placed within their proper limits; and to whom all are subject, the heavens and the things that are therein, the earth and the things that are therein, the sea and the things that are therein, the things which are in the heights, the things which are in the depths, and the things which lie between. This Messenger He sent to us. Was it then, as one might conceive, for the purpose of exercising tyranny or of inspiring fear and terror? By no means, but under the influence of clemency and meekness. As a king sends his son, who is also a king, so sent He Him; as God He sent Him; as a Saviour He sent Him, and as seeking to persuade, not to compel us. As calling us He sent Him, not as vengefully pursuing us; as loving us He sent Him, not as judging us. For He will yet in the future send Him to judge.

Mathetes (130)

O holy Child of Bethlehem, descend to us we pray;
Cast out our sin, and enter in – be born in us today
Phillips Brooks (1813-1893)

December 14th

Behold, a virgin shall conceive and bear a son, and shall call his name Immanuel.
Isaiah 7:14

What we need is God brought near. Immanuel brings God near to us, near in His own incarnate person, near in His loving life, near in His perfect sympathy. Immanuel touches humanity, the creature, at His cradle; He reaches down to humanity, the sinner, at His cross -- the end of His descent to us, the beginning of our ascent to God. There we meet Him; and saved from sin, we know Him as our Jesus the Saviour; and reconciled to God, we have Him with us as Immanuel, God with us, always with us, with us through all life's changes, with us in death and in the life to come.

Biblical Illustrator (1887)

Jesus Christ has come to be with people, not only during the brief years of His earthly ministry, but to be with all who love and trust Him, in a far closer, more real, more deep, more precious, more operative Presence than when He dwelt here. Through all the ages Christ Himself is with every soul that loves Him; and He will dwell beside us and bless us and keep us. God's presence means God's sympathy, God's knowledge, God's actual help.... Instead of staggering at the apparent improbability that so transcendent and mighty a Being should stoop from His throne, where He lords it over the universe, and enter into the narrow room of our hearts, let us rather try to rise to the rapture of the astonished Psalmist, *The Lord of hosts is with us.*

Alexander Maclaren (1826-1910)

> Christ, by highest heaven adored, Christ, the everlasting Lord,
> Late in time behold Him come, offspring of a virgin's womb.
> Veiled in flesh the Godhead see; hail, the incarnate Deity,
> Pleased as Man with man to dwell, Jesus, our Emmanuel!
>
> Charles Wesley (1707-1788)

December 15th

Thanks to the tender mercy of our God,
who will cause the Dawn to visit us from on high.
Luke 1:78 (Moffatt)

God's great visit to us is the incarnation of our blessed Lord and Saviour Jesus Christ. What but tender mercy, hearty mercy, intense mercy, could bring the great God to visit us so closely that He actually assumed our nature? The Lord so visited us as to become a babe, and then a child, who dwelt with His parents.... The Lord so visited us as to become the carpenter's son, and to know all about our toil, and our weariness, even to hunger and faintness. Jesus Christ has visited us so as to be tempted in all points like as we are, though without sin. He really assumed our nature, and thus paid to us a very close visit. He took our sickness and bare our infirmities. This was a kind of visit such as none could have thought of granting save the infinitely tender and merciful God. The Man is our next kinsman, a Brother born for adversity; in all our affliction He was afflicted. He was bone of our bone and flesh of our flesh; and His visit to us was therefore of the most intimate kind.

The visitation of the Lord to us is as the dayspring. Day, when it first breaks in the east, has not the blaze of burning noon about it; but it peeps forth as a grey light and gradually increases to perfect day. So did the Lord Jesus come: dimly as it were, at first at Bethlehem, but by-and-by He will appear in all the glory of the Father.... He shows us just as much of Himself as to delight us without utterly overwhelming us with the excess of brightness. The Lord visits us as the dayspring, and He brings us hope of greater glory yet to come. The dayspring is not the noon; but it is the sure guarantee of it; and so the First Advent is the pledge of the glory that is to be revealed.

C.H. Spurgeon (1834-1892)

December 16th

The people that walked in darkness have seen a great light.
Isaiah 9:2

When these words were written, this great light had not appeared; these people were still walking in darkness. 700 years were to pass before the light should shine upon them.... Who was He? The great Deliverer, the promised Messiah come at last, the Lord Jesus Christ. He came very differently from what had been expected; not as a great prince, but as a poor man, a wanderer, a humble teacher. Yet it was the Son of God in human form. Far lower in outward appearance than had been thought, but really far higher; not a mere temporal deliverer and restorer of the Jewish nation, but the Redeemer of souls, the Saviour of sinners, "the true Light," who should shine into thousands of hearts, and make them wise unto salvation. He was the great Light, the true Light, the Sun of righteousness....

We know Him in His finished work; not only as coming but as dying, and not only as dying but as rising again and ascending into heaven. We know the Lord Jesus as our complete Saviour, coming in our nature, living in this world, atoning for our sins by His blood, rising again for our justification, ascending up on high to be our Mediator, and ever living to make intercession for us. If this light of the gospel had not come to us, we should have been a dark land still. We might, like ancient Greece and Rome, have been highly civilized, learned, polished, and refined; but spiritually we should have been in darkness. For there is no spiritual light but from God. Christ is the only true light of the world. Each heart is in darkness till Christ be received, and only a work of grace can open the heart to receive Him, and cause the true light to shine within. Happy are they to whom He is indeed the Light of life.

Sunday at Home Magazine (1870)

December 17th

So the Word became human and lived a little while among us, and we actually saw His glory, the glory of One who is an only Son from His Father.
John 1:14 (Williams)

Ideas are often poor ghosts; our sun-filled eyes cannot discern them; they pass in their vapour and cannot make themselves felt. But at times they are made flesh; they breathe upon us with warm breath, they touch us with a soft responsive hand, they look at us with sincere eyes and speak to us in appealing tones; they are clothed in a living human soul, with all its conflicts, its faith and its love. Then their presence is a power, then they shake us like a passion, and we are drawn after them with gentle compulsion, as flame is drawn to flame. If this be true of words, how could the greatest, grandest, holiest Word of all have been expressed except in the same way? *The Word was made flesh*, says God. Bethlehem, Olivet, Galilee, Calvary made it plain.

George Eliot (1819-1880)

It was the Person of God wearing a human coat and shoes, walking freely amongst us that we might get our tangled up ideas about God, ourselves and life straightened out. He was God Himself wrapped up in human form coming close that we might get acquainted with Him all over again. We had grown deaf to the music of God's voice, blind to the beauty of His face, slow-hearted to the pleading of His presence. His hand was touching us but we didn't feel it. So He came in a new way, in a very close-up way and walked down our street into our own doors that we might be caught by the beauty of His face, and thrilled by the music of His voice, and by the spell of His presence.

S.D. Gordon (1859-1936)

We would have been afraid... had it not been a 'Face like my face.'

Robert Browning (1811-1889)

December 18th

Christ Jesus... took upon Him the form of a servant,
and was made in the likeness of man.
Philippians 2:5-7

L et all mortal flesh keep silence,
     and with fear and trembling stand;
Ponder nothing earthly minded,
     for with blessing in His hand
Christ our God to earth descendeth,
     our full homage to demand.

King of kings yet born of Mary,
     as of old on earth He stood,
Lord of lords in human vesture,
     in the Body and the Blood
He will give to all the faithful
     His own self for heav'nly food.

Rank on rank the host of heaven
     spreads its vanguard on the way,
As the Light of Light descendeth
     from the realms of endless day,
That the pow'ers of hell may vanish
     as the darkness clears away.

At His feet the six-winged seraph;
     cherubim with sleepless eye,
Veil their faces to the Presence,
     as with ceaseless voice they cry,
"Alleluia, Alleluia, Alleluia, Lord most high!"
Traditional French carol

We cannot understand Christmas without Good Friday, the meaning of the cradle unless we see the shadow of the cross. He stooped down that thereby He might befit us to be like Him. Where He is, He will lead us. What He is, He will make us.
Alexander Maclaren (1826-1910)

The Word became flesh, and dwelt among us.
John 1:14

The pure Godhead is terrible to behold; we could not see it and live; but clothing Himself with our flesh makes the Divine more amiable and delightful to us. Now we need not be afraid to look upon God, seeing Him through Christ's human nature. It was a custom of old among the shepherds to clothe themselves with sheep-skins to be more pleasing to the sheep; so Christ clothed Himself with our flesh that the Divine nature may be more pleasing to us. The human nature is a glass through which we may see the love and wisdom and glory of God clearly represented to us. Through the lantern of Christ's humanity we may behold the light of the Deity shining.

Christ did not gain one perfection more by becoming a person, nor could He lose anything of what He possessed as God. The almightiness of God now moved in a human arm; the infinite love of God now beat in a human heart; the unbounded compassion of God to sinners now glistened in a human eye; God was love before, but Christ was now love covered over with flesh.

Robert Murray M'Cheyne (1813-1843)

We could not tell what God's thoughts about us were until He showed us them in a way we could understand. And He let us know them by sending Jesus Christ into the world. He took a body like ours in order that we might know God's thoughts about us; and the more we know Jesus the more we know of God's mind. He is the Word, God's thought made flesh....

Christ came down to the tabernacle of our nature which had broken down and become a ruin, to raise it up and repair it, making it fit for the habitation of God by His own indwelling.

Biblical Illustrator (1887)

I do not wonder at any miracle, but I do marvel at this, which is a miracle among miracles, that God should become human.

Cyprian of Carthage (200-258)

December 20th

Let the very spirit which was in Christ Jesus be in you also. From the beginning He had the nature of God. Yet He did not regard equality with God as something at which He should grasp. Nay, He stripped Himself of His glory, and took on Him the nature of a bondservant by becoming a man. And being recognized as truly human, He humbled Himself and even stooped to die; and that too a death on a cross. It is because of this also that God has so highly exalted Him, and has conferred on Him the Name which is supreme above every other name, in order that in the Name of Jesus every knee should bow, of beings in the highest heavens, of those on the earth, and of those in the underworld, and that every tongue should confess that Jesus Christ is Lord, to the glory of God the Father.

Philippians 2:5-11 (Weymouth)

The Sons of the morning had sung in joy over a new-born world. Attendance at the birth of earth! They now hail with intense wonder, and praise in loftier strains, the birth in a stable, the appearance of a babe in Bethlehem. They had seen suns blazing into light; they had seen worlds start into being, and watched them as, receiving their first impulse from the Creator's hand, they rolled away into the far realm of space; but never had they followed world or sun with such interest as they follow the weary steps of this Traveler from His humble cradle to the cross of Calvary. What draws all their eyes to that sacred spot? What keeps them gazing on it with looks of such solemn interest? The Son of God dies beneath His Father's hand. Innocence bleeds for guilt; divine innocence for human guilt; a spectacle at which, in the mysterious language of the Apocalypse, *There was silence in heaven*. Love would have spared the pains of a beloved Son, but it is mastered by God's hatred of sin.

Thomas Guthrie (1803-1873)

The human race would have perished utterly had not the Lord and saviour of all, the Son of God, come among us to put an end to death. This great work was, indeed, supremely worthy of the goodness of God.

Athanasius of Alexandria (296-373)

December 21st

And she shall bring forth a son, and thou shalt call His name Jesus:
for He shall save His people from their sin.
Matthew 1:21

Jesus was His mother's maker, and His mother's child; He formed the living womb that gave Him birth, and ten thousand ages before that, the dead rock that gave Him burial. A child, yet Almighty God; a son, yet the everlasting Father; His history carries us back into eternity; and the dignities which He left, those glories which He veiled, how should they lead us to adore His transcendent love, and kneel the lower at His cross to cry, Jesus! Your love to me was wonderful. *My soul does magnify the Lord, and my spirit has rejoiced in God my Saviour.*

Thomas Guthrie (1803-1873)

Mary, you did not bear this Child for yourself alone. The Child is not yours; you did not bring Him forth for yourself, but for me, even though you are His mother, even though you held Him in your arms and wrapped Him in swaddling clothes and picked Him up and laid Him down.... I know none, neither people nor angels, who can help me except this Child whom you, O Mary, held in your arms.

If a person could put out of their mind all that they are and have except this Child, and if for them everything – money, goods, power, honor – fades into darkness and they despise everything on earth compared with this Child, so that heaven with its stars and earth with all its power and all its treasures become as nothing to them, that person would have the true gain from this message of the angel....
To you is born the Savior. Then ought you to say, Amen, I thank Thee, dear Lord.

Martin Luther (1483-1546)

Still to the lowly soul He doth Himself impart,
And for His cradle and His throne chooseth the pure in heart.

John Keble (1792-1866)

Bethlehem… out of there shall He come forth unto me that is to be ruler in Israel;
whose goings forth have been from of old, from everlasting.

Micah 5:2

Caesar Augustus, while sending forth his edicts to the utmost limits of the East, little knew that he was obeying the decrees of the King of Kings. God had foretold that the Saviour should be born in Bethlehem. In order that this might be accomplished He made use of Augustus, and through this prince the order was given for the census of the whole people.

Dean Stanley (1815-1881)

There was nothing great about Bethlehem. It was but a shepherd village, yet here the great purpose of God became a fact. It is in facts that God's purposes come to us that we may take hold of them as realities. The city is poor, but its lowliness makes it more suitable as a birthplace of Him who though He was rich, yet for our sakes became poor. It is the house of bread, fit dwelling for Him who is the Bread of God…. At Bethlehem our world's history began, for His birth has influenced all history, sacred and secular, before and behind. Christ, Immanuel, Jesus, are our Lord's names in time; but Word and Son are expressive of His eternal standing. The inaccessible Godhead becomes approachable; the incomprehensible becomes comprehensible. All the nations of the earth God has made of one blood, and of the one blood the Word was made partaker. Thus Bethlehem becomes a link between heaven and earth. Would you learn the way to God? Go to Bethlehem; the Infant in the manger is the Way. Would you learn the vanity of earth? Go to the manger where the Lord of Glory lies. Would you have a safeguard against worldliness, sin and error? Seek the Child's companionship. Would you learn to be humble? Go to Bethlehem; there the Highest became lowest. Would you learn self-denial? See the Word made flesh.

Horatius Bonar (1808-1887)

December 23rd

Fear not: for, behold, I bring you good tidings of great joy,
which shall be to all people. For unto you is born this day
in the city of David a Saviour, which is Christ the Lord.

Luke 2:10-11

If you can sing: "The Son, who is proclaimed to be a Lord and Savior, is my Savior"; and if you can confirm the message of the angel and say yes to it and believe it in your heart, then your heart will be filled with assurance and joy and confidence, and you will not worry much about even the costliest and best that this world has to offer.... For if it is true that the Child was born of the virgin and is mine, then I have no angry God, and I must know and feel that there is nothing but laughter and joy in the heart of the Father and no sadness in my heart. For if what the angel says is true, that He is my Lord and Savior, what can sin do against me? *If God is for us, who is against us?* Greater words than these I cannot speak....

Faith is not only to believe in Mary's Son, but rather that He who lies in the virgin's lap is our Savior, that we accept this and give thanks to God who so loved us that He gave us a Savior who is ours. And for a sign He sent the angel from heaven to proclaim Him, in order that nothing else should be preached except that this Child is the Savior and far better than heaven and earth. Him we should acknowledge and accept; confess Him as our Savior in every need, call upon Him and never doubt that He will save us.

Martin Luther (1483-1546)

Though Christ a thousand times in Bethlehem be born,
if He's not born in thee, thy soul is still forlorn.

Angelius Silesius (1624-1677)

December 24th

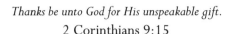

Thanks be unto God for His unspeakable gift.
2 Corinthians 9:15

Break forth, O beauteous heavenly light and usher in the morning. O shepherds, shudder not with fright, but hear the angels' warning: this child, now weak in infancy, our confidence and joy shall be, the power of Satan breaking, our peace eternal making.

Johann Rist (1641)

Joy to the world! the Lord is come:
Let earth receive her King;
Let every heart prepare Him room,
And heaven and nature sing.

Joy to the earth! the Saviour reigns;
Let men their songs employ;
While fields and foods, rocks, hills and plains,
Repeat the sounding joy.

No more let sins and sorrows grow
Nor thorns infest the ground.
He comes, to make His blessing flow
Far as the curse is found.

He rules the earth with truth and grace,
And makes the nations prove
The glories of His righteousness,
And wonders of His love.

Isaac Watts (1674-1748)

How silently, how silently, the wondrous gift was given! So God imparts to human hearts the blessings of His heaven. No ear may hear His coming, but in this world of sin, where meek souls will receive Him still, the dear Christ enters in.

Phillips Brooks (1813-1893)

December 25th

She brought forth her firstborn son, and wrapped Him in swaddling clothes, and laid Him in a manger; because there was no room for them in the inn.

Luke 2:7

Christians awake, salute the happy morn whereon the Saviour of the world was born. Rise to adore the mystery of love, which hosts of angels chanted from above; with them the joyful tidings first begun of God Incarnate and the Virgin's Son.

John Byrom (1692-1763)

O come, all ye faithful, joyful and triumphant,
O come ye, O come ye to Bethlehem;
Come and behold Him, born the King of Angels;
O come, let us adore Him, Christ the Lord.

God of God, Light of Light,
Lo! He abhors not the Virgin's womb;
Very God, begotten, not created;
O come, let us adore Him, Christ the Lord.

Sing, choirs of angels, sing in exultation,
Sing, all ye citizens of heaven above:
'Glory to God in the highest':
O come, let us adore Him, Christ the Lord.

Yea, Lord, we greet Thee, born this happy morning;
Jesus, to Thee be glory given;
Word of the Father, now in flesh appearing;
O come, let us adore Him, Christ the Lord.

John Francis Wade (1711-1787)

Who is He in yonder stall, at whose feet the shepherds fall? 'Tis the Lord! O wondrous story! 'Tis the Lord, the King of Glory. At His feet we humbly fall: crown Him, crown Him, Lord of all!

Benjamin Hanby (1833-1867)

December 26th

Almighty God, who hast given us Thy only-begotten Son to take our nature upon Him, and as at this time to be born of a pure virgin; grant that we, being regenerate and made Thy children by adoption and grace, may daily be renewed by the Holy Spirit; through our Lord Jesus Christ, who liveth and reigneth with Thee and the same Spirit, ever one God, world without end. Amen.

Book of Common Prayer (1822)

In the beginning was the Word, and the Word was with God, and the Word was God. The same was in the beginning with God. All things were made by Him; and without Him was not any thing made that was made. In Him was life; and the life was the light of men. And the light shineth in darkness; and the darkeness comprehended it not.... He was in the world, and the world was made by Him, and the world knew Him not. He came unto His own, and His own received Him not. But as many as received Him, to them gave He power to become the sons of God, even to them that believe on His name; which were born, not of blood, nor of the will of the flesh, nor of the will of man, but of God. And the Word was made flesh, and dwelt among us, and we beheld His glory, the glory as of the only begotten of the Father, full of grace and truth.

John 1:1-14

Almighty God, give us grace that we may cast away the works of darkness, and put upon us the armour of light, now in the time of this mortal life, in which Thy Son Jesus Christ came to visit us in great humility; that in the last day, when He shall come again in His glorious Majesty, to judge both the quick and dead, we may rise to the life immortal, through Him who liveth and reigneth with Thee and the Holy Ghost, now and ever. Amen.

Book of Common Prayer (1822)

In old times God was known by names of power, of nature, of majesty; but his name of mercy was reserved for now.

Jeremy Taylor (1613-1667)

December 27th

I have given you an example that you should do as I have done to you.
John 13:15

The first reason for the gift of the Incarnate Son to a perishing world is that He might be a sacrifice for its sin. The second reason is that He might be an example of godly life to those who believe in Him. We sinners cannot invert the order, and say that He was given, first as our example, and secondly as our sin-offering before God. We cannot imitate Him until He has redeemed us from the power and guilt of sin; the first need of a sinner is pardon and moral freedom, the second, the ideal of a new life.

Canon Lidden (1829-1890)

St Wenceslaus (903-935), going to his devotions in a remote church, was barefooted in the snow and ice. His servant endeavored to imitate his devotions, but grew faint through the violence of the snow and cold, whereupon King Wenceslaus commanded him to walk in the same footsteps which his feet should mark for him.... In the same manner does the blessed Jesus. He commands us to mark His footsteps, to tread where His feet have stood, and not only invites us forward by His example, but He has trodden down much of the difficulty, and made the way easier and fit for our feet.

Jeremy Taylor (1613-1667)

O let me see Thy footmarks, and in them plant my own,
My hope to follow duly is in Thy strength alone.
O guide me, call me, draw me, uphold me to the end;
And then in heaven receive me; my Savior and my Friend!
O Jesus, Thou hast promised, to all who follow Thee,
That where Thou art in glory there shall Thy servant be;
And, Jesus, I have promised to serve Thee to the end;
O give me grace to follow, my Master and my Friend.

E. John Bode (1816-1874)

December 28ᵗʰ

And others had trial of cruel mockings... were slain with the sword...
of whom the world was not worthy....
Hebrews 11:36-38

No blaze of glory shone on Paul's last hours. No multitudes of admiring brethren surrounded his last days with the halo of martyrdom. Near the spot where he was martyred it is probable that they laid him in some nameless grave -- in some spot remembered only by the one or two who knew and loved him. How little did they know, how little did they even understand, that this apparent earthly failure would in reality be the most infinite success!

F. W. Farrar (1831-1903)

When Polycarp (69-155) was brought to trial, the pro-consul asked if he was Polycarp; to which he assented. He then exhorted him,

"Have pity on your own great age: swear by the fortune of Caesar; repent; say, 'Take away the Atheists'" (the Christians were considered atheists because they didn't worship the gods). Polycarp responded,

"Eighty and six years have I served Him, and He has never wronged me, and how can I blaspheme my King who has saved me?"

"I have wild beasts," said the proconsul, "and I will expose you to them unless you repent."

"Call them!" said the martyr.

"I will tame your spirit by the fire," said the Roman.

"You threaten me," said Polycarp, "with the fire which burns only for a moment, but are yourself ignorant of the fire of eternal punishment, reserved for the ungodly?" Soon after, being bound on the burning stake, he exclaimed, "O Father of Thy beloved and blessed Son, Jesus Christ. O God of all principalities and of all creation! I bless Thee that Thou has counted me worthy of this day, and of this hour, to receive my portion in the number of martyrs, in the cup of Christ."

Gray & Adams Commentary (1951)

December 29th

Maranatha... the Lord is at hand.
1 Corinthians 16:22

He shall come not in lowliness but in His proper glory; no longer in humiliation but in majesty; no longer to suffer but to bestow on us all the fruit of His cross -- the resurrection and incorruptibility. No longer will He then be judged, but rather will Himself be Judge, judging each and all according to their deeds done in the body, whether good or ill. Then for the good is laid up the heavenly kingdom, but for those that practice evil outer darkness and the eternal fire. So also the Lord Himself says, *I say unto you, hereafter you shall see the Son of Man seated on the right hand of power, coming on the clouds of heaven in the glory of the Father.* For that Day we have one of His own sayings to prepare us, *Get ready and watch, for you know not the hour in which He comes.* And blessed Paul says, *We must all stand before the judgment seat of Christ, that each one may receive according as he practiced in the body, whether good or ill....* Of that reward it is written: *Eye has not seen nor ear heard, neither has entered into the heart of man the things that God has prepared* for them that live a godly life and love the Father through Christ Jesus our Lord. To the Father, Son and Holy Spirit be honor and might and glory to ages of ages. Amen.

Athanasius of Alexandria (296-373)

The Lord will come and not be slow;
　　His footsteps cannot err;
Before Him righteousness shall go,
　　His royal harbinger.
Rise, Lord, judge Thou the earth in might,
　　This longing earth redress;
For Thou art He Who shall by right
　　The nations all possess.

John Milton (1608-1674)

December 30ᵗʰ

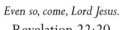

Even so, come, Lord Jesus.
Revelation 22:20

The book of Revelation from end to end reminds us of eternal realities and immeasurable hopes. The visions of Christ which precede each crisis of horrible judgment, the psalms and harp-notes of heaven which are heard amid the cries and the fury of people, all teach the same lesson. Fear not, even in the midst of anguish and persecution, you true saints of God. Christ shall triumph! Christ's enemies shall be overthrown! All who hate Him shall be hurled into ruin; all who love Him shall, after this brief spasm of anguish, be blessed everlastingly…. *Maranatha – the Lord is at hand! Even so, come, Lord Jesus!* This book encourages us to endurance by the lessons of Hope. It is to keep us faithful. It is a precious vessel in which the treasury of Christian hope has been deposited for all ages of the Church.

F. W. Farrar (1831-1903)

> Come then, and added to Thy many crowns,
> Receive yet one, the crown of all the earth,
> Thou who alone art worthy! It was Thine
> By ancient covenant ere nature's birth,
> And Thou has made it Thine by purchase since,
> And overpaid its value with Thy blood.
> William Cowper (1731-1800)

O, the joy to see Thee reigning, Thee, my own beloved Lord! Every tongue Thy name confessing, worship, honour, glory, blessing, brought to Thee with one accord; Thee, my Master and my Friend, vindicated and enthroned, unto earth's remotest, and glorified, adored and owned.

Anonymous

December 31st

Now unto the King eternal, immortal, invisible, the only wise God,
be honour and glory for ever and ever. Amen.

1 Timothy 1:17

Praise God from whom all blessings flow;
Praise Him, all creatures here below;
Praise Him above, ye heav'nly host;
Praise Father, Son and Holy Ghost.

> All people that on earth do dwell,
> Sing to the Lord with cheerful voice,
> Him serve with mirth, His praise forth tell;
> Come ye before Him and rejoice.

Know that the Lord is God indeed;
Without our aid He did us make;
We are His folk, He doth us feed,
And for His sheep He doth us take.

> O enter then His gates with praise,
> Approach with joy His courts unto;
> Praise, laud, and bless His Name always,
> For it is seemly so to do.

For why? The Lord our God is good;
His mercy is for ever sure;
His truth at all times firmly stood,
And shall from age to age endure.

> To Father, Son, and Holy Ghost,
> The God whom heav'n and earth adore,
> From men and from the angel host,
> Be praise and glory evermore. Amen.

Thomas Ken (1637-1711) (first verse)
William Kethe (1530-1594)

All laud to God the Father be;
All praise, eternal Son, to Thee;
All glory, as is ever meet,
To God the Holy Paraclete.

Ambrose (340-397)

Sources

Quotations were drawn from many primary and secondary sources. Some are as follows:

Baxter, Richard (1825). *A Call to the Unconverted*. New York: American Tract Society.

Bevan, Frances (n.d.). *Hymns of Ter Steegen, Suso and Others*. London: Nisbet & Co.

Biblical Illustrator. Volumes 1-28 (1887). (Joseph Exell, ed.). London: James Nisbet & Co.

Boreham, F. W. (1917). *The Other Side of the Hill* (pp. 98, 99, 100, 186); (1923). *Rubble and Roseleaves* (pp. 124, 132, 215). New York: The Abingdon Press (Used by permission of Dr Geoff Pound, principal of The Baptist College of Victoria, Australia).

Broughton, Rosemary (1990). *Praying with Teresa of Avila*. Winona, MN: Saint Mary's Press (pp. 54, 64). From *The Collected Works of St. Teresa of Avila*, translated by Kieran Kavanaugh and Otilio Rodriguez; copyright Volume 1 (1976), Volume II (1980), Volume III (1985) by Washington Province of Discalced Carmelites ICS Publications (Used by permission of ICS Publications, 2131 Lincoln Rd. N.E., Washington, DC).

Bunyan, John (1870). *Pilgrim's Progress*. Philadelphia: Presbyterian Board of Publishing.

Carmichael, Amy (1933). *Rose from Brier* (pp. 18-24, 140); (1955). *Edges of His Ways* (pp. 12, 149). London: SPCK Holy Trinity Church (Used by permission of Christian Literature Crusade, Fort Washington, PA).

Cowper, William (n.d.). *Poems of Cowper*. London: Thomas Nelson & Sons.

Doddridge, P. (n.d.). *The Rise and Progress of Religion in the Soul*. London: The Religious Tract Society.

Drummond, Henry (1891). *Addresses by Professor Henry Drummond*. New York: Fleming H. Revell.

Drummond, Henry (n.d.). *The Greatest Thing in the World and Other Addresses*. London: Collins Clear Type Press.

Faber, George S. (1837). *The Primitive Doctrine of Justification Investigated*. London: R.B. Seeley and W. Burnside.

Farrar, Frederic W. (1903). *The Life and Work of St Paul*; (1904). *The Life of Christ*. London: Cassell and Company.

Gray, James Comper & Adams, George M. (1951). *Gray & Adams Bible Commentary*. Volumes 1-5. Grand Rapids: Zondervan Publishing House [Formerly *The Biblical Museum* (1879) and *The Biblical Encyclopedia* (1903)].

Gordon, S. D. (1904). *Quiet Talks on Prayer* (pp. 76-77, 109-11, 158). New York: Grosset & Dunlap; (1915). *Quiet Talks on John* (pp. 51, 196, 198). London: Fleming H. Revell (Used by permission of Baker Book House, Grand Rapids).

Guthrie, Thomas (n.d.). *Christ and the Inheritance of the Saints.* Grand Rapids: Zondervan Publishing House.

Havergal, Frances Ridley (n.d.). *Kept for the Master's Use.* Chicago: The Bible Institute Colportage Association.

Henry, Matthew (1935). *Bible Commentary.* New York: Fleming H. Revell.

Jones, E. Stanley (1926). *The Christ of the Indian Road* (pp. 181-2). Toronto: McClelland & Stewart (Used by permission of Abingdon Press, Nashville).

Jowett, J.H. (1905). *The Passion for Souls.* New York: Fleming H. Revell Company.

Kempis, Thomas à (n.d.). *The Imitation of Christ.* London: Collins; (1910). *The Imitation of Christ.* London: J.M. Dent & Sons.

Krummacher, F. W. (1872). *The Suffering Saviour.* Boston: Gould & Lincoln.

Lear, Sidney H.L. (1907). *Fenelon. Archbishop of Cambrai.* London: Longman's, Green & Co.

Macbeath, John (1933). *The Face of Christ;* (n.d.). *The Second Watch.* London: Marshall, Morgan & Scott.

Macaulay, J. C. (1941). *The Gospel of John* (pp. 60, 260). Grand Rapids: Wm. B. Eerdmans Publishing (Used by permission of publisher).

Mackintosh, C. H. (1880). *Notes.* Volumes 1-5. New York: Loizeaux Brothers Bible Truth Depot.

Maclaren, Alexander (1871). *Sermons Preached in Manchester.* London: Macmillan and Co.

Maclaren, Alexander (1952). *Expositions of Holy Scripture.* Volumes 1-11. Grand Rapids: Wm. B. Eerdmans Publishing.

McCheyne, Robert Murray (1975). *A Basket of Fragments.* Fearn, Ross-shire, Scotland: Christian Heritage / Christian Focus Publications.

Meyer, F. B. (1896). *The Secret of Guidance.* New York: Fleming H. Revell.

Meyer, F. B. (n.d.). *Paul. A Servant of Jesus Christ.* London: Morgan and Scott.

Miller, J.R. (1900). *The Golden Gate of Prayer.* London: Hodder and Stoughton.

Morgan, G. C. (1912). *Living Messages of the Books of the Bible.* New York: Fleming H. Revell.

Murray, Andrew (n.d.). *Absolute Surrender.* London: Marshall Brothers.

Murray, Andrew (n.d.). *Like Christ*. New York: Grosset & Dunlap.

Owen, John (2005). *The Glory of Christ*. Fearn, Ross-shire, Scotland: Christian Heritage / Christian Focus Publications.

Pulpit Commentary (1890).(H. D. Spence & J. S. Exell, eds.) London: Funk & Wagnalls.

Roberts, Alexander & Donaldson, James (Eds.).(1896). *Ante-Nicene Fathers. Translations of the Writing of the Fathers down to A.D. 325. Volume V*. Buffalo, NY: Christian Literature Co.

Robertson, Frederick (1870). *Life, Letters, Lectures, and Addresses*. New York: Harper & Brothers.

Rutherford, Samuel (n.d.). *Religious Letters*. London: Religious Tract Society.

Rutherford, Samuel (1955). *The King in His Beauty. Extracts from the Letters and Sermons of Samuel Rutherford* (selected by J. Cyril Downes). London: The Epworth Press.

Sauer, Erich (1951). *The Triumph of the Crucified* (pp. 13-14). Grand Rapids: Wm. B. Eerdmans Publishing; (1962). *The King of the Earth* (p. 148). London: The Paternoster Press (Used by permission of The Paternoster Press, United Kingdom).

Smith, Hannah Pearsall (1888). *The Christian's Secret of a Happy Life*. London: Nisbet and Co.

Stalker, James (1890). *Imago Christi. The Example of Jesus Christ*; (1893). *The Preacher and His Models*. London: Hodder and Stoughton.

Spring, Gardiner (1850). *The Mercy Seat*. New York: W.M. Dodd.

Spurgeon, C. H. (n.d.). *The Treasury of David*. Volumes 1-6. London: Marshall Brothers.

Spurgeon, C. H. (n.d.). *The Treasury of the Old Testament*. Volumes 1-3. London: Marshall, Morgan & Scott.

Stanford, Derek (Ed.).(1957). *Fenelon's Letters to Men and Women*. London: Peter Owen Limited (H. L. Sidney Lear, translator, 19th century).

Tozer, A. W. (Ed.).(1963). *The Christian Book of Mystical Verse*. Camp Hill, PA: Christian Publications.

Uptam, T.C. (1908). *The Life of Madame Guyon*. London: Allenson & Co.

Wesley, John (1939). *Wesley's Sermons*. Kansas City, Mo: Beacon Hill Press.

Whyte, Alexander (1905). *Jesus Christ Our Lord. His Walk, Conversation and Character*. London: Oliphants Ltd.

Winslow, Octavius (n.d.). *The Preciousness of Christ*. Shiloh Online Library: www.shilohonline.org

Christian Focus Publications

publishes books for all ages
Our mission statement –

STAYING FAITHFUL

In dependence upon God we seek to help make His infallible Word, the Bible, relevant. Our aim is to ensure that the Lord Jesus Christ is presented as the only hope to obtain forgiveness of sin, live a useful life and look forward to heaven with Him.

REACHING OUT

Christ's last command requires us to reach out to our world with His gospel. We seek to help fulfill that by publishing books that point people towards Jesus and help them develop a Christ-like maturity. We aim to equip all levels of readers for life, work, ministry and mission.

Books in our adult range are published in three imprints.

Christian Focus contains popular works including biographies, commentaries, basic doctrine and Christian living. Our children's books are also published in this imprint.

Mentor focuses on books written at a level suitable for Bible College and seminary students, pastors, and other serious readers. The imprint includes commentaries, doctrinal studies, examination of current issues and church history.

Christian Heritage contains classic writings from the past.

Christian Focus Publications, Ltd
Geanies House, Fearn,
Ross-shire, IV20 1TW, Scotland, United Kingdom
info@christianfocus.com

For details of our titles visit us on our website
www.christianfocus.com